BASIC MANAGEMENT
An experience-based approach

BASIC MANAGEMENT

An experience-based approach

HYLER J. BRACEY
Development Consultants, Inc.

and

AUBREY SANFORD
Department of Management
University of Southern Mississippi

1977

BUSINESS PUBLICATIONS, INC. Dallas, Texas 75231
Irwin-Dorsey Limited Georgetown, Ontario L7G 4B3

Sold and Distributed Exclusively By:

Development Consultants, Inc.
3707 MONTAGUE BLVD • HATTIESBURG MS • 39401 • 601-544-3946
2060 EAST 54TH STREET • SUITE #1 • INDIANAPOLIS IN • 46220 • 317-253-7119

© BUSINESS PUBLICATIONS, INC., 1977

All rights reserved. No part of this publication may be reproduced, stored in a retrieval system, or transmitted, in any form or by any means, electronic, mechanical, photocopying, recording, or otherwise, without the prior written permission of the publisher.

First Printing, January 1977

ISBN 0-256-01933-9
Library of Congress Catalog Card No. 76-28901

Printed in the United States of America

To

JOE FRANK SANDERSON, SR.

*Executive Vice President
Sanderson Farms, Inc.*

One of our best teachers

Introduction

... the managers' effectiveness is significantly influenced by his insight into his own work.*

This book deals with management in general and the basic management process in particular. It is in some important ways like most other management books and in other ways like no other management book. It is similar to most other books on management in that it has the overall objective of developing and improving skills which increase managerial effectiveness. And like most other books on the subject, it attempts to achieve this objective by helping develop a better understanding of the management process and its functions.

The approach is unlike most other management books in that it focuses on the real world management situations faced by most managers rather than the situations faced primarily by high level corporate executives. Many books dealing with the management process are concerned primarily with high level management in large organizations. We believe that these books are, for the most part, not helpful in the situations in which most managers find themselves. While it is true that high level executives and supervisors are all managers performing the same basic management process, the problems, concerns, and activities of the two groups are entirely different. The great majority of managers are not concerned with developing long-run corporate strategy, nor with how the entire organization should be structured. They are more concerned with planning and getting out next week's or next month's work. We have tried to make this book both understandable and helpful to the great majority of managers.

The second important way in which this book differs from other books on management is that it focuses on developing skill through experience. We have found that managerial effectiveness at any level depends on skills which can be developed. Most books concentrate primarily on learning *about* management. The unique aspect of this book is that it provides the opportunity to learn new concepts of management and to gain experience in their use in a classroom setting.

THE PROCESS OF SKILL DEVELOPMENT

The development of managerial skill is essentially a process of learning new knowledge (ideas, information, concepts, and/or techniques) and then learning through experi-

---

*Henry Mintzberg, "The Manager's Job: Folklore and Fact," *Harvard Business Review*, vol. 53 (July–August 1975), p. 60.

FIGURE 1
Process of skill development

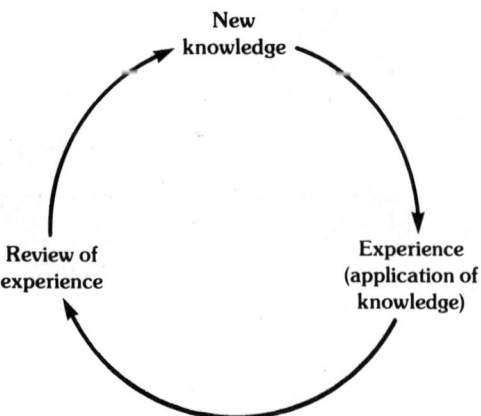

ence to apply the new knowledge. Figure 1 illustrates the process of skill development. It is in fact a circular process; it can begin at any place in the cycle.

For the sake of explanation, we can assume that the process starts with the learning of new knowledge about the process of management—what it is, what its major parts are, and how the parts fit together. While such knowledge is potentially valuable, it is of little value until it can be put into practice, and this must be learned through experience. The second stage of skill development, then, involves application of this knowledge in practical situations. This is really where true skill and ability begin to develop. The things you learn in this book will be of little value until you consciously try to use them in a practical situation. Rarely, however, are people able to apply newly acquired knowledge very effectively the first few times that they try. If you are to truly improve your skill in application, you must learn from your experience. Learning from experience requires conscious reflection on that experience—it means asking and answering questions such as the following: *What happened and why; What was good and why; What was bad and why;* and *What could I have done differently?* From such reflection, true understanding can develop, and with it, skill. Additionally, new knowledge about the management process itself is generated from the experience, thus completing the cycle. This new knowledge again is tested through experience and the cycle continues.

It is this cycle which must be followed to develop your managerial skill and improve your managerial effectiveness. There are opportunities built into the book to allow you to practice and learn through experience to apply the ideas and concepts presented. The responsibility for learning and development rests squarely on you. No one can develop your skills for you.

THE APPROACH OF THIS BOOK

This book has the following four specific objectives:

1. Enhance awareness of the impact of management practices on results.
2. Broaden understanding of the managerial process.
3. Improve skills in planning, organizing, directing, and controlling.
4. Improve leadership, motivation, and teamwork skills.

To achieve these objectives, nineteen "learning blocks" (chapters or sections) are included. Each of the nineteen blocks is complete enough to be used independently of the others.

Consequently, the learning blocks can be used selectively to emphasize one or more of the four objectives.

Each of the topic areas—communication, planning, organizing, directing, motivation, leadership, and control—are covered by blocks which contain both text material and classroom experience in managing. The pattern of learning for each of the topics begins with an experience designed to increase awareness of the importance of the topic. Next, individual prework and in-class teamwork designed to increase understanding of important concepts, ideas, and approaches is done. At times, this is followed by an additional classroom experience associated with the topic to provide the opportunity to apply learnings and improve skills in the area. Thus, each of the learning blocks associated with each topic provides the opportunity to experience managerial concepts.

Each learning block includes the following sections:

GOALS:

A short statement of the learning goals of the block.

PREWORK ASSIGNMENT:

A statement of what needs to be done by each person before starting a work session. This typically involves reading the materials in the block and for some blocks answering multiple choice questions to be used in the learning work session. Doing the prework before the session is important for the greatest learning to occur.

SESSION INTRODUCTION:

A brief explanation of the concepts to be covered in the work session.

SESSION OVERVIEW:

A brief explanation of what is going to take place during the work session.

STEPS:

Detailed instructions for each part of the work session.

This experience-based approach to learning has been very rewarding and exciting to us. Its effectiveness in developing managers far exceeds anything else we have tried, or witnessed, to date. We sincerely hope that your experience with this book is rewarding.

December 1976   **Hyler J. Bracey**
                                                                                                       Aubrey Sanford

Acknowledgments

We are deeply indebted to many people for their contributions and influence—too many to give an exhaustive listing. We would, however, like to express sincere appreciation to a special group of people without whose contributions this book would not have become a reality.

We have been highly influenced by and are deeply indebted to University Associates, Inc., of La Jolla, California, for the basic learning model. Their impact on our personal and professional development greatly influenced our thinking and writing. Several experiences draw on and are adaptations of various structured experiences published in the Pfeiffer and Jones Series in Human Relations Training: the Get Acquainted in the first block was adapted from "Peter-Paul," the communication exercise in Block III was adapted from "Listening Triads," the International Office Building is an adaptation of "The Lego Person," the Microwave Towers is adapted from the "Towers," and Shipping Containers was adapted from "Greeting Cards."

We also wish to acknowledge the support of Roy Moore, Chairman of the Management Depargment; Joseph A. Greene, Jr., Dean of the College of Business Administration; Charles Moorman, Vice President of Academic Affairs; all of the University of Southern Mississippi.

Special thanks go to Joe Frank Sanderson, Sr., Executive Vice President; Odell Johnson, Vice President and Director of Operations; and the employees of Sanderson Farms, Inc. Their encouragement and willingness to experiment were invaluable.

We are grateful to Barbara Salmon who typed portions of the manuscript innumerable times and to Tony Cain and Marty Pritchard who developed some of the models.

Last but not least, we are deeply indebted to the students who were our inspiration and guinea pigs.

Much of what follows that is good is due to the people mentioned above. We take sole responsibility for that which is incorrect or inadequate.

H. J. B.
A. S.

Contents

BLOCK I: ORIENTATION 1

BLOCK II: UNDERSTANDING THE MANAGEMENT PROCESS 5
Reading, prework, and small group discussion of management and
management process.

BLOCK III: UNDERSTANDING COMMUNICATION 21
Reading, prework, and small group discussion to learn communication
concepts; structured experience to improve communication skills.

BLOCK IV: PLANNING EXPERIENCE—INTERNATIONAL OFFICE BUILDING 39
Structured experience in which participants have the opportunity to
plan and carry out a task to learn the impact of planning on results.

BLOCK V: UNDERSTANDING THE PLANNING FUNCTION 43
Reading, prework, and structured small discussion of planning concepts.

BLOCK VI: PLANNING EXPERIENCE—PLANNING AND CONSTRUCTING A
MICROWAVE TOWER 67
Structured experience in which participants have the opportunity to
apply planning concepts by planning and carrying out a task.

BLOCK VII: PRODUCTION ORGANIZATION SIMULATION—SHIPPING
CONTAINERS 73
Structured experience in which participants plan and organize a firm
that will later (Block XIII) actually produce a product.

BLOCK VIII: UNDERSTANDING THE ORGANIZING FUNCTION 81
Reading, prework, and small group discussion of organizing concepts.

BLOCK IX: DIRECTING EXPERIENCE—PATTERN ASSEMBLY 105
Structured experience in which participants direct, and are directed by
others, in the performance of a task.

BLOCK X: UNDERSTANDING THE DIRECTING FUNCTION 109
Reading, prework, and small group discussion of directing process.

BLOCK XI: DIRECTING EXPERIENCE—PROBLEM SOLVING 123
Structured experience in which all participants have the opportunity to
try to help others solve a real problem.

BLOCK XII: UNDERSTANDING MOTIVATION AND BEHAVIOR 127
Reading, prework, and small group discussion of motivation and behavior concepts.

BLOCK XIII: PRODUCTION ORGANIZATION SIMULATION—SHIPPING CONTAINERS (continued) 147
Structured experience which allows participants to experience motivation and commitment to job and organization.

BLOCK XIV: UNDERSTANDING LEADERSHIP 151
Reading, prework, and small group discussion of directing process and leadership concept.

BLOCK XV: FEEDBACK ON LEADERSHIP STYLE 173
Instrument which provides feedback on participants' leadership styles.

BLOCK XVI: CONTROL EXPERIENCE—THE BRANCH OFFICE 177
Structured experience which allows participants to experience the control function of management.

BLOCK XVII: UNDERSTANDING THE CONTROL FUNCTION 181
Cognitive material, prework, and small group discussion of control concepts.

BLOCK XVIII: CONTROL EXPERIENCE—PERFORMANCE REVIEW 197
Role-playing experience where participants have the opportunity to review the performance of others and have their own performance reviewed.

BLOCK XIX: INTEGRATING THE MANAGEMENT FUNCTION 203
A comprehensive structured experience designed to help participants integrate their learnings associated with each of the management functions and help focus development goals for future appreciation.

Index 207

Construction materials for Blocks VII and XIII

Construction materials for Blocks IV, VI, and IX

Block I

Orientation

GOALS

1. Get acquainted with team members.
2. Become oriented to the program.

PREWORK ASSIGNMENT

None.

SESSION INTRODUCTION

This session will involve you in operating as a member of a team. During this work session, you will have the opportunity to get to know your team members. Later, an orientation and introduction to the program will be given.

SESSION OVERVIEW

Step 1: Form into teams (10 min.).
Step 2: Interview a partner (10 min.).
Step 3: Introduce your partner to the team (15 min.).
Step 4: Getting acquainted with the instructor (15 min. optional).
Step 5: Orientation to the program (10-30 min.).
Step 6: Self-evaluation and individual learnings.

Step 1: Form into teams (10 min.)

(Teams are formed by the instructor.)

Step 2: Interview a partner (10 min.)

(Each person is to join one of the other team members to form a pair; in case of odd numbers form one triad.)

During the next 10 minutes, each partner is to get to know the other partner by interviewing them (5 minutes for each partner interview). During the interview there is to be no note taking. Try to avoid questions such as: *Where were you born? How many children do you have?* etc. Rather, try to find out what kind of person your partner is—what are her or his characteristics?

The person being interviewed is to make the other person work to get to know them. Be open and honest but don't volunteer information.

Step 3: **Introduce your partner to the team** (15 min.)

On a voluntary basis each person is to introduce his or her partner in one or two minutes. Each team member is to stand behind the partner (it's helpful if they put their hands on the partner's shoulders) and begin the introduction with "I am (your partner's name). I . . ." Continue to assume you are your partner for the remainder of the introduction. The partner being introduced is to remain silent while being introduced. After the introduction they may add or clear up any matters they wish.

When all team members have been introduced, the team may ask each other questions, talk about reactions to the experience, etc.

Step 4: **Getting acquainted with your instructor** (15 min.—optional)

Step 5: **Orientation to the program** (10–30 min.)

    A. Goals of the program.

        1. Enhance awareness of the impact of management practices on results.
        2. Broaden understanding of the management process.
        3. Increase skills in planning, organizing, directing, and controlling.
        4. Improve leadership, motivation, and teamwork skills.

    B. Learning model.

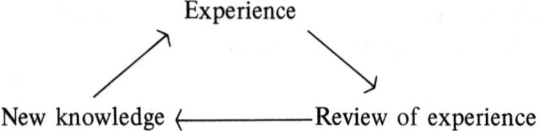

    C. Norms.

        1. Participation.
        2. Responsibility.
        3. Openness.
        4. Experimentation.
        5. Focus on useful skills.

    D. Administrivia.

Step 6: **Self-evaluation and individual learnings**

Spend some "alone" time and think about what occurred during the last experience. Focus in on two or three things that affected you or that seemed significant to you. These may be positive or negative elements of the experience. What learnings can you draw from this reflection and what does this mean to you? Don't be concerned about what you ought to have learned but rather focus on what you did learn and what it means to you. Based on your reflection of the experience, jot down your responses to the following questions:

1. What were your major learnings from the experience?

2. What implications do your learnings have for you as an individual?

3. What implications do your learnings have for you as a manager?

4. What questions do you have as a result of your experience, reflection, and learnings?

5. What implications will your learnings have on your future experiences?

Block II

Understanding the management process

GOALS

1. Create an understanding of the overall managerial process.
2. Increase awareness of the communication process.

PREWORK ASSIGNMENT

Read the following material on "Management—An Overview" for understanding. Answer the 10 prework questions at the end of the material.

MANAGEMENT—AN OVERVIEW

Managers, executives, and administrators are responsible for the proper use of enormous resources, both human and material—their decisions, their power, and their leadership have vital consequences for society as a whole.[1]

This reading is intended to be an overview of and introduction to management. Consequently, the remainder of this reading is devoted to identifying the role of management in organizations, introducing the concepts of management process and managerial effectiveness. The information is organized under the following three topic headings:

Management in organizations.
The nature of management.
Managerial effectiveness.

Each topic is discussed in detail.

MANAGEMENT IN ORGANIZATIONS

Managing and *management* are terms which are familiar to almost everyone, but both terms tend to be used rather loosely in practice. People speak of managing time, managing people, managing warehouses, etc. Additionally, management is sometimes used to refer to a basic process, a group of people and a body of knowledge.

[1] Rosalind C. Barnett and Renatu Tagiuri, "What Young People Think About Managers," *Harvard Business Review* (May–June 1973), p. 106.

In this book, managing and management are generally used to refer to the process of accomplishing objectives with and through others. Occasionally the term *management* is used to refer to a group of people (people who perform the management process) or to knowledge (theory) about what the management process involves and how it is performed. In all cases, the meaning of the terms will be apparent.

What is a manager?

A manager is a person in an organization who tries to accomplish the objectives of the organization with and through the efforts of other people. In the broad sense, anyone in an organization who has authority over other people is a manager. Managers direct the work of other people. From this viewpoint, managers manage people, not physical resources such as buildings and machines.

There are usually many different managers at different levels in an organization, and it is sometimes useful to distinguish between them. As Figure II-1 indicates, the total management group is usually divided into three groups by level in the organization. Those at the top are referred to as executives. Those in the middle are called managers. And those at lower levels are called supervisors. The important point to remember is that all three groups manage people and are in fact managers.

FIGURE II-1
Categories of managers

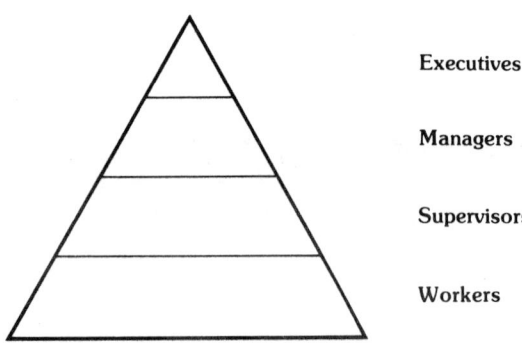

This book focuses generally on all levels of management and specifically on the middle and lower levels.

The importance of management

General opinion concerning the role and importance of managing has changed in the recent past. Not too long ago it was believed that while organizations and the managing of them were important, there was little need to study management because it was just "good common sense."

Today, even more than ever, it is recognized that organizations are critical to the success of our society. Our society is limited in what it can accomplish only by the effectiveness of its organizations. Managing determines the effectiveness and efficiency of organizations. It is the role of management to guide and direct organizations so that organizational objectives that serve the needs of society and various groups within society are achieved as efficiently as possible.

Management is still recognized as an important activity, but it is no longer believed that managing is just "good common sense." Organizations today operate in very complex situations and managing has become an extremely difficult job. It is now recognized that managing requires high levels of skills which must be learned and can be taught. It is an assumption of this book that managing is a process performed by all managers and that understanding this process promotes effective managerial performance.

THE NATURE OF MANAGEMENT

Because their prime function is to get work accomplished with and through others, all managers perform the same management process. An understanding of the management process and skill in its performance is essential for effective managerial performance. In this section, the management process is introduced and described briefly. Each part of the process is discussed in depth in later readings.

The management process

Management is believed to be a universal process. That is, the basic process of accomplishing work through others is the same for all management jobs at all levels in all organizations. This is not to say that all managers do the same things, nor that all managerial jobs require the same level of ability. It is to say that the basic *nature* of all managerial jobs is the same.

The management process is complex and it is not very meaningful to talk about all of it at one time. What is more useful is to divide the subject into its most important parts or elements and discuss each of the parts and how each of the parts fits with the other parts to form the total.

Consider that the circle in Figure II-2 represents the entire management process. Dividing this circle into several slices makes it much easier and more meaningful to talk about. Each of these slices represents a major part or element of the management process and each part is related to every other part and, therefore, to the total management process.

Dividing the management process into parts can be done by asking: *What are the things that must be done to get work accomplished with and through others?* The most useful answer is that people's activities must be planned, organized, directed, and controlled. Thus, the major parts of the management process are planning, organizing, direct-

FIGURE II-2
The management process

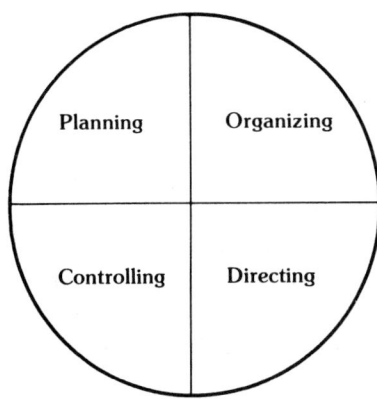

ing, and controlling. These parts or elements of the management process are usually referred to as *functions* and that is the name that is used for them throughout the remainder of the book.

One thing needs to be emphasized. Since the management process is a universal process, management functions are also universal. All managers perform the same basic functions of planning, organizing, directing, and controlling. The discussion in the book is organized around these functions. Each of the four managerial functions is described briefly below and in greater detail in subsequent sections of the book.

One other distinction needs to be made clear. The terms management process, functions, and management processes are all used at various places. *Management process* is almost always used to refer to the total management task of getting work done with and through others. *Functions* (planning, organizing, etc.) refer to characteristic parts of the total management process. *Management processes* is sometimes used to refer to activities associated with performance of management functions. Thus, management processes refer to such things as decision making, communicating, delegating, etc. These distinctions will be clear from the context of their use.

Planning. Planning refers to that part of the managerial process having to do with deciding what will be achieved and how it will be achieved. It consists of establishing the objectives or goals that will be striven for and deciding the path that will be followed to achieve the objectives. Thus, planning is oriented toward the future.

As a managerial function, planning is an attempt to deal with the uncertainty of the future. Managers try to anticipate the future so that they can influence it or at least be prepared to react to it. In this sense, planning is a means of fire prevention and also preparation for fire-fighting. Without good planning, managers are at the mercy of whatever conditions arise.

Realistically, most managers do not have complete freedom in establishing their own objectives. In almost all cases managers operate within limits imposed from some higher level of authority. This does not mean that objective setting is unimportant for most managers. Setting realistic objectives within general guidelines from above is an important part of all managerial jobs. Even in cases where managers have little or no freedom in objective setting, they still need to understand the objective setting process so that they can effectively engage in it and systematically determine what needs to be done to achieve the objectives.

In summary, planning is basically a two-part process:

1. Setting objectives.
2. Planning to achieve objectives.

Organizing. Organizing refers to the development of a system that promotes the performance of activities in a coordinated manner. It is essentially a matter of deciding who will do what and who reports to whom. Thus, organizing involves grouping activities into jobs, assigning activity groupings, and delegating the authority necessary to perform the activities. The result of the organizing process is an organization structure—a system of activity-authority relationships. It is largely through this activity-authority structure that activities are coordinated and controlled.

As the above paragraph implies, organizing proceeds logically from planning. The entire purpose of organizing is to facilitate achievement of objectives. Activities can be grouped and assigned in different ways and there are different kinds and amounts of authority that can be delegated. These things need to be decided in light of the objectives and people involved. So effective performance of the organizing function requires good performance of the planning function and an understanding of the different ways activities can be grouped and related to each other with authority.

Again it is unrealistic to believe that most managers have complete freedom to organize their department in any way they see fit. Most operate within limits imposed from above. However, all managers have some influence on how the activities they direct are organized and all have a responsibility to challenge the limits within which they operate when these limits get in the way of achieving objectives. So organizing is a function performed by all managers.

In summary, the organizing function is an attempt to create order in the performance of necessary activities and it involves the following two steps:

1. Grouping of activities necessary to achieve objectives.
2. Delegation of authority necessary to perform activities.

Directing. The function of directing refers to those activities involved with activating the organization structure. Thus, it focuses on leading and motivating subordinates in the day-to-day performance of their jobs.

While the performance of all of the management functions involves communicating with other people, the directing function is performed almost entirely through communicating. Much of directing occurs in an interpersonal context; that is, it takes place on a face-to-face basis. Effective communication is a necessary, but insufficient, condition for good performance of the directing function. Managers need to be able to communicate effectively, but they also need to communicate the right things.

In summary, the directing function involves influencing and helping subordinates to do their jobs through interpersonal interaction.

Controlling. The function of controlling involves those activities designed to assure that what is actually achieved is what was intended or planned. The process of controlling performance involves measuring what is actually achieved, comparing it to some previously set objective, and making corrections for deviations. Thus, controlling involves deciding what will be measured, how it will be measured, and developing criteria for determining when performance is in control or out of control.

In the final analysis, controlling means the control of people. It is true that the achievement of objectives is what is important and that is the purpose of controlling, but people perform activities. Controlling involves locating the responsibility for the activities out of control and getting people to alter their performance so they contribute what they should to the objectives. A large part of managerial control is exercised through performance evaluation, problem solving, and counseling. Understanding of these control techniques is essential for effective performance of the controlling function. In summary, controlling is comparing actual results to desired results and taking any corrective action needed.

It is helpful to divide the total management process into the above described functions to develop understanding, but it should be pointed out that in practice there are no clear dividing lines between the functions. At any given time, a manager's activities might involve any one or more of the four functions.

In theory, the four functions are performed in a particular order. It is useful to think of the performance of the functions as a continuous circular process. Starting with planning, each of the functions builds upon the preceding ones. However, in practice, this may be difficult to observe because no managers plan all of their activities, organize them, direct them, and finally control. At any given time, a manager may be in the process of planning some things, organizing others, directing others, etc. Nevertheless, with

FIGURE II-3
Sequence and performance of function

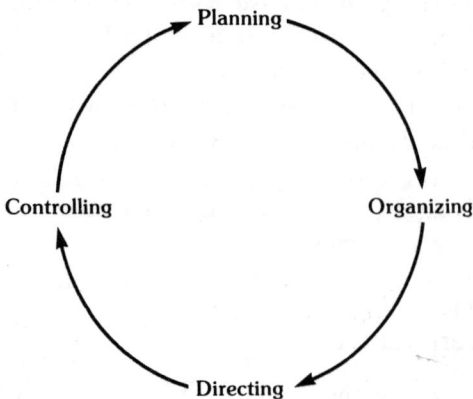

respect to the order of performance for any given part of the management job, the sequence shown in Figure II-3 tends to prevail.

All managers at all levels in all organizations perform the same management process and functions, but this does not mean that all management jobs are alike. The relative importance of the functions and the proportion of time spent on their performance tends to vary at different organizational levels. Additionally, while the basic process is the same, activities—the actual things that managers do—vary widely with both the level of management and nature of the specific job.

Relative importance of the functions

The relative importance and the proportion of time devoted to performance of each of the management functions varies with the level of management. Generally, the lower the level of the managerial job, the greater the importance of and the greater the proportion of time spent in performance of the directing and controlling functions. These general statements are illustrated in Figure II-4.

It is important to keep in mind that Figure II-4 does not imply that planning and organizing are unimportant functions in supervisory jobs. It implies only that directing and controlling are relatively more important than the planning and organizing functions at that level. Good directing and controlling cannot overcome extremely poor planning

FIGURE II-4
Importance of functions at different levels

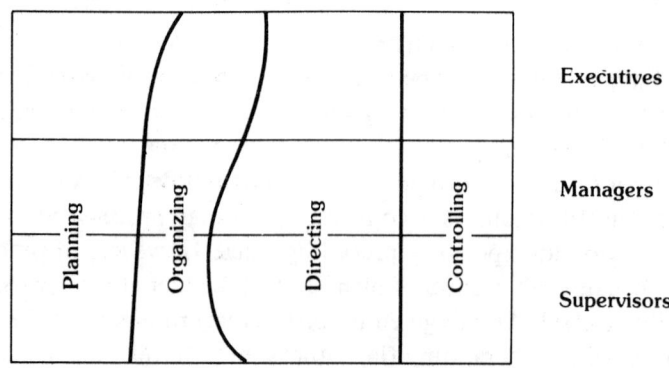

and organizing in any managerial job. Some functions are more important than others, but we should not fall into the trap of thinking that some of the management functions are not important enough to worry about. In this book, considerable attention is devoted to each of the four functions.

Activities differ

Just as the relative importance of functions differs at different levels, the actual activities involved in the performance of the management functions vary with both the level and nature of the job.

Managers at high levels tend to be more concerned with long-range activities of broad focus, while managers at lower levels are more concerned with short-range activities of narrower focus. For example, the executive concentrates on long-range planning and overall control of organizational performance. In contrast, supervisors are more likely to concentrate on planning and organizing the work of a department for the next week, month, or six months.

These differences in activities are necessary because of the differences in the levels of management. Long-range planning does little good if managers do not manage the present work of the organization effectively. On the other hand, good supervision cannot compensate for poor long-range planning. Managers at any level need to recognize that activities at different levels vary, but that many different kinds of activities are required for effective organizational performance.

It is obvious that the activities involved in management jobs reflect the nature of the job and therefore differ. All managers plan, but the actual planning activities of sales managers differ from those of production line managers, office managers, or educational managers. The functions and purpose of the activities are the same, but the activities themselves are different.

Because the functions and their purpose are the same in all management jobs, it is important for all managers at all levels to understand the basic management process.

MANAGEMENT EFFECTIVENESS

Throughout the discussion above we have implied that a manager's effectiveness is determined largely by how well one performs the four functions of the management process. The important question is, what is it that determines the quality of the performance of the functions? Are particular personality traits necessary for effective managerial performance, and if not, just what does determine a manager's effectiveness?

In the past it was rather widely believed that good managers were born and not made. The assumption was that particular personality traits resulted in effective managers and that little could be done to alter personality traits. Put very simply, people either had what it took to be good managers or they didn't; there was little that they could do to improve managerial ability.

Today there is a lot of evidence that indicates that managers are made, not born. Both research and practical experience indicate that effective performance of the management process rests upon particular skills. As used here, skills refer to abilities that can be developed and that can be exercised in practice. We believe that effective performance of the management process depends heavily on three basic skills—technical skill, managerial skill, and communication skill. Further, these three skills can be improved and developed through education and training.

Technical skill

Technical skill refers to an understanding of and proficiency in the performance of a particular type of activity. It is made up of knowledge and understanding of the concepts, processes, and methods of the particular technical area. It is exercised in practice as the ability to identify and analyze problems and the ability to use the tools and techniques of the technical area.[2]

All managers manage people performing technical activities of some kind. Managers do not just manage people; they manage people performing some particular type of activity such as marketing activities, clerical activities, religious activities, engineering activities, production activities, nursing activities, educational activities, etc. Moreover, most managers manage people performing even more specialized types of activities. For example, rather than just production activities, it may be stitching, assembling, painting, packaging, grading, shipping, etc.

Certainly, managers' abilities to plan, organize, direct, and control the technical activities of other people are influenced by their own skill in the particular area. Effective performance of the management process would be impossible without knowledge of the technical nature of the activities involved. So all managers need some technical skill in their particular area of activity.

Management skill

Management skill refers to an understanding of and proficiency in the performance of the management process itself. It includes knowledge and understanding of the concepts and functions involved in the basic managerial process, knowledge and understanding of what is involved in the performance of each function and how each of the functions is related to the other functions.

Effective managerial performance requires technical knowledge but it also requires knowledge of the management process itself. While both technical skill and managerial skill influence the quality of the performance of the management process, management skill is a separate and distinct skill in its own right. Technical skill does not make a manager skillful in planning and organizing the activities of others to achieve objectives. Conversely, managerial skill by itself does not make one skillful in a technical area. Put very simply, both skills are needed for effective managerial performance.

Communication skill

Communication skill refers to the ability to relate to and interact effectively with other people. It refers to a person's ability to actually communicate to others what they mean by their behavior and to understand what others really intend to communicate by their behavior. More simply, communication skill refers to peoples' ability to express themselves through their behavior so that they are understood and to the ability to understand the behavior of others. It involves interacting with other people, and communication is the basis of all human interaction. Neither technical skill nor management skill are of much value unless a manager can relate to other people effectively through communication. Technical skill is of little value unless it can be communicated to others. And the actual exercise of much of managerial skill takes place through communication and interaction with others. Communication skill itself does not necessarily make a manager effective, but without it, effectiveness is almost impossible.

[2] Robert L. Katz, "Skills of an Effective Administrator," *Harvard Business Review* (September–October 1974), p. 91

Relative importance of the skills

While all three skills are important for effective performance, their relative importance tends to vary with the level of the management job, as shown in Figure II-5. Generally, the higher the level of the management job, the managerial skill is more important and the technical skill is less important. Conversely, the lower the level of the management job the less important managerial skill is. Communication skills are important at all managerial levels.[3]

FIGURE II-5
Relative importance of skills

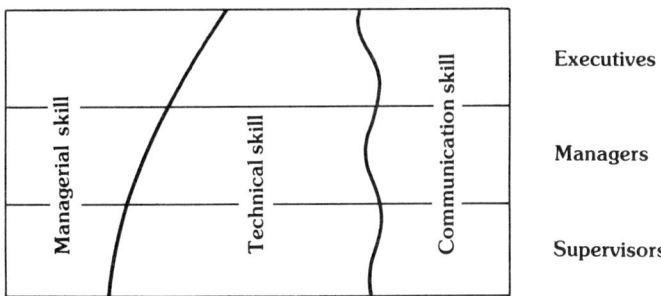

Keep in mind that the above statements are in relative terms. All three skills are important determinants of effectiveness at all levels. From a management standpoint no one skill is very effective without the others to complement it. The three skills are relatively equal in importance at middle and lower managerial levels.

Improving managerial performance

Improving managerial performance and effectiveness is a matter of improving and developing the three skills described above. This book focuses primarily on managerial skill and secondarily on communication skill, not because they are the most important but because they are the skills in which the majority of managers need development. Managers tend to have higher levels of technical skill than either managerial or communication skills. There are several reasons for this. Most managers have been technically educated either through formal training or through experience. Second, most managers start out as operative employees in some technical area and then move up into management jobs. In summary, most managers have had relatively little education and training in management and communication skills compared to the training that they have had in their respective technical area.

It is with the development of managerial and communication skills that this book is concerned. The primary focus of this book is managerial skill. However, communication skill is so important to managerial skill that we have included a discussion of it also. The truth is that we would have liked to have included a more extensive discussion of communication skill, but not everything can be included in a single book. So only the following learning block, Block III, is devoted to communication specifically. We believe that this will make the material on managerial skill more meaningful and will improve learning.

[3]Ibid., p. 101.

SUMMARY

Management is the basic process of accomplishing objectives with and through others. It is a universal process which involves four universal functions—planning, organizing, directing, and controlling. Planning involves setting objectives and planning to achieve objectives. Organizing involves grouping activities and delegating authority. Directing is influencing and helping subordinates do their jobs, and controlling is assuring that achievements are what was planned.

Managerial effectiveness is influenced by three interrelated skills—technical skill, managerial skill, and communication skill. Technical skill refers to knowledge and understanding of the technical nature of the activities engaged in. Managerial skill refers to knowledge and understanding of the management process. Communication skill refers to the ability to relate to other people effectively. Technical and managerial skills are both important and are exercised through the vehicle of communication.

Skills can be developed and improved. The process of skill development involves learning new knowledge, learning to apply knowledge through experience, and reviewing the experience in application to learn even more new knowledge.

PREWORK QUESTIONS

MANAGEMENT—AN OVERVIEW

Based on the reading, select the best and most complete answer for the following questions. Select only one answer even though others are not wrong. If you are unsure of your choice, it is better to leave it blank. Once you have completed the questions transfer your individual answers to the Prework Answer Sheet (p. 19) under the column marked *Individual answers*.

Individual answers　　*Team answers*

_____　　1. Managing is:　　_____

    a. A basic process which is the same everywhere.
    b. Something that some managers do.
    c. More important at higher organizational levels than at lower organizational levels.
    d. Best when it is impersonal.

_____　　2. Managerial jobs today:　　_____

    a. Are less important because of automation.
    b. Require different approaches at different levels.
    c. Are probably harder to do and require highly developed management skills.
    d. Require that people be experts in several different fields.

_____　　3. Planning is:　　_____

    a. Something that only some managers do.
    b. The beginning point of managerial performance.
    c. Deciding what is to be achieved and how.
    d. The most important management function.

_____　　4. Organizing:　　_____

    a. Is a function performed primarily at the top of the organization.
    b. Can normally be done before planning occurs.
    c. Extends on planning to create an environment for orderly performance.
    d. Is determining who is to be whose boss.

_____　　5. Directing:　　_____

    a. Is giving orders and checking on subordinates' work.
    b. Is guiding and helping subordinates to do their jobs.
    c. Should be impersonal.
    d. Primarily is influencing subordinates to do their work.

_____　　6. Controlling:　　_____

    a. Winds up being the control of people.
    b. Is not necessary if direction is good.
    c. Is a negative management function because it involves discipline and evaluation.
    d. Is the end point of the management process.

_____ 7. Technical skill: _____

        a. Is the most important skill in managing.
        b. Refers primarily to job knowledge.
        c. Is not related to managerial skill.
        d. Is not required on some managerial jobs.

_____ 8. Managerial skill is: _____

        a. Something many people are born with.
        b. Just as important for supervisors as for executives.
        c. More important than communication skill for supervisors.
        d. A skill that can be learned through experience.

_____ 9. Communication skill: _____

        a. Cannot be learned.
        b. Is unimportant if managers have managerial and technical skill.
        c. Is the ability to understand others and be understood by others.
        d. Is the ability to say what you mean.

_____ 10. Managerial effectiveness: _____

        a. Means that managers are effective.
        b. Refers to managerial behavior.
        c. Depends on managerial skill.
        d. Is determined by improvable skills.

SESSION INTRODUCTION

This session will focus on creating an understanding of the management process. This will be done through team discussion and lecture.

SESSION OVERVIEW

Step 1: Teamwork on prework (20 min.).
Step 2: Scoring individual and team answers, and comparing these team effectiveness scores (15 min.).
Step 3: Critique of team discussion (10 min.).
Step 4: Lecture and discussion (35 min.).
Step 5: Self-evaluation and individual learnings.

Step 1: Teamwork on prework (20 min.)

As prework you answered a 10-item multiple-choice test on "Management—An Overview." Each team is to identify the single best answer for each question. The text material is not to be used during the discussion but you may use your prework answers. Team answers are to be recorded on the Prework Answer Sheet (p. 19) under the column *Team answers*.

You will have 20 minutes to arrive at the team answers through thinking and analysis. At that time, the individual and team answers will be scored to determine how effectively each team operated. The scoring system reflects the degree of commitment to team answers. Each correct answer results in +10 points. Any item left unanswered receives 0 points. An incorrect answer results in -10 points. Thus, the score is calculated by taking the number of correct answers, subtracting the number of incorrect answers, and multiplying by 10.

This step should be completed by _____ .

Step 2: Scoring individual and team answers, and comparing these team effectiveness scores (15 min.)

Using the Prework Answer Sheet, score your individual and team answers based on the correct responses distributed to you. A simple procedure to follow is to record the correct answers in the column *Correct answers*. Where the given and correct answers match, put +10 in the *Points* column. Where no answer is given, record 0 points and where the given and correct answer do not match, put -10 in the *Points* column. By totaling the points, the individual and team score can be determined.

Individuals and teams can be compared based on their scores. However, individuals come to teams with varying degrees of preparation and knowledge. As a result the final score may not reflect how information was shared and how decisions were made during the team discussion. To take this into account a *Team effectiveness score* can be determined.

At least one team member should complete the Team Effectiveness Score sheet (p. 20), according to the following steps:

a. Determine the average individual score by adding the individual scores and dividing by the number of team members.
b. Subtract the average individual score from the team score to determine a gain or loss. A positive number indicates the team arrived at a higher score than the

average of what each individual arrived at working separately. A loss, or negative number, indicates that team discussion and agreement resulted in a lower score than the individuals did working alone.

c. Determine what the possible improvement was by subtracting the average individual score from the perfect score of 100. This number represents how many points of improvement were possible through team discussion and agreement.

d. Determine team effectiveness by dividing the gain (+) or loss (−) by the possible improvement and multiplying by 100. Once all teams have completed the scoring, the average individual, team, and team effectiveness scores will be collected and posted.

Step 3: **Critique of team discussion** (10 min.)

Each team is to discuss the following question: *What does the difference in the average individual scores and team scores say about the learning that took place in the discussion?*

Step 4: **Lecture and discussion** (35 min.)

Lecture and discussion on the management process.

Step 5: **Self-evaluation and individual learnings**

Spend some "alone" time and think about what occurred during the last experience. Focus in on two or three things that affected you or that seemed significant to you. These may be positive or negative elements of the experience. What learnings can you draw from this reflection and what does this mean to you? Don't be concerned about what you ought to have learned, but rather focus on what you did learn and what it means to you. Based on your reflection of the experience, jot down your responses to the following questions:

1. What were your major learnings from the experience?

2. What implications do your learnings have for you as an individual?

3. What implications do your learnings have for you as a manager?

4. What questions do you have as a result of your experience, reflection, and learnings?

5. What implications will your learnings have on your future experiences?

PREWORK ANSWER SHEET

Questions	Individual answer	Individual points*	Correct	Team points*	Team answer
1					
2					
3					
4					
5					
6					
7					
8					
9					
10					
Individual score			Team score		

*Blanks—(no answer given)—receive 0 points; where correct and given answers match +10 points; where correct answer and given answers do not match −10 points.

TEAM EFFECTIVENESS SCORE SHEET

Individual scores

1. _____

2. _____

3. _____

4. _____

5. _____

6. _____

7. _____

8. _____

(A) (_____) ÷ (_____) = [Average individual score]
    Total individual scores   No. members

(B) Team score Less average individual score

(C) Perfect score 100 Less average individual score

(D) (_____) ÷ (_____) = (_____) × 100 = _____ %   Team effectiveness
    Gain (+) or loss (−)   Possible improvement

Block III

Understanding Communication

GOALS

1. Create an understanding of the communication process.
2. Increase individual communication skills.

PREWORK ASSIGNMENT

Read the following material on "Communication" for understanding. Answer the 10 prework questions at the end of the material.

COMMUNICATION

A manager's number one problem . . . can be summed up in one word: Communication.[1]

Communication is the basis of all human interaction. It is how we interact with and relate to other people. It is a complex process which at its best is never perfect. Communication effectiveness does, however, rest on skills that can be improved and developed. The purpose of this reading is to describe and explain some of the more important communication concepts. The reading is organized into the following three sections:

Communication and management.
Barriers to effective communication.
Elements of effective communication.

The first section focuses on what communication is, how it takes place, its importance in managing, and the most important skills influencing its effectiveness. In the second major section two critical barriers to effective interpersonal communication are identified and the last section describes the major components of effective communication.

COMMUNICATION AND MANAGEMENT

What it is

Communication is the means through which people interact and relate to one another. It is generally defined as the process of transferring information and understand-

---

[1] "The Number One Problem," *Personnel Journal,* vol. 40 (April 1966), p. 237.

ing from one person to another person. The degree to which communication is effective then depends upon the degree to which the intended understanding develops. A humorous example of ineffective communication and misunderstanding is illustrated in the following incident.

> "Mother, I wish I didn't look so flat-chested," said my 15-year-old daughter as she stood before the mirror in her first formal dress.
>
> I remedied the matter by inserting puffs of cotton in strategic places. Then I hung around Mary's neck a string of seed pearls—just as my grandmother had done for my mother and my mother for me.
>
> At midnight her escort brought her home. The moment the door closed behind him Mary burst into tears.
>
> "I'm never going out with him again," she sobbed. "Mother, do you know what he said to me? He leaned across the table and said, 'Gee, you look sharp tonight, Mary. Are those real?' "
>
> "I hope you told him they were," I said indignantly. "They've been in the family for three generations!"
>
> My daughter stopped sobbing. "Oh, the pearls. Good heavens, I'd forgotten all about them."[2]

No communication is ever perfect but managers (and all people) can increase their effectiveness by improving their communication skill.

Communication in management

At the risk of being repetitious, we want to emphasize that managers do their job of accomplishing objectives with and through other people mainly via the communication process. As mentioned before, the ability to communicate effectively is a necessary, but insufficient condition for effective management. Consider the relationships indicated in Figure III-1. Even extremely high levels of technical and managerial skill are of little value unless managers can communicate with others. On the other hand, being able to communicate effectively does not necessarily make a person a good manager; effective management also requires technical skills and communication skills. Managers need to be able to plan, organize, direct, and control people performing technical activities and they do all these things through communication.

FIGURE III-1
All management passes through the bottleneck of communication

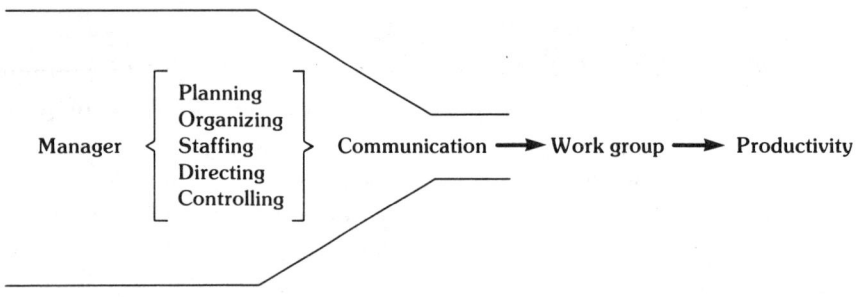

Source: Keith Davis, *Human Behavior at Work,* 4th ed. (New York: McGraw-Hill Book Co., 1972), p. 380.

[2]William V. Haney, *Communication and Organizational Behavior,* 3d ed. (Homewood, Ill.: Richard D. Irwin, Inc., 1973), p. 220.

The communication process

The model in Figure III-2 illustrates how communication takes place. The communication process begins with people who have reasons for communicating. The purpose of communication is to influence other people in some way. The influence is attempted by sending some information to the other person. Thus, the communication process always starts with people who have purposes for communicating and some information to communicate.

FIGURE III-2
The communication process

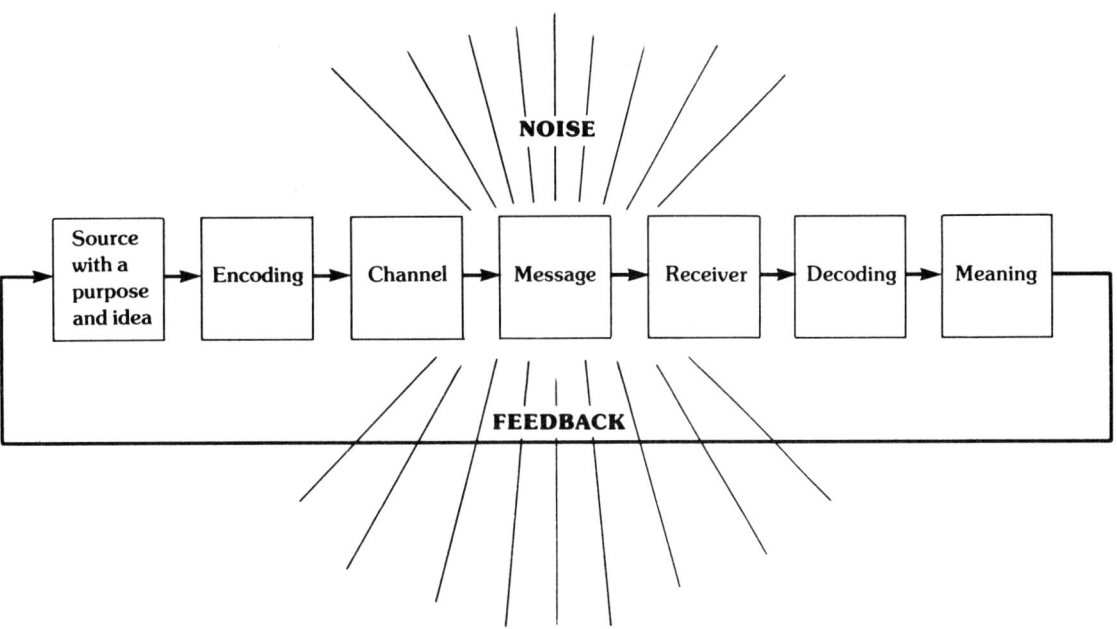

Most people are not capable of communicating directly. It is impossible for most people simply to transfer their thoughts and ideas to others; they must use some code or symbols to represent their ideas or information and then transfer these codes and symbols to others. The formulation of ideas into a particular code is known as encoding. Language and words are by far the most important set of codes and symbols used to communicate, but they are by no means the only ones available. Facial expressions, pictures, tones of voice, and gestures also are important symbols used to communicate. Most communication makes use of a combination of different types of symbols. Communicators select a set of symbols to represent their ideas or information and they transfer, not their ideas, but the set of symbols which stands for their ideas.

This set of symbols, when placed in some channel, becomes a message. Channels are the mediums or carriers of messages. Channels and messages are highly interrelated. Human beings have five distinct senses—sight, sound, taste, touch, and smell—thus, they have a total of five possible channels for sending messages. By far the most important channels are sight and sound. Once a set of symbols is placed into some channel it becomes a message. A message is the physical product of the encoding process in a channel. The message might consist of symbols (words and/or pictures) written on a piece of paper (visual channel) or it might be oral (in which case a combination of symbols, such as words, gestures, facial expressions, and tone of voice, are placed in the sound channel). Messages are received by other people and they must be translated back in meaning as ideas or information. The receivers of messages reverse the encoding process and attach meaning to symbols and messages. The product of the decoding process is the meaning receivers attach to messages. This meaning or understanding may or may not be that intended by the communication source; and the meaning, therefore, may or may not have the intended effect.

Another element always present in the communication process is feedback. Feedback is the response that the receiver-decoder makes as a result of the communication. It always is present, although it may not always be recognized easily. The feedback element can be thought of as a reversal of the communication process in which receivers now become the sources. The important point is that feedback represents responses to messages, and it always occurs. It is through feedback that people find out how effective their communication has been; therefore, feedback provides potential for changes in future communication efforts to make them more effective.

The final element which always is present when communication takes place is noise. Noise is anything that interferes with the effectiveness of communication. Literally, it can be noise in the sound channel, but it also can be present in the other four channels and in any of the processes. Thus, noise can be a poorly encoded or decoded message. Noise of some type always exists; therefore, no human communication is ever perfect. When managers (or anyone else) communicate, all elements of the model are involved. Communication may be oral, written, or some combination of the two; it may be in the form of memos or letters, or it may be informal, but no shortcut can be made in the process.

Communication skills

The degree to which any person's communication efforts are effective is significantly influenced by what one authority calls human skills. According to Katz,

> The person with highly developed human skill is aware of his own attitudes, assumptions, and beliefs about other individuals and groups; he is able to see the usefulness and limitations of these feelings. ... He is equally skillful in communicating to others, in their own context, what he means by his behavior.[3]

It seems that Katz is saying that communication skill is actually a composite of two more basic skills—the ability to make one's self understood by others (sending skills) and the ability to understand others (listening skills). Sending and receiving skills are influenced by several things. One is ability in the use of language and other important communication symbols. A second element is awareness and understanding of the different modes (such as verbal, symbolic, and body language) through which communication takes place. A third important element is perception of the other person's frame of reference—the ability to empathize. Thus, communication skills involve more than *just* telling people things clearly.

One approach to improving communication skill is to understand the process of communication, the major barriers to effective communication, and the elements of effective communication.

BARRIERS TO EFFECTIVE COMMUNICATION

While there are innumerable barriers to effective interpersonal communication, there

---

[3] Robert L. Katz, "Skills of an Effective Administrator," *Harvard Business Review,* 33 (September–October 1974), p. 91.

are two major ones—the tendency to take communication for granted and the tendency to evaluate before understanding.

Taking it for granted

There is, we believe, a natural human tendency to simply take communication for granted. We grow up and learn how to talk and write with some degree of effectiveness and all too often we fail to recognize that communicating effectively is a difficult process at which we must work hard. The complexity of the communication process described above takes on additional meaning when we consider that people communicate through three different modes or channels.[4] We communicate verbally, symbolically, and nonverbally.

Verbal communication

The most familiar and most often used mode of communication is the verbal mode. This mode of communication is so familiar to us that we tend to forget that words do not always mean the same thing to everyone. Sattler points out that the 500 most commonly used words in the English language have an average of 28 different meanings in the *Oxford Dictionary*.[5] Probably even more important than the fact that words have different common meanings is the fact that words do not have meaning; meaning exists in peoples' minds.[6] There are as many different meanings for any word as there are people who are aware of the word. The meaning people attach to a word depends primarily on their past experiences with the word and no two people ever have the same experiences. So words mean different things to different people.

Symbolic communication. People surround themselves with symbols and these symbols communicate a great deal of information to other people. We wear certain types of clothes, live in particular neighborhoods in some type of residence, drive an automobile, wear our hair a certain way, either do or do not have a beard or mustache, etc.[7] These are all symbols that whether we are aware of it or not communicate things to other people. In fact, we tend to stereotype people according to their symbols. Beyond the well-known stereotypes associated with certain common symbols, it is impossible to generalize about what particular symbols communicate to people. Symbols can and do communicate different things to different people. This is what causes much of the complexity and problem.

People can communicate more effectively if they are aware of and understand this important mode of communication. Unless you are aware of what your symbols are communicating, then you may be *saying* one thing while your symbols are communicating something else. One of the authors recently had a conversation with a man who stated that he did not need such status symbols as an expensive pleasure boat, but admitted that he drove a black Cadillac automobile. The man's symbols did not fit his words. Another example of symbolic communication familiar to many people is the situation illustrated by the statement, "Stay away from the boss today; he has his red tie on." The symbol (tie) is communicating something to other people.

When words and symbols do not match up, mixed messages are communicated to

---

[4] John E. Jones, "Communication Modes; An Experiential Lecture," in J. William Pfeiffer and John E. Jones, eds., *The 1972 Annual Handbook For Group Facilitators* (Iowa City, Iowa: University Associates, 1972), pp. 173–77. The discussion in this section draws heavily on this source.

[5] William M. Sattler, "Talking Ourselves into Communication Crisis," *Michigan Business Review* (July 1957), p. 30.

[6] S. I. Hayakawa, *Language in Thought and Action* (New York: Harcourt, Brace and World, Inc., 1949), p. 292.

[7] Jones, "Communication Modes."

people. Mixed messages confuse rather than communicate effectively. The most effective communication results when both the words and the symbols send the same messages. For effective communication the moral seems clear—find out from other people what your symbols are communicating. They may or may not be communicating what you intend. Align your symbolic communication with your verbal communication.

Nonverbal communication. Much is being learned today about what people communicate to other people with their bodies. While not everything is fully clear, the evidence is overwhelming that peoples' bodies do, in fact, communicate things to other people. One form of body language with which most people are familiar is pointing of the finger. Often people do not think about it, but it does communicate. This mode of communication is known as body language. Body language is made up of several different elements. Some of the more common elements are: (1) how people carry their body, (2) how much and where people touch each other, (3) how the body is postured, (4) subvocal verbal communication, and (5) gestures and the physical distance people keep between themselves and other people.[8] Exactly what particular forms of these elements of body language communicate is still a large unknown.[9]

About the most that can be said is that communication effectiveness is increased the more we learn about what our body language communicates and what other peoples' body language communicates. This mode of communication is especially important because most body language is unconsciously exhibited and is therefore "honest" communication of what we think and feel. There is only one place to find out what our body language says—from other people.

Human communication is indeed complex when we consider that verbal, symbolic, and nonverbal modes all communicate. The most effective communication occurs when all these forms send out the same message. This usually means that we align our verbal and symbolic communication with our body language.

The tendency to evaluate

One authority in the field of communication believes that one of the biggest barriers to effective communication is the natural tendency to evaluate the communication before it is understood;

> I should like to propose, as a hypothesis for consideration, that the major barrier to mutual interpersonal communication is our very natural tendency to judge, to evaluate, to approve (or disapprove) the statement of the other person or the other group. Let me illustrate my meaning with some very simple examples. Suppose someone, commenting on this discussion makes the statement, "I didn't like what that man said." What will you respond? Almost invariably your reply will be either approval or disapproval of the attitude expressed. Either you respond, "I didn't either; I thought it was terrible," or else you tend to reply, "Oh, I thought it was real good." In other words, your primary reaction is to evaluate it from your point of view, your own frame of reference.

* * * * *

> Is there any way of solving this problem of avoiding this barrier? I feel that we are making exciting progress toward this goal, and I should like to present it as simply as I can. Real communication occurs, and this evaluative tendency is avoided, when we listen with understanding.

---

[8] Ibid.

[9] See Gerald I. Nierenberg and Henry H. Calero, *How To Read a Person Like a Book* (New York: Hawthorn Books, Inc., 1971), for a detailed discussion of body language.

What does that mean? It means to see the expressed idea and attitude from the other person's point of view, to sense how it feels to him, to achieve his frame of reference in regard to the thing he is talking about.[10]

While it might not solve all communication problems, listening for understanding would certainly improve most people's communication skill and increase most managers' effectiveness. Many times, the authors have experienced trying to relate an idea to a person whose response in so many words was, "Hurry up and tell me what your idea is so I can tell you what is wrong with it." The lesson is clear—try to *understand* what other people are communicating before evaluating it.

ELEMENTS OF EFFECTIVE COMMUNICATION

Five interpersonal elements significantly influence both sending and receiving skills. The five elements are the self-concept, self-disclosure, clarity of expression, listening, and coping with emotions.[11]

The self-concept

Probably the most important factor affecting interpersonal communication is the self-concept. As we are using the term, self-concept refers to how one sees oneself. It includes beliefs about who the person is, what they stand for, what they do, and what they value. A person's self-concept is who they are. "It is his own filter on the world around him."[12] The self-concept is the "star" in all communication.

The self-concept has a tremendous influence on a person's ability to communicate—generally the degree to which people are aware of themselves and think of themselves as being okay, the more effectively they can communicate.

In the language of TA (Transactional Analysis), people who see themselves as being o.k. people can communicate more effectively because they are less guarded, more open, and express themselves more clearly. Additionally they are likely to be more accepting of others and as a result better able to understand others. People who see themselves as not o.k. tend to see themselves as unworthy, uninteresting, and without ability; they generally lack confidence as a person, are more guarded, and are likely to have difficulty expressing their true thoughts and feelings for fear that others will think that something is wrong with them as people.[13]

Ironically, the most significant determinant of the self-concept is communication. People learn who they are from other people—from the ways others react to their behavior in significant situations. That is, people's ideas about themselves are formed from their perceptions of what others think and do in response to them. When people are responded to as if they are o.k., they are likely to see themselves that way. When people are responded to as if they are not o.k., they are likely to see themselves that way and feel bad about themselves. Thus, communication is influenced by the adequacy of the self-concept and the self-concept is significantly influenced by communication.[14]

---

[10] Carl R. Rogers and Fritz Roelhlesberger, "Barriers and Gateways to Communication," *Harvard Business Review* (July-August 1952), pp. 46–52.

[11] Myron R. Chartier, "Five Components Contributing To Effective Interpersonal Communications," in J. William Pfeiffer and John E. Jones, eds., *The 1974 Annual Handbook for Group Facilitators* (La Jolla, CA: University Associates, 1974), pp. 125–28. This section draws heavily on this source.

[12] Ibid., p. 125.

[13] Ibid.

[14] Ibid.

Self-disclosure

A second important element influencing communication is the degree to which people reveal their true thoughts and feelings.[15] Generally, the more people are willing to disclose of themselves the more effectively they can communicate.

The simple model in Figure III-3 helps illustrate the effects of self-disclosure on communication. People can communicate effectively only within a common frame of reference. The more we disclose to you, the more you know about us and the more you disclose to us, the more we know about you. The more we know about each other, the larger is our common frame of reference.[16] Common frames of reference allow senders of communication to better frame their message in terms the receiver will understand.

FIGURE III-3

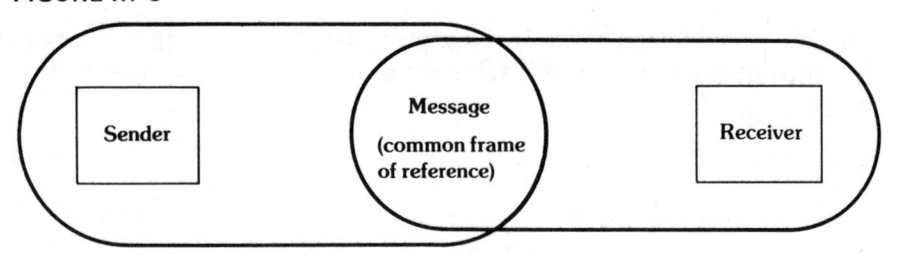

```
  ┌─────────────┐   ┌──────────┐   ┌─────────────┐
  │   Sender    │───│ Message  │───│  Receiver   │
  │             │   │(common   │   │             │
  │             │   │ frame of │   │             │
  │             │   │reference)│   │             │
  └─────────────┘   └──────────┘   └─────────────┘
```

Self-disclosure is risky business for most people. It is risky because we fear that if others really know and understand us, they will not accept and like us.[17] So we wait until we can trust others with significant information about ourselves before we really disclose very much. Jourard contends that trust develops from self-disclosure.[18] His point is that very little is going to happen to cause one person to trust another with information about oneself unless one discloses something of oneself to the other. Thus, trust is built upon self-disclosure. Whether you agree or disagree with Jourard, it seems clear to us that self-disclosure has a significant impact on communication.

The moral is to recognize the effect of disclosure on communication effectiveness and make conscious choices. Make up your own mind about what you will and will not disclose to whom, but make that decision based on recognition of its effect on your ability to communicate with others. We would, however, encourage you to test out the effects of greater self-disclosure on your ability to communicate effectively before you form any hard and fast conclusions on the subject.

Clarity of expression

The degree to which people are able to express what they think and *feel* is also an essential element in good communication.[19] This is the element of communication that most of us have received the most training in; we study language and speaking extensively through formal education. Maybe because of this we tend to assume that when we express ourselves, others know or should know exactly what we mean. The natural human

---

[15] Ibid., p. 127.

[16] Phillip C. Hanson, "The Johair Window: A Model for Soliciting and Giving Feedback," in J. William Pfeiffer and John E. Jones, eds., *The 1973 Annual Handbook for Group Facilitators* (Iowa City, Iowa: University Associates, 1973), pp. 114-19 for a more detailed explanation of their concepts.

[17] Chartier, "Five Components," p. 127.

[18] Sidney Jourard, *Self-disclosure* (New York: Wiley-Interscience, 1971).

[19] Chartier, "Five Components," p. 126.

tendency is to assume that since we know what we mean, others do also. Unfortunately, all too often this is not the case.

Several suggestions can be made about effective expression. Be sure yourself of what you want to communicate. Frame your communication with the receiver and the receiver's frame of reference in mind. Last, check out through feedback what you actually did communicate.

Listening

Almost everyone is familiar with the argument over whether a tree falling in the woods with no one around to hear it makes any noise. In interpersonal communication, the argument makes little sense. If no one listens there is no communication. Someone must receive the communication—hear it—before communication is possible. But effective communication depends not just on hearing, but on active listening for understanding.[20] Listening for understanding is practicing empathy in communication. It means really listening to what is being said to fully understand it. Effective listening requires what Reik calls the "third ear."[21] It means listening to what is not being said as well as what is being said—listening between the lines.

Several suggestions can be made about good listening. Listen to understand. Check out what you think you are hearing. Summarize what you hear. And above all, be conscious of your listening behavior.

Coping with emotions

Emotions also influence the ability to communicate. The single fact is that all people have emotions (anger, fear, joy, etc.) and when they repress their emotions, it interferes with their ability to communicate. When people attempt to hide emotions, they are rarely successful and others must guess exactly what we think and feel. When this happens, communication is less effective than it could be. Generally, the degree to which people accept their emotions as natural and express them is the degree to which they can communicate effectively.[22] It is, in our opinion, unfortunate that society generally teaches people to hide their emotions.

For effective communication, Chartier recommends the following:

1. *Be aware* of your emotions.
2. *Admit* your emotions. Do not ignore or deny them.
3. *Own* your emotions. Accept responsibility for what you do.
4. *Investigate* your emotions. Do not seek for a means of rebuttal to win an argument.
5. *Report* your emotions. Congruent communication means an accurate match between what you are saying and what you are experiencing.
6. *Integrate* your emotions with your intellect and allow yourself to learn and grow as a person.[23]

SUMMARY

Communication is relating to other people. It is an important essential skill for managers because it is the vehicle through which other skills are exercised. It is a com-

---

[20] Ibid.
[21] T. Reik, *Listening with the Third Ear* (New York: Pyramid Publications, 1972).
[22] Chartier, "Five Components," p. 127.
[23] Ibid.

plex process that requires high levels of sending and receiving skills for effectiveness.

The major barriers to effective communication are the tendency to take it for granted and the tendency to evaluate before understanding. The three main modes of communication are the verbal mode, the symbolic mode, and the nonverbal mode. Complexity is increased and misunderstanding more likely because people are not always aware of what the three modes are communicating.

Effective interpersonal communication depends on five major elements—an adequate self-concept, self-disclosure, clarity of expression, active listening, and coping with emotions.

PREWORK QUESTIONS

COMMUNICATION

Based on the reading, select the best and most complete answer for the following questions. Select only one answer even though others are not wrong. If you are unsure of your choice it is better to leave it blank. Once you have completed the questions transfer your individual answers to the Prework Answer Sheet (p. 37) under the column marked *Individual answers.*

Individual answers   *Team answers*

_____ 1. Communication is the process of: _____

    a. Passing information from one person to another person.
    b. Creating understanding in other people.
    c. Relating to other people.
    d. Interacting with other people.

_____ 2. Symbolic communication refers to: _____

    a. Status symbols.
    b. What our symbols communicate.
    c. What other people think about us.
    d. Stereotyping.

_____ 3. Verbal communication: _____

    a. Is usually the most accurate and honest.
    b. Depends heavily for effectiveness on common word meanings.
    c. Would be no problem if people would only define their terms.
    d. Should be used rather than symbolic communication.

_____ 4. Body language: _____

    a. Is the language of bodily movement.
    b. Refers to what our bodies communicate to other people.
    c. Is often misinterpreted.
    d. Means little because people usually do not notice it.

_____ 5. Listening for understanding: _____

    a. Means letting others get their "piece" said.
    b. Means agreeing with the other person's point of view.
    c. Is mostly a matter of politeness.
    d. Is trying to see things from the other person's point of view.

_____ 6. The self-concept: _____

    a. Is formed by what others say.
    b. Filters our world and affects our ability to communicate.
    c. Is either o.k. or not o.k.
    d. Probably should be ignored since it is so little understood.

_____ 7. Self-disclosure as an element of communication: _____
   a. Means that people should "spill their guts" to each other.
   b. Improves communication by enlarging the common frame of reference.
   c. Is related to trust.
   d. Means "telling it exactly like it is."

_____ 8. Active listening: _____
   a. Means second-guessing the sender's motives.
   b. Means trying to hear what is really intended.
   c. Means listening for and confronting dishonesty.
   d. Means being sure to hear exactly what is said.

_____ 9. As a communication variable, clarity of expression: _____
   a. Is usually little problem because people receive a great deal of training in it.
   b. Refers to the ability to convey thoughts and feelings accurately.
   c. Refers to being sure of what you are saying.
   d. Refers to expressing ideas simply and clearly.

_____ 10. Effective communication is facilitated when people: _____
   a. Act on all of their emotions.
   b. Accept and express their emotions constructively.
   c. Express their constructive emotions.
   d. Have the right emotions.

SESSION INTRODUCTION

This session will focus on creating an understanding of the communication process through experience, discussion, and lecture. The first activity will give you the opportunity to engage in a communication skill-building exercise. Later in the session you will have the opportunity to put what you have learned into practice during discussions of the communication process.

SESSION OVERVIEW

Step 1: Communicating for understanding (30 min.).

Step 2: Discussion of learning (10 min.).

Step 3: Teamwork on prework (25 min.).

Step 4: Scoring individual and team answers, and comparing these team effectiveness scores (10 min.).

Step 5: Increasing team effectiveness (20 min.).

Step 6: Lecture and discussion (30 min.).

Step 7: Self-evaluation and individual learnings.

Step 1: **Communicating for understanding** (30 min.)

(Participants join others to form triads.)

One of the biggest barriers to effective communication between people is the natural tendency to judge or evaluate the communication before it is understood. More effective communication will result if a clear message is sent and one listens for understanding. To gain skills in sending and receiving messages, each member will assume the role of the sender, receiver, or observer.

A. The sender and receiver are to carry on a 5-minute discussion while observing the following rules:

1. The sender chooses one of the following topics and begins a discussion on that topic.

    a. Job opportunities for women.
    b. Promotion policies.
    c. Cost of living.
    d. A current political issue.
    e. Pornography.
    f. Interracial marriage.
    g. Premarital sex relations.
    h. Any other issues.

2. Before either the sender or receiver may speak they must summarize to the other what the previous one said. They must keep summarizing until it meets the satisfaction of the one who spoke last. No new statement or any other response may be given until the last person who spoke is satisfied that the other has understood what was said. The observer is to serve as a referee and enforce the above rules.

B. At the end of 5 minutes, the sender, receiver, and observer spend 3 minutes reviewing the discussion by answering the following questions:

1. Did you have trouble listening? Why?
2. Did you find yourself wanting to interrupt the other person?
3. Did you decide what the other person was saying was right or wrong before you heard it all?
4. What did you learn about your own listening ability?

C. The triad members change roles (observer becomes sender, sender becomes receiver and receiver becomes observer) and conduct the 5-minute discussion and 3-minute review again.

D. The roles are changed again for another round so that everyone has an opportunity to be in all three roles.

Step 2: Discussion of learnings (10 min.)

Summarization of learnings by participants and instructor.

Step 3: Teamwork on prework (25 min.)

As prework you answered a 10-item multiple-choice test on "Communication." Each team is to identify the single best answer for each question. The text material is *not* to be used during the discussion but you may use your prework answers. Team answers are to be recorded on the Prework Answer Sheet (p. 37) under the column *Team answers*.

You will have 25 minutes to arrive at team answers through thinking and analysis. At that time the individual and team answers will be scored to determine how effectively each team operated. The scoring system reflects the degree of commitment to team answers. Each correct answer receives 10 points. Items unanswered are worth 0 points. An incorrect answer results in −10 points. Thus, the score is calculated by taking the number correct, subtracting the number incorrect, and multiplying by 10.

This step should be completed _____ .

Step 4: Scoring individual and team answers, and comparing these team effectiveness scores (10 min.)

Using the Prework Answer Sheet, score your individual and team answers based on the correct responses distributed to you. A simple procedure to follow is to record the correct answers in the column *Correct answers*. Where the given and correct answers match, put +10 in the *Points* column. Where no answer is given, record 0 points and where the given and correct answers do not match, put −10 in the *Points* column. By totaling the points the individual team score can be determined.

Individuals and teams can be compared, based on their scores. However, individuals come to teams with varying degrees of preparation and knowledge. As a result the final score may not reflect how information was shared and how decisions were made during the team discussion. To take this into account, a Team Effectiveness Score can be determined.

At least one team member should complete the Team Effectiveness Score Sheet (p. 38), according to the following steps:

a. Determine the average individual score by adding the individual scores and dividing by the number of team members.

b. Subtract the average individual score from the team score to determine a gain or loss. A positive number indicates the team arrived at a higher score than the average of what individuals arrived at working separately. A loss, or negative number, indicates that team discussion and agreement resulted in a lower score than the individuals did working alone.

c. Determine the possible improvement by subtracting the average individual score from the perfect score of 100. This number represents how many points of improvement were possible through team discussion and agreement.

d. Determine team effectiveness by dividing the gain (+) or loss (−) by the possible improvement and multiplying by 100. Once all teams have completed the scoring, the average individual, team, and team effectiveness scores will be collected and posted.

Step 5: **Increasing team effectiveness** (20 min.)

A. Individual work.

To get maximum learning from experience we must review our experiences and draw conclusions from them. To prepare for a team discussion allocate 100 percent among the five statements under "Communication" that describes how you assess the team's work on the ten-item multiple-choice test on planning.

Individual answers   Communication: *Team answers*

_____ a. Members expressed their ideas but did not stand up for them.   _____

_____ b. Members presented their ideas and also kept the discussion polite and friendly.   _____

_____ c. Members expressed different ideas but were willing to compromise in order to complete the task.   _____

_____ d. Members presented their views and would not change their minds.   _____

_____ e. Discussion was aimed at getting the best answer, ideas were expressed openly, and differences of opinion were resolved through discussion and understanding.   _____

B. Teamwork.

The responses to the above question are to be discussed to achieve team agreement that represents how the team operates. Discuss and examine the reasons for variations in percentage allocation. Examining the reasons and giving examples of behavior can serve as the basis for team-wide understanding and agreement. Avoid averaging answers to get the team response.

Step 6: **Lecture and discussion** (30 min.)

Step 7: **Self-evaluation and individual learnings**

Spend some "alone" time and think about what occurred during the last experience. Focus in on two or three things that affected you or that seemed significant to you. These may be positive or negative elements of the experience. What learnings can you draw from this reflection and what does this mean to you? Don't be concerned about what you ought to have learned, but rather focus on what you did learn and what it means to you. Based on your reflection of the experience, jot down your responses to the following questions:

1. What were your major learnings from the experience?

2. What implications do your learnings have for you as an individual?

3. What implications do your learnings have for you as a manager?

4. What questions do you have as a result of your experience, reflection, and learnings?

5. What implications will your learnings have on your future experiences?

PREWORK ANSWER SHEET

Questions	Individual answer	Individual points*	Correct	Team points*	Team answer
1					
2					
3					
4					
5					
6					
7					
8					
9					
10					
	Individual score		Team score		

*Blanks—(no answer given)—receive 0 points; where correct and given answers match +10 points; where correct answer and given answers do not match −10 points.

TEAM EFFECTIVENESS SCORE SHEET

Individual scores

1. _____
2. _____
3. _____
4. _____
5. _____
6. _____
7. _____
8. _____

Average individual score

(A) (   ) ÷ (   ) =
Total individual scores   No. members

Team score
Less average individual score

(B)

Perfect score 100

(C)

Less average individual score

Team effectiveness

(D) (   ) ÷ (   ) = (   ) × 100 =   %
Gain (+) or loss (−)   Possible improvement

Block IV

Planning experience—International office building

GOALS

1. Experience the importance of planning and its impact on results.
2. Increase one's awareness of the value of effective planning.

PREWORK ASSIGNMENT

None.

SESSION INTRODUCTION

Planning involves determining where you are, where you would like to be, and how to get there. It involves setting objectives and determining how to reach the objectives. This exercise gives you the opportunity to engage in a planning experience and see the results of your efforts.

SESSION OVERVIEW

Step 1: Preparing for the exercise (10 min.).
Step 2: Planning and constructing the International Office Building (45 min.).
Step 3: Posting of planning and construction times (5 min.).
Step 4: Reviewing the experience (20 min.).
Step 5: Cross-team exchange and discussion (10 min.).
Step 6: Self-evaluation and individual learnings.

Step 1: Preparing for the exercise (10 min.)

This experience will involve your team planning for and assembling an exact replica of the International Office Building model out of construction panels. The model will be displayed and available for viewing later.

Punch out the first sheet of construction panels provided at the end of the book. Keep the construction panels in front of your work station.

Step 2: Planning and constructing the International Office Building (45 min.).

You are to plan and assemble these pieces exactly like the model which is displayed.

A maximum of 45 minutes is allowed for *both* planning and constructing. You are to spend a maximum of 30 minutes planning and preparing to assemble your pieces. Once you have completed your planning stage you will *not* be allowed to look at the model again. The team with the smallest amount of planning and assembly time will be considered the most effective in accomplishing the task. You can work together as a group in any way which you think will be most helpful in planning and assembling the pieces.

There are some ground rules, however:

1. Only one person may leave the table at a time to look at the International Office Building model. The model may not be handled in any way. Your construction panels may not be taken from the table you are working on.
2. Until you are ready to start the assembly, you may not exchange your construction panels with other team members or put any two pieces together. The panels must stay in front of each person. They can be handled by that one person, but not fitted together nor lined up in any orderly arrangement.
3. Advise your observer when you are ready to start assembling so that you can be timed. Once you notify the observer that you are finished with the planning stage, you may NOT look at the model again.
4. When you are finished assembling, your observer will note the time.
5. The observer will determine whether the assembly has been completed properly. If the observer finds an error when the assembly is completed, the team will be advised that the model is not correct, but will not be told what the error is. The observer will start time again, adding to the original time.
6. Remember, you have a maximum of 45 minutes for *both* planning and constructing. You have a maximum of 30 minutes to prepare as a group for the assembly, but let your observer know when you are ready to start assembling. The most effective team is the one with the smallest planning and assembly time.

Step 3: Posting of planning and construction times (5 min.)

The planning and construction time for each team is posted.

Step 4: Reviewing the experience (20 min.)

A. Individual work.

To get maximum learning from our experience we must review our experiences and draw conclusions from them. To prepare for a team discussion, complete the following questions or statements as an individual during the next few minutes. Allow all team members to finish individually before moving to the teamwork.

1. Think about what occurred during the planning experience. Focus on two or three things that affected you or that seemed significant to you. These may be positive or negative elements of the experience. What learnings can you draw from this reflection and what does this mean to you? Don't be concerned

about what you ought to have learned, but rather focus on what you did learn and what it means to you.

2. As a team we would have been more effective if we had planned:

1	2	3	4	5	6	7	8	9
Much less								Much more

3. The time we spent on planning was:

1	2	3	4	5	6	7	8	9
Fully ineffective								Fully effective

4. Assume that you could repeat the experience.
   a. What is one thing that you would recommend you or your team not do that was done?

   b. To improve planning what is one thing that you would recommend you or your team do that was not done?

B. Teamwork.

As a team, discuss and complete the following items. The best learning will occur if all team members will share their ideas and feelings in the discussion.

1. Once everyone has completed the above individual work discuss the individual responses as a team.
2. The team is to discuss and come to a team-wide understanding and agreement on two things they learned about planning from the experience. Select a spokesperson to present the team's learnings in the next step.

Step 5: Cross-team exchange and discussion (10 min.)

Each team makes a report to the other teams and open discussion follows.

Step 6: Self-evaluation and individual learnings

Spend some "alone" time and think about what occurred during the last experience. Focus in on two or three things that affected you or that seemed significant to you. These may be positive or negative elements of the experience. What learnings can you draw from this reflection and what does this mean to you? Don't be concerned about what you ought to have learned, but rather focus on what you did learn and what it means to you. Based on your reflection of the experience, jot down your responses to the following questions:

1. What were your major learnings from the experience?

2. What implications do your learnings have for you as an individual?

3. What implications do your learnings have for you as a manager?

4. What questions do you have as a result of your experience, reflection, and learnings?

5. What implications will your learnings have on your future experiences?

Block V

Understanding the planning function

GOAL

Create an understanding of the planning function.

PREWORK ASSIGNMENT

Read the following material on "Planning" for understanding. Answer the ten prework questions at the end of the material.

PLANNING

An objective without a plan is a dream.[1]

The most basic purpose of all managerial jobs is the achievement of organization objectives with and through the efforts of other people. Some have said, "Planning is at least half the job of achievement." Planning *is* one of the more important parts of the management process. It does tend to be at least half of the management job since the performance of all of the other functions stem from it. In this sense, planning is both the beginning and end-point in the management process.

Planning is not an addition to any managerial job—it is a part of all managerial jobs. All managers plan. It is not a matter of whether managers do or do not plan; it is a matter of how well they plan. So this chapter is not about something that managers normally don't do; it is about something that you and all managers do.

The objective of this reading is to help you understand the planning part of management better, so that you can improve your planning skill. The information is organized into four major sections:

The nature of planning.
Setting objectives.
Planning to achieve objectives.
Planning in practice.

The first section defines planning as a management function, points out its importance, identifies responsibility for its performance, and introduces the steps in the plan-

---

[1] W. J. Reddin, *Effective Management by Objectives* (New York: McGraw-Hill Book Co., 1972), p. 15.

ning process. The next section describes the first part of the planning process, setting objectives, in detail. The following section focuses on the second major part of the planning—planning to achieve objectives. The fourth section looks at managerial planning in practice. As you read and study the chapter it will be helpful if you try to relate your understanding of planning to your own experience.

THE NATURE OF PLANNING

Planning is essentially mental work. It involves selecting and developing courses of action for the future. It is not necessarily complicated and hard to understand. In many respects it is fairly simple, but good planning is hard work because it involves facing and preparing for the uncertainty of the future.

The true nature of planning can best be understood by looking closely at what planning actually is, its importance, and the basic steps in the process.

What planning is

In a very important sense, planning is problem solving. Whenever a manager realizes that what he is achieving is not what he should be achieving, a problem exists. The problem is how to get from the present level of achievement to the desired level. As Figure V-1 indicates, planning involves determining what the current level of performance is, what performance should be, and what must be done to get there.

FIGURE V-1
What planning is

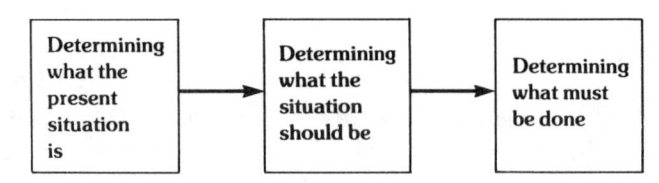

Determining what the present situation is → Determining what the situation should be → Determining what must be done

So a plan is a statement of what is to be achieved and how. Planning, simply, is deciding in advance what will be achieved, when it will be achieved, and how it will be achieved.

The importance of planning

Planning is an important part of the managerial process for at least two reasons. First of all, it is the only useful way of reducing the uncertainty and risk associated with the future. Second, effective performance of the other three management functions is dependent on good planning.

Reducing Uncertainty. One of the biggest problems facing managers (and all people for that matter) is that they cannot predict the future with certainty. One thing is certain, and that is that the future is uncertain. Such uncertainty makes it hard to plan—to decide what should be achieved and how—but it also makes good planning that much more important.

Many managers spend a great deal of their time "fighting fires." They barely succeed in settling one crisis before another one arises and they never seem to know where the next one will break out. Much of this constant "fire-fighting" is the result of inadequate planning—of not anticipating and preventing crises before they start or of not preparing for the ones that cannot be eliminated.

Only by effective planning can a manager hope to influence what happens in the future. Planning is itself an attempt to influence and control what the future will hold. It is an attempt to make sure that particular things do happen (the activities necessary for achievement of objectives and therefore the achievement of objectives themselves) and that certain things (things which interfere with achievement of the objective) do not happen. Through good planning, many of the "fires" of the future can be anticipated and prevented.

Planning is also the only effective means of being prepared to react to the uncertainties of the future. Unless managers plan, they are at the mercy of the future and they can only react to things as they occur. Not all managerial crises can be prevented, but many can be anticipated and prepared for so that reactions to what does happen are in the best interests of achieving organization objectives.

Importance to other functions. Planning is the primary management function. The management process and each of its four functions is performed to accomplish organizational objectives. Performance of the process is not an end in itself, but is the means to the end of objective achievement. Since planning is concerned with the selection of these objectives and the determination of the activities necessary for their achievement, the performance of the organizing, directing, and controlling functions is based on the planning function. Consequently, good planning is a prerequisite for effective performance of the other functions.

In practice, planning and each of the other three functions are inseparable. As Figure V-2 indicates, each builds upon the others. Performance of the organizing function begins with and uses the products (objectives and activities) of the planning function. Directing sets the organization structure in motion so that the activities that are planned are performed. Good performance of the controlling function is impossible without good objectives to use as standards. In short, effective performance of the management process must begin with good planning.

FIGURE V-2
Importance of planning

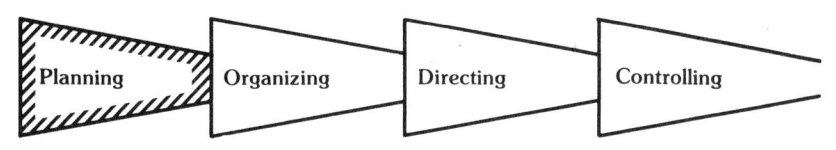

Responsibility for planning

Planning is a basic part of the management process, and it is every manager's responsibility to plan; but the scope and character of planning vary depending on the level and authority of the manager. Executives have a great deal of freedom in planning; they are restricted only by very broad policies from the board of directors and by governmental regulation. Supervisors have much less freedom and authority to decide what they will achieve and how it will be achieved, because their objectives and activities have to fit within the objectives and policies of their superiors. It is, however, almost impossible for superiors to spell out objectives and policies so completely that their subordinates have no further need of and responsibility for planning. The scope of the planning function varies, but planning is always a part of the management job.

While most managers do not have unlimited freedom and authority in planning, they are nevertheless responsible for planning within the limits imposed on them. It is every manager's duty to do what is necessary to achieve their part of the organization's objectives. This means that within their authority and within overall policy, it is their responsibility to plan—to set more specific and meaningful performance objectives and to decide in detail what they must do to achieve the objectives. People who have absolutely no freedom to plan and therefore no responsibility for planning are not really managers.

The planning process

From what has been said, it is probably obvious that there is logic and order to the planning process. If not, there would be little reason to study planning. Figure V-3 illustrates that the planning process essentially involves two major steps—setting objectives and planning to achieve objectives.

FIGURE V-3
Major parts of planning

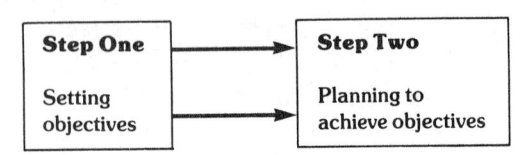

```
┌─────────────┐      ┌─────────────────┐
│ Step One    │─────▶│ Step Two        │
│             │      │                 │
│ Setting     │─────▶│ Planning to     │
│ objectives  │      │ achieve objectives│
└─────────────┘      └─────────────────┘
```

Just as the overall management process is universal, the planning process is universal. No matter what the level or type of job, planning involves the same steps or elements identified above. The actual issues and activities involved in planning differ from job to job; but the fundamental process is always the same.

SETTING OBJECTIVES

Setting objectives is essentially a three-step process. Each of the three steps is described and related to the total planning process and one useful approach to the performance of the three steps is explained.

Assessing the present situation

The first step in setting objectives is a careful study of the present performance situation. How can managers decide where they want to go unless they know where they are at the present time? How can managers begin to determine what needs to be achieved until they know what they are and are not achieving right now? As Figure V-4 indicates, the first step in planning and objective setting is a thorough analysis of all areas of performance to determine what actually is and is not being achieved.

FIGURE V-4
Steps in setting objectives

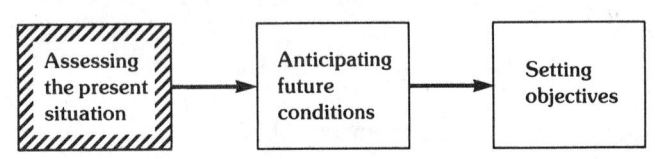

```
┌─────────────┐   ┌─────────────┐   ┌─────────────┐
│ Assessing   │──▶│ Anticipating│──▶│ Setting     │
│ the present │   │ future      │   │ objectives  │
│ situation   │   │ conditions  │   │             │
└─────────────┘   └─────────────┘   └─────────────┘
```

The basic framework described below has been found useful by many managers in studying their current performance. This framework breaks the analysis of the present situation down into three steps—identification of performance areas, determination of performance standards, and evaluation of current performance.

Identification of performance areas. Managerial jobs exist to produce output or results needed to achieve overall organizational objectives. Therefore, the vital first step for managers in assessing their present level of performance is to identify the major performance areas and results needed from their job. How can managers meaningfully judge their level of performance except in terms of the results or output their job needs to contribute to the achievement of organization objectives?

For example, suppose we were going to evaluate the performance of a piece of equipment. Our first task would be to identify the major elements of the operation and performance of the equipment that are important, i.e., speed of operation, skill required to operate, cost of operation, reliability, etc. We could then evaluate each of these areas of operation and performance to get a pretty good idea of what the equipment's overall performance is.

As in the example of the equipment above, the identification of performance areas in managerial jobs is a matter of identifying the major areas or aspects of performance that are important. Performance areas, then, are the specific unique areas of output or results that a managerial job produces; they are the reasons that the job exists.

Identifying the performance areas of a job is a matter of deciding what output or results the job should contribute to its unit. One authority suggests asking and answering the following questions as a guide to identifying the performance areas in any managerial job.[2]

1. What is the unique contribution of my job?
2. Why is my position needed at all?
3. What would change if my position were eliminated?
4. What thing would be different if I were highly effective in my job?
5. What things would I look at to see how effective I am?
6. How much authority do I have?
7. What are the most important things my job affects?
8. On what do I spend my time?
9. To make the biggest improvement in my performance next year, what would I concentrate on?

Using these questions as a guide, managers should be able to identify from three to eight performance areas which fully describe their job. Figure V-5 contains a hypothetical set of performance areas for a supervising job in production. Notice that the perform-

FIGURE V-5
Sample supervisory performance areas

1. Production level
2. Labor cost
3. Materials cost
4. Quality level
5. Supplies cost

[2] Reddin, *Management by Objectives*, p. 47.

ance areas are actually outputs of the job that affect the achievement of organizational objectives.

Determining performance standards. Before managers can meaningfully appraise their present performance they need some way of measuring their performance.

Generally, the more specific the feedback on performance, the more meaningful it is to the manager. To plan effectively, managers need to know how they are doing in a specific area, rather than how they are performing generally.

Performance *standards* are scales or yardsticks that can be used to measure performance or output in a particular performance area. So what is needed is one or more performance standards to measure performance in each performance area. Without such standards, assessment of performance is virtually meaningless.

It is difficult but not impossible to develop performance standards for all true performance areas in managerial jobs. Sometimes it is argued that certain aspects of managerial performance cannot be measured. Not all aspects of performance can be measured objectively, but all true managerial performance areas produce outputs or results which can be meaningfully measured by some method. If there is simply no way that performance in a given area can be measured, it may as well be forgotten because no one will ever know what results are in that area anyway.

At least one standard exists for measuring output and performance in all true performance areas. One way to approach the development of a standard for a given performance area is through asking and answering questions like the following:

1. What is the output or results of the area?
2. What are the units of output or results?
3. What does the output of the area look like?
4. What type of information gives an indication of performance in the area?
5. How could I tell if performance was good in the area?
6. How could I tell if performance was poor in the area?

Through this type of thinking, managers should be able to develop at least one standard which can be used to measure performance in each of their areas of output. Figure V-6 contains a sample set of standards that can be used to sample performance areas in Figure V-5.

FIGURE V-6
Sample performance standards

Performance areas	Standards
1. Production level	Units produced total
2. Labor cost	Cost per unit
3. Materials cost	Cost per unit
4. Quality level	Percent defective
5. Supplies cost	Cost per unit

Evaluating present performance. With performance areas identified and performance standards for each area developed, assessment of performance is a matter of collecting the information needed to determine what performance is in each area and coming to some conclusions concerning the level of performance. The question is: *Is 10¢ a unit labor cost good or bad and to what degree?* Comparative information which shows how performance has changed through time or how performance in the area compares to the performance of others is extremely helpful in determining the quality or level of performance in a given area.

As a result of this assessment, process managers should have a fairly clear idea of what their present performance level is in each of their performance areas. And it is this type of specific information that managers need to decide where and how much performance needs to improve and to plan for such improvement.

Anticipating future conditions

Figure V-7 indicates that the second step in the objective setting process is predicting or systematically anticipating future conditions. Whatever objectives are set must be achieved in the future under conditions of uncertainty. Before a manager can set realistic objectives and develop specific plans for their achievement, one needs to know "what's the future going to bring."

FIGURE V-7
Steps in setting objectives

Assessing the present situation → Anticipating future conditions → Setting objectives

The conditions under which managers operate in the future will affect not only the objectives they set but also what has to be done to achieve the objectives that are set. For example, suppose that a manager was fairly certain that the wage rates of employees were going to increase in the near future; this would influence any objective set with respect to labor cost and it might have a big influence on how the objective could be achieved.

No one can predict the future with certainty, but managers should identify those conditions having the most effect on their particular performance areas and make a conscious attempt to determine what these conditions will be. Only through anticipating "what's in the future" in each of their performance areas can managers try to by-pass roadblocks and/or be prepared to deal with the roadblocks that they will face.

Such forecasting may involve the collection and analysis of predictive information or it may involve only some serious thinking about how things are likely to be in the future. What managers need to do is to identify the conditions that affect performance in each of their performance areas and then try to determine what these conditions are likely to be. One useful approach to this step in planning is the use of the questions below:

1. What conditions affect performance in the area?
2. What type of information do I need to determine what these conditions will be?
3. Where can the information needed be found?
4. How can I get the information needed?
5. What does the information mean?

These questions should be answered for each important condition affecting each performance area. The main thing is for managers to set objectives and develop plans for achieving them, based on some assumptions about the future that seem realistic to them in light of available information.

Setting objectives

The final step in objective setting, emphasized in Figure V-8, is deciding where you want and need to go—actually setting objectives. Objectives are the performance results desired; they are the real beginning point of the planning and management process, and at the same time the desired end result of the management process. Objectives provide the direction necessary for achievement and without them there is little to keep a manager from simply wandering in all directions. Objectives then are the "guiding light" for the entire management process.

FIGURE V-8
Objective setting in planning

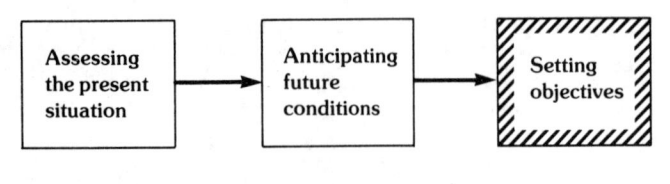

Assessing the present situation → Anticipating future conditions → *Setting objectives*

Hierarchy of objectives. Organizations do not have one set of objectives which each manager attempts to achieve. They have a complex hierarchy of objectives in which almost all managers have different and more specific objectives. This hierarchy of objectives begins at the top of the organization with overall organizational objectives and proceeds downward with narrower and more specific objectives for each manager, derived from the objectives at the level above. Figure V-9 illustrates a part of the hierarchy of objectives for an organization.

FIGURE V-9
Organizational hierarchy of objectives

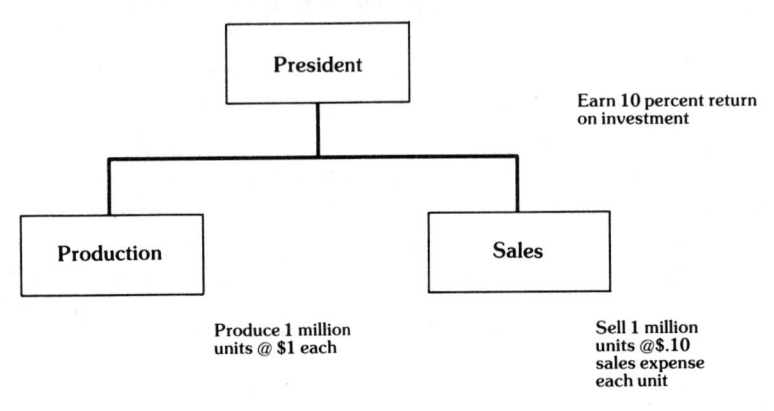

President — Earn 10 percent return on investment

Production — Produce 1 million units @ $1 each

Sales — Sell 1 million units @ $.10 sales expense each unit

Objectives for each manager at each level are a part of the objectives at the level above. They are in reality only specific points on a performance standard that can be used to measure performance in the area. So the real task of setting performance objectives for any job begins with the identification of the performance areas and standards discussed above. At this stage in planning the task of setting specific objectives is a matter of determining what level of performance will be sought in each area, in light of anticipated future conditions. So a specific objective should be set on each performance standard in each performance area of the management job.

Characteristics of good objectives. Objectives need to have several characteristics to be fully useful as a guide to the rest of the planning process and the performance of the other three management functions. They should be measurable by some means, have a time dimension, and be realistically attainable but challenging. Establishing objectives with these characteristics is not difficult if performance areas and standards have been developed properly.

If at all possible, all objectives should be stated in measurable terms. It is generally more meaningful to state that costs should be reduced by 5 cents a unit than it is to say that costs should be reduced. This does not mean that all objectives must be stated in number; it means that the objectives should be stated in terms that allow a manager to tell to what degree the objective is achieved.

A second characteristic of a good objective is that it be bounded by time. Rather than reduce cost by 5 cents a unit, reduce costs by 5 cents a unit by the end of six months is more meaningful. It is usually easy to specify the time that an objective should be achieved. Without this dimension, objectives have much less meaning and provide less incentive and guidance.

The level of performance called for by a specific objective should be challenging but achievable. Generally objectives should be set that call for a significant improvement in the level of performance in the area, considering the conditions that will be prevailing in the future.

Last, it is helpful for managers to determine the relative importance of each of their objectives. This is a simple matter of allocating 100 percent among objectives based on the effect that the achievement of the objectives will have on the achievement of overall organizational goals. This ordering of objectives helps managers concentrate their efforts on the more important things.

It is only fair to say that setting the type of objectives discussed above is not an easy task. It cannot be done well if performance areas and standards are not well thought out and developed. If the general approach described above is used, it should be possible for almost all managers to develop objectives similar in nature to the sample areas, standards, and objectives illustrated in Figure V-10.

FIGURE V-10
Sample performance objectives, standards, and areas

	Areas	Performance Standards	Objectives	Rank
1.	Production level	Units produced	1,000,000 next year	30%
2.	Labor cost	Cost per unit	$1.00	30
3.	Materials cost	Cost per unit	$ .50	20
4.	Quality level	Percent defective	1%	10
5.	Supplies cost	Cost per unit	$ .05	10

PLANNING TO ACHIEVE OBJECTIVES

Objectives by themselves accomplish little. They are like New Year's resolutions; they are of little value until action is taken to achieve them. Thus, the second major phase of planning is deciding how objectives will be achieved. This is a difficult part of planning. In many cases, setting objectives is relatively easy; but deciding what needs to be done to achieve the objectives is more difficult. As Figure V-11 shows, planning to

FIGURE V-11
Planning to achieve objectives

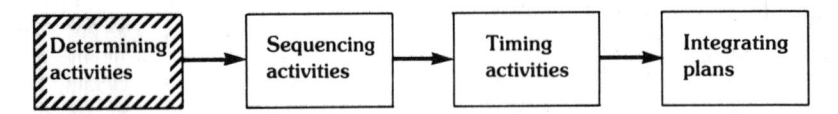

```
┌─────────────┐    ┌─────────────┐    ┌─────────────┐    ┌─────────────┐
│ Determining │ →  │ Sequencing  │ →  │   Timing    │ →  │ Integrating │
│  activities │    │ activities  │    │ activities  │    │    plans    │
└─────────────┘    └─────────────┘    └─────────────┘    └─────────────┘
```

achieve objectives is a matter of determining what activities must be performed in light of anticipated future conditions and then developing an integrated overall plan of action.

Determining activities

The first step in planning to achieve any objective is deciding what activities must be performed for the objective to become a reality. An activity is work done to achieve an objective.

Deciding what activities are necessary to achieve a specific objective involves analyzing the objective in light of anticipated future conditions. It is asking and answering the question: *What activities must be performed for the objective to be achieved?* The result of this process should be a list of activities whose performance will lead to the achievement of the objective. Figure V-12 contains a sample set of activities for two of the objectives in Figure V-10.

FIGURE V-12
Sample activities associated with an objective

Objective:	Realize supply cost of $.05 per unit	Objective:	1 percent defective units produced
Activities:		**Activities:**	
1. Establish requisition system for supplies		1. Study to see where and what type of training is needed	
2. Put requisition system into force		2. Develop training program	
		3. Train employees	

While the process of determining activities seems fairly simple, it is not an easy job to do well. It is extremely easy to fall into the trap of selecting platitudes such as the following instead of true activities:

Try harder.

Work harder.

Work long hours.

Make better use of time.

Be better organized.

Get subordinates to work harder.

These may be desirable things for a manager to do, but they are not the type activities usually required for the achievement of specific objectives. Well set objectives usually require the performance of more specific activities.

To test whether or not the activities decided on for the achievment of an objective are specific enough, managers might ask themselves the following questions:

1. How will I know if the activity is being performed?
2. Can I tell when the activity is finished?
3. How does the activity affect the objective?
4. Does this activity apply only to this objective?

Answers to these types of questions will provide an indication of the quality of the activities selected. Unless an activity has a definite beginning and ending point, it is probably a poor activity, and activities which seem appropriate and necessary for almost *all* objectives are rarely specific enough to be of much value in achieving any one objective.

Sequencing activities

As many managers know, the achievement of many managerial objectives requires not only that certain activities be performed but that the activities be performed in a particular order. That is, certain activities need to be performed before other activities are performed. As illustrated in Figure V-13 the next part of the planning process involves deciding on the order in which the activities need to be performed that are required to achieve the objective.

FIGURE V-13
Sequencing activities

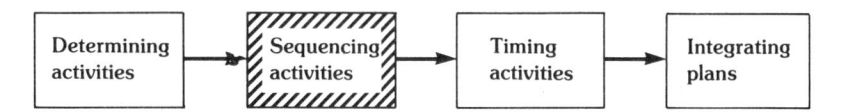

Determining activities → Sequencing activities → Timing activities → Integrating plans

It is probably an unusual situation when the order of performance of activities makes little or no difference in the achievement of the objective. Most managerial objectives, even fairly simple ones, require the performance of more than one specific activity, and these activities are usually related to each other in some fashion. It is not unusual for many of the activities associated with an objective to be highly interrelated, so that the performance of some of the activities influence or depend on the performance of other activities. Thus the order of performance of activities has a definite influence on the achievement of many objectives.

Ordering or sequencing the activities associated with a particular objective is really a matter of deciding what needs to be done when. Therefore, this phase of planning to achieve objectives involves studying the activities associated with a particular objective and determining what needs to be done first, what needs to be done next, and so on. This is not a particularly difficult thing to do, but it does require careful study of the activities involved.

When sequencing the activities associated with an objective, it is often useful to lay out a diagram of the activities. This type of diagram is called an activity network and is fairly simple to construct. It consists of numbers and arrows. The numbers represent activities and their order of performance and the arrows indicate how the activities are related sequentially. For example, the activity network in Figure V-14 indicates that activity 1 must be completed before activity 2 is started.

Figure V-15 illustrates a different type of relationship between activities. It indicates that activities 1 and 2 are unrelated and can be performed at the same time, but that both must be completed before activity 3 is started.

FIGURE V-14
Sample activity network with two related activities

FIGURE V-15
Sample activity with both related and unrelated activities

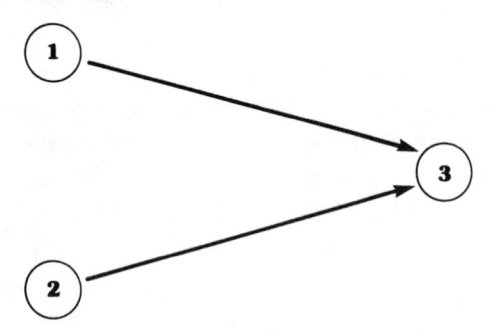

FIGURE V-16
Possible activity relationships

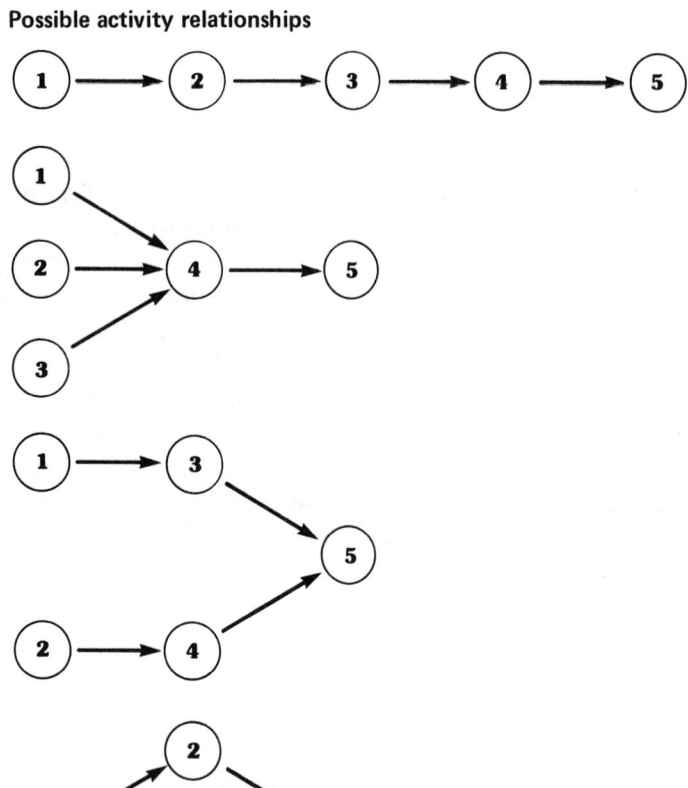

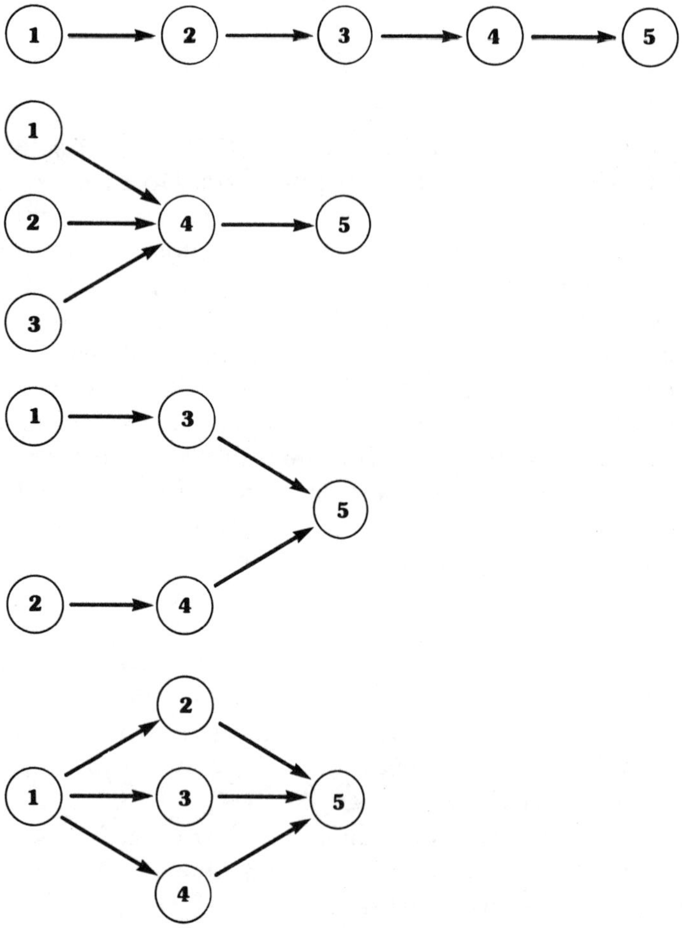

54   Basic management: An experience-based approach

Figure V-16 illustrates four possible networks for five activities. In network one, each activity must precede the next activity. In network two, activities 1, 2, and 3 can proceed together, but all must be completed before activity 4 is begun, and activity 4 must occur before activity 5 is begun. In network three, activities 1 and 2 and activities 3 and 4 can take place simultaneously, but activity 1 must precede activity 3 and activity 2 must precede activity 4. In turn, activities 3 and 4 must be completed before activity 5 is began. In network four, activity 1 must precede activities 2, 3, and 4 and these must precede activity 5. These four sample networks illustrate the majority of relationships which exist between the activities associated with most objectives.

It is important to understand that the activity network itself does not determine the order of performance of activities. It is merely a helpful way of showing how activities are related in their performance. For objectives with more than two or three activities, it may be helpful to draw an activity network for the objective. These activity networks make it easier to time the activities associated with an objective and then to integrate the activities for all objectives into a master plan.

Timing activities

Closely related to the sequencing of activities is the actual timing of activities. Once the order of performance of the activities associated with an objective has been determined, the next logical step is to place time frames on the activities. This is really a matter of deciding how long an activity will take and therefore when it should be started and completed.

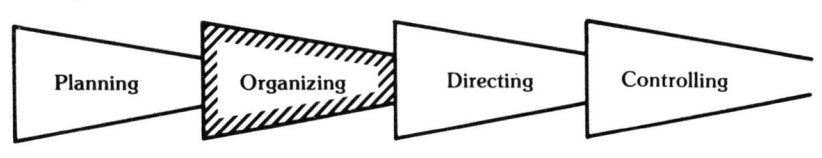

FIGURE V-17
Timing activities

Planning — Organizing — Directing — Controlling

One way to approach this task is to work backward from the objective with the activity network. Since the objective has a time frame, all activities required for its achievement must be completed in the time alloted for the achievement of the objective. Using this approach, a manager simply determines how long the last activity in the network will take and sets a starting date for the activity accordingly. As in Figure V-18, if

FIGURE V-18
Activity network with time frames

Objective: 1 percent defective units
Activities:

		Dec. 15 start	Jan. 1 start	Feb. 1 start
1.	Study to see where training is needed			
2.	Develop training programs			
3.	Train employees			
		Dec. 31 complete	Jan. 31 complete	March 1 complete

the objective is to be achieved by March 1 and the last activity will take a month to complete, then it must be started on or before February 1. In this manner, starting and ending dates for each activity in each network for each objective can be determined.

The timing of activities should be done carefully. The future can hardly ever be predicted with certainty and often activities take either more or less time than that alloted for them. One way of dealing with this uncertainty is to build some reasonable amount of slack into the time frame. This can be done by considering the practical maximum and minimum times that activities could require and then setting frames based on realistic estimates.

Integrating plans

A plan is composed of an objective and a set of timed activities that will achieve the objective. Therefore, managers have a plan for each of their objectives. The last step, indicated in Figure V-19 in the planning process, is the integration of all of the plans into an overall master plan. If the previous steps in the planning process have done well, this is not a difficult task. It is a matter of checking each of the plans against the others to determine if the plans themselves or any of their activities are interrelated.

FIGURE V-19
End point of planning process

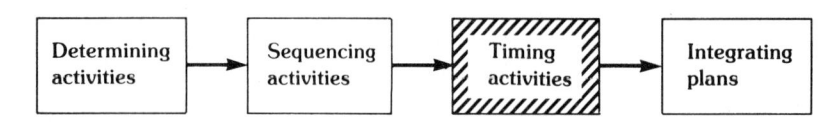

Determining activities → Sequencing activities → Timing activities → Integrating plans

As a final step in planning, it is often useful to develop a master time schedule showing all of the major activities and their beginning and ending times. This master schedule and the more detailed schedules like those in Figure V-18 then become a "roadmap" of activity to guide the manager in day-to-day activities and to check progress toward objectives.

Special purpose plans

Most managers are aware that their managerial job includes both routine everyday performance and the occasional performance of one-time special projects. The above discussion of planning has focused on planning for routine job performance, because this is the type of planning that supervisors spend the greatest amount of time on. One-time special projects also have to be planned, however, and the approach described above is applicable to this type of planning as well. The basic approach in either case is the same. The difference with planning special projects is that they are harder to plan because there is usually less information available and little direct experience with the project. If anything, this only makes the approach more valuable for planning special projects.

The basic planning process and the approach described above are equally applicable to all managerial levels of all organizations. The nature of the activities, their scope and breadth, and their importance vary, but the process is the same everywhere. With this in mind the next section focuses on some of the more important practical considerations in using this approach.

PLANNING IN PRACTICE

We believe that almost all managers can understand and learn to use the above concepts to increase their planning skills and effectiveness. In this last major section of the chapter, two of the more important practical considerations in planning and in the use of this approach are discussed.

Planning constraints

Any discussion of managerial planning would be incomplete unless some attention was devoted to the constraints or limits within which planning takes place. There are always limits within which managers have to plan. Certainly there are few managers at any level not subject to financial and legal constraints. Even top level executives must plan within the limits that owners, society, government, and the physical environment place on them.

Certainly no manager has complete planning freedom. All managers must plan within the general boundaries imposed on all managers. In addition to these constraints, however, most managers must operate within guidelines imposed by upper level managers.

One of the most important sets of constraints on management planning includes the policies, rules, and procedures established at higher levels to guide managerial action at lower levels. The achievement of most organization objectives requires that there be at least some uniformity of decision-making and action throughout the organization. To bring about the uniformity necessary, policies are established as guidelines to decision-making. They allow for uniformity with some flexibility. Procedures are established to handle particular matters and certain rules are imposed where a required course of action is necessary.

While policies, rules, and procedures are (or should be) formulated to help the organization achieve its objectives, they nevertheless may be important constraints on planning. These constraints need to be taken into consideration when a manager plans. And any future changes in the policies, rules, and procedures need to be anticipated. Thus, as was indicated above, a big part of anticipating future conditions involves trying to determine what policies, rules, and procedures will be during the period being planned for.

Last, all managers have a responsibility to the organization and to themselves to try to get changes or exceptions made to those policies, rules, and procedures that actually get in the way of doing their job. After all, the purpose of organizational policies, rules, and procedures is to help managers do their job of achieving organizational objectives.

Some suggestions about the use of this planning approach

We are aware that this discussion has not answered all of the questions a manager might have about this approach to planning. Questions such as: *Where do I start? What part does my boss play?* etc. are still unanswered. We could never answer all of these questions, but we will make some brief comments.

Certainly, the place to start is with a good understanding of the planning process. Second, no manager should attempt to use the approach who does not believe in the approach enough to at least experiment with it. If you really don't believe it will work, then it probably won't. Third, before going very far, you should fully inform your boss and seek the boss' help. Much of the rest depends on learning from actual experience.

One point deserves to be emphasized. The real skill of planning is developed slowly through planning on the job. Mistakes will be made and not everything will work out as "rosy" as the discussion implies, but experience is still one of the better teachers of skill. The manager who uses the concepts described to become a more skillful planner is highly likely to be the one who learns from *both* failures and successes. Learning from experience requires conscious reflection on the experience. This is simply an application of the learning model described in the introduction.

SUMMARY

Planning is a universal management function. The basic process of planning is the same at all levels in all types of organizations. Planning is an important part of management because it determines what performance is attempted. Only through planning can a manager attempt to limit and influence the uncertainty of the future.

Planning is basically a two-part process of setting objectives and planning to achieve objectives. One useful approach to setting managerial performance objectives is to assess present performance, anticipate future conditions, and then set performance objectives.

Planning to achieve objectives involves determining the activities necessary for achievement of objectives, sequencing and timing these activities, and integrating all objective plans into an overall performance plan.

PREWORK QUESTIONS

PLANNING

Based on the reading "Planning," select the best and most complete answer for the following questions. Select only one answer even though others are not wrong. If you are unsure of your choice it is better to leave it blank. Once you have completed the questions transfer your individual answers to the Prework Answer Sheet (p. 64) under the column marked *Individual answers*.

Individual answers   *Team answers*

1. Performance areas:
   a. Should be established mainly from job descriptions.
   b. Should be fairly broad in scope.
   c. Are identifiable output needed to achieve organizational objectives.
   d. Are impossible to develop in some supervisory jobs.

2. Performance standards:
   a. Should be established before performance can be measured.
   b. Are the "yardsticks" by which performance can be measured.
   c. Should be established for most performance areas.
   d. Are more or less the same thing as objectives.

3. Good performance objectives:
   a. Are only specific points on a performance standard.
   b. Cannot be set unless performance areas and standards are well-defined.
   c. Should call for levels of performance that are challenging.
   d. Are always stated in numbers.

4. Planning is important because:
   a. It focuses on objectives.
   b. It deals with future uncertainties.
   c. It influences what is achieved.
   d. It helps prevent "fire-fighting."

5. In the planning process:
   a. Managers decide what they should achieve and how it will be achieved.
   b. The very first step is to set objectives.
   c. Setting good objectives is the most important thing.
   d. Most of the real work is "thinking" type work.

6. The objective setting process:
   a. Is really a way of deciding what a job should contribute to the organization.
   b. Focuses on what has been achieved in the past.
   c. Focuses on managerial behavior.
   d. Differs from job to job.

7. Planning to achieve objectives is:
   a. Relatively easy if good objectives have been set.
   b. Really a matter of getting everyone to do their job.
   c. Mostly developing activity networks.
   d. Basically a matter of determining what needs to be done to achieve objectives.

8. When determining the activities necessary to achieve an objective:
   a. It is better to develop general activities in order to leave the plan flexible.
   b. It is usually better to assume that future conditions will be very similar to the past and present.
   c. Managers should pick activities in light of their effect on the achievement of the objectives.
   d. Managers should modify the objectives to fit the activities.

9. In sequencing the activities associated with an objective:
   a. The main consideration is how the activities are related to each other.
   b. The idea is to spread the work out so there are few idle periods and few busy periods.
   c. It is important to place emphasis on the major activities rather than the minor ones.
   d. Managers should always start with what needs to be done first and work forward.

10. Activity networks:
    a. Reveal what needs to be done when.
    b. Should not be used if the activities are complicated.
    c. Are really control charts rather than planning aids.
    d. Are ways of sorting out and keeping track of what needs to be done when.

SESSION INTRODUCTION

This session will focus on creating an understanding of the planning function by drawing on the planning experience, the text material and a lecture.

SESSION OVERVIEW

Step 1: Teamwork on prework (25 min.).
Step 2: Scoring individual and team answers, and comparing these team effectiveness scores (10 min.).
Step 3: Increasing team effectiveness (30 min.).
Step 4: Lecture and discussion (20-40 min.).
Step 5: Self-evaluation and individual learnings.

Step 1: Teamwork on prework (25 min.)

As prework you answered a 10-item multiple-choice test on "planning." Each team is to identify the single best answer for each question. The text material is *not* to be used during the discussion but you may use your prework answers. Team answers are to be recorded on the Prework Answer Sheet (p. 64) under the column "Team answers."

You will have 25 minutes to arrive at team answers through discussion and analysis. At that time the individual and team answers will be scored to determine how effectively each team operated. The scoring system reflects the degree of commitment to team answers. Each correct answer receives 10 points. Items unanswered are worth 0 points. An incorrect answer results in -10 points. Thus, the score is calculated by taking the number correct, subtracting the number incorrect and multiplying by 10.

This step should be completed by _____ .

Step 2: Scoring individual and team answers, and comparing these team effectiveness scores (10 min.)

Using the Prework Answer Sheet, score your individual and team answers based on the correct responses distributed to you. A simple procedure to follow is to record the correct answers in the column *Correct answers*. Where the given and correct answers match, put +10 in the *Points* column. Where no answer is given, record 0 points and where the given and correct answers do not match, put -10 in the *Points* column. By totaling the points, the individual and team score can be determined.

Individuals and teams can be compared, based on their scores. However, individuals come to teams with varying degrees of preparation and knowledge. As a result the final score may not reflect how information was shared and how decisions were made during the team discussion. To take this into account, a Team Effectiveness score can be determined.

At least one team member should complete the Team Effectiveness Score Sheet (p. 65), according to the following steps:

a. Determine the average individual score by adding the individual scores and dividing by the number of team members.
b. Subtract the average individual score from the team score to determine a gain or loss. A positive number indicates the team arrived at a higher score than the average of what individuals arrived at working separately. A loss, or negative number, indi-

cates that team discussion and agreement resulted in a lower score than the individuals did working alone.

c. Determine the possible improvement by subtracting the average individual score from the perfect score of 100. This number represents how many points of improvement were possible through team discussion and agreement.

d. Determine team effectiveness by dividing the gain (+) or loss (−) by the possible improvement and multiplying by 100. Once all teams have completed the scoring, the average individual, team, and team effectiveness scores will be collected and posted.

Step 3: Increasing team effectiveness (30 min.)

A. Individual work.

To get maximum learning from our experience we must review our experiences and draw conclusions from them. To prepare for a team discussion allocate 100 percent among the five statements under each major concept that describes how you assess the team's work on the 10-item multiple-choice test on planning.

Individual answers / *Team answers*

1. Communication:
   a. Members expressed their ideas but did not stand up for them.
   b. Members presented their ideas and also kept the discussion polite and friendly.
   c. Members expressed different ideas but were willing to compromise in order to complete the task.
   d. Members presented their views and would not change their minds.
   e. Discussion was aimed at getting the best answer, ideas were expressed openly, and differences of opinion were resolved through discussion and understanding.

2. Planning:
   a. Discussion was adequately planned before it began.
   b. Specific objectives were set for the discussion.
   c. Discussion followed the plan set forth.
   d. The objectives set for the discussion were reached.
   e. Better planning would have improved the discussion.

B. Teamwork.

The responses to the above questions are to be discussed to achieve team agreement that represents how the team operates. Discuss and examine the reasons for variations in percentage allocation. Examining the reasons and giving examples of behavior can serve as the basis for team-wide understanding and agreement. Avoid averaging answers to get the team response.

Step 4: Lecture and discussion (20–40 min.)

Step 5: Self-evaluation and individual learnings

Spend some "alone" time and think about what occurred during the last experience. Focus in on two or three things that affected you or that seemed significant to you. These may be positive or negative elements of the experience. What learnings can you draw from this reflection and what does this mean to you? Don't be concerned about what you ought to have learned, but rather focus on what you did learn and what it means to you. Based on your reflection of the experience, jot down your responses to the following questions:

1. What were your major learnings from the experience?

2. What implications do your learnings have for you as an individual?

3. What implications do your learnings have for you as a manager?

4. What questions do you have as a result of your experience, reflection, and learnings?

5. What implications will your your learnings have on your future experiences?

PREWORK ANSWER SHEET

Questions	Individual answer	Individual points*	Correct	Team points*	Team answer
1					
2					
3					
4					
5					
6					
7					
8					
9					
10					
	Individual score	_____	Team score	_____	

*Blanks—(no answer given)—receive 0 points; where correct and given answers match +10 points; where correct answer and given answers do not match −10 points.

TEAM EFFECTIVENESS SCORE SHEET

Individual scores

1. _____
2. _____
3. _____
4. _____
5. _____
6. _____
7. _____
8.

Average individual score

(A) (　　　) ÷ (　　　) =
Total individual scores   No. members

Team score
Less average individual score

(B)　　　　　　　　　　(C)　　Perfect score 100
　　　　　　　　　Less average individual score

Team effectiveness

(D) (　　　) ÷ (　　　) = (　　　) × 100 = 　　%
Gain (+) or loss (−)   Possible improvement

Block VI

Planning experience—Planning and constructing a microwave tower

GOALS

1. Gain practical skills in planning.
2. Explore individual and group objective setting and its impact on outcomes.
3. Increase awareness of the value of effective planning and its impact on task completion.

PREWORK ASSIGNMENT

None.

SESSION INTRODUCTION

Planning involves determining where you are now, establishing where you would like to be, and determining how to get there. It entails establishing objectives and developing a plan to accomplish the objectives. During this next exercise you will have the opportunity to engage in the objective setting process as an individual and as a member of a group, determine how to accomplish the objective, and perform the tasks for which you have set an objective.

SESSION OVERVIEW

Step 1: Individual objective setting and tower assembly (15 min.).
Step 2: Team objective setting and tower assembly (20 min.).
Step 3: Posting the results of the planning and assembling (5 min.).
Step 4: Reviewing the experience (25 min.).
Step 5: Cross-team exchange and discussion (15 min.).
Step 6: Self-evaluation and individual learnings.

Step 1: Individual objective setting and tower assembly (15 min.)

During this experience you will set an objective on how high you believe that you can construct a microwave tower out of the assembly panels contained at the end of this book. To gain some skills in planning and assembling the microwave tower you will operate as an individual for the next two rounds of objective setting and tower construction. You will be operating as a member of a team in the last part of the activity.

Punch out the 27 assembly panels provided at the end of the book and practice joining them for purposes of building a tower. Spend about three minutes doing this.

Round 1. Silently estimate the height of the microwave tower that you believe you can assemble with the panels during a 3-minute period. Cut the provided string to the length which represents your height goal. When you have established the goal, lay the string on the table in front of you.

(The instructor tells the participants to begin and calls time after 3 minutes.)

Determine whether you over- or under-estimated your ability by comparing the length of your string to the height of the tower you constructed.

Disassemble your tower and prepare for another round of objective setting and microwave tower assembly.

Round 2. During this round you will determine an assembly height goal for the microwave tower and announce it and compare it to the goals set by your team members. The winner of the round will be the person who has the highest goal *and* completes the microwave tower successfully during a 3-minute period. To repeat, the winner will be the person who both sets the highest goal *and* builds the tower that high. The tower must stand on its own with no outside support.

Determine your goal and cut off a length of string which represents your tower height goal. When all the team members have cut their piece of string, compare your goal with the other team members' goals.

(The instructor tells the participants to begin and calls time after 3 minutes.)

Each team table is to determine who set the highest goal and accomplished it. That person is the winner.

Disassemble your towers and prepare for another round of objective setting and microwave tower assembly.

Step 2: Team objective setting and tower assembly (20 min.)

The previous activities were primarily to gain skills in planning and assembling the tower as an individual. The next activity will be to work with your team members in planning and assembling the microwave tower. To put focus on the goal setting and planning to achieve the goal, certain rules must be followed:

1. Only 20 minutes may be used for both planning, and assembling.
2. During the planning stage the team members may talk with one another.
3. At the end of the planning stage notify the observer of your height goal.
4. During the assembly stage you may *not* talk with one another.

The team which sets the *highest* goal *and* builds their tower that high successfully during the 20-minute period will be considered the winner. At the end of the planning and assembly time, the tower *must* stand on its own with no outside support, i.e., you cannot use your hands, string, chairs, etc. to support it. It is important to remember to tell the observer your tower goal when you complete the planning phase. And after that point there may be no talking among team members.

(The instructor tells the participants to begin and calls time after 20 minutes.)

Step 3: Posting the results of planning and assembling (5 min.)

The observer collects the goals from each of the teams and announces which team set the highest goal *and* accomplished it.

Step 4: Reviewing the experience (25 min.)

    A. Individual work.

To get maximum learning from our experience we must review our experiences and draw conclusions from them. To prepare for a team discussion, complete the following questions or statements as an individual during the next few minutes. Allow all team members to finish before moving to the teamwork.

1. During the first part of the experience you operated as an individual in setting an objective for and building the tower.

    a. What impact did the objective have on your performance?

    b. What does your learning in this part of the experience say about objective setting and the planning process?

2. During the latter part of the experience you operated with your team to set an objective for and build the tower. Answer the following based on that part of the experience.

    a. I thought the objective was:

1	2	3	4	5	6	7	8	9
Much too low								Much too high

    b. I thought the planning to achieve the objective was:

1	2	3	4	5	6	7	8	9
Completely ineffective								Extremely effective

    c. Before you started assembling the tower, how clear was your understanding of what you were to contribute?

1	2	3	4	5	6	7	8	9
Completely unclear								Extremely clear

VI/Planning experience—Planning and constructing a microwave tower

d. My commitment to reach the goal was:

| 1 | 2 | 3 | 4 | 5 | 6 | 7 | 8 | 9 |

Extremely   Extremely
weak   strong

e. How can you use what you learned in this part of the experience in the real world?

3. Think about what occurred during the last experience on planning. Focus in on two or three things that affected you or that seemed significant to you. These may be positive or negative elements of the experience. What learnings can you draw from this reflection and what does this mean to you? Don't be concerned about what you ought to have learned but rather focus on what you did learn and what it means to you.

B. Teamwork.

As a team discuss and complete the following items. The best learning will occur if all team members will share their ideas and feelings in the discussion.

1. Discuss the individual responses to the above questions.
2. a. The team is to discuss and come to a team-wide understanding and agreement on two things they learned.
   b. Select a spokesperson to present the team's learnings in the next step.

Step 5: **Cross-team exchange and discussion** (15 min.)

Each team makes a report to the other teams and open discussion follows.

Step 6: **Self-evaluation and individual learnings**

Spend some "alone" time and think about what occurred during the last experience. Focus in on two or three things that affected you or that seemed significant to you. These may be positive or negative elements of the experience. What learnings can you draw from this reflection and what does this mean to you? Don't be concerned about what you ought to have learned, but rather focus on what you did learn and what it means to you. Based on your reflection of the experience, jot down your responses to the following questions:

1. What were your major learnings from the experience?

2. What implications do your learnings have for you as an individual?

3. What implications do your learnings have for you as a manager?

4. What questions do you have as a result of your experience, reflection, and learnings?

5. What implications will your learnings have on your future experiences?

Block VII

Production organization simulation—Shipping containers

GOALS

1. Experience the organizing function by creating a production organization.
2. Assess variables that influence organizational effectiveness.

PREWORK ASSIGNMENT

None.

SESSION INTRODUCTION

Organizations are activity-authority structures utilized to coordinate groups of people toward the accomplishment of the goals established in the planning process. This experience will give you the opportunity to create and later operate a production-centered organization.

SESSION OVERVIEW

Step 1: Organizing for production (50 min.).
Step 2: Reviewing and assessing the organizing activity (20 min.).
Step 3: Report to the organization (10 min.).
Step 4: Understanding of organization position (5 min.).
Step 5: Self-evaluation and individual learnings.

Step 1: Organizing for production (50 min.)

Your group (10–28 members) will create and operate a business organization which will manufacture four types of shipping containers. The positions in the organization are to be filled by the members of the group. Be sure your organization can meet emergencies and shifting market demands, since these will be introduced into the exercise.

This exercise is focused primarily on problems of manufacturing productivity. Consequently, you do not need to be concerned about problems of capital, retained earnings, balance sheets, budget controls, purchasing, pay scales, etc. You will be told what market conditions exist at the time your plant begins operating (8:00 a.m. today).

The products are shipping containers (square top, square bottom, sets—top and bottom put together, oval) manufactured out of sheets of paper. Instructions for manufacturing the shipping containers are provided later in this section and the materials are at the end of the book. You will need to work out some way of making sure that the specifications are met, and that data are gathered on (1) total volume of output, (2) proper product mix (i.e., meeting the market demand for certain kinds of containers), and (3) number not marketable. Be sure that your records are set up to keep these data current. In determining volume and product mix figures, you can count only finished products in inventory at the end of any production period. Goods in process are not to be counted. Thus, you will need a place to store finished inventory.

The goal of the organization is to maximize gross profits. Each marketable shipping container has the following price, cost, and margin:

	Price		Costs		Margin
Square top	$10	−	$ 6	=	$4
Square bottom	9	−	5	=	4
Sets	18	−	10	=	8
Oval	8	−	5	=	3

Any containers left over in inventory at the end of each production period suffer a carrying cost penalty of $2. Rejects cost the organization $4. Thus, gross profit is determined as follows:

Gross Profit Statement

Gross sales:
    Number of marketable shipping containers
        Square top .... × $10 =
        Square bottom .... × $ 9 =
        Sets .... × $18 =
        Oval .... × $ 8 =
        Total sales .... =(a)

Costs:
    Number of marketable shipping containers
        Square top .... × $ 6 =
        Square bottom .... × $ 5 =
        Sets .... × $10 =
        Oval .... × $ 5 =
        Total .... =(b)

Total number of items carried over in inventory
    ——— × $ 2 = (c)

Total number of rejects
    ——— × $ 4 = (d)

Total costs (b+c+d) .... = (e)
Gross profit (a−e) ....

You will not need a sales force, but you will need some person to get market requirements from Brasan Brokerage Co. An example of market requirements is as follows:

8:00 a.m. Bulletin—The Brasan Brokerage Co. buys all the containers manufactured by your company. Between 8:00 a.m. and 8:15 a.m. we will purchase any number of containers in the following percentages:

- 10% Square tops
- 30% Square bottoms
- 40% Sets—top and bottom put together
- 20% Oval

You have 50 minutes from the time you begin organizing to complete this step. You may go about the task in any fashion. During this step there is no need to go into production but you may wish to have a test run to see how the organization is running.

In summary, create an organization that will:

1. Produce a large volume of shipping containers that meet specifications and are of the types required to meet market demand.
2. Maintain flexibility needed to deal with changes in market demand.
3. Try to be creative in designing the organization.

You have 50 minutes to get organized for production. At the end of that time the organizing experience will be reviewed for learnings and recommended changes. *In a later session*, you will have 15 minutes to make changes and prepare for production. Your organization will then have two 15-minute production periods back-to-back.

The instructions for manufacturing the shipping containers are at the end of this block. Six pages of practice material are at the end of this book.

This step should be completed by _____ . At that time begin Step 2.

Step 2: Reviewing and assessing the organizing activity (20 min.)

To extract the learnings from the previous activity, return to your original teams and complete the following individual and team work.

This step should be completed by _____ .

A. Individual work.

To get maximum learning from our experience we must review our experiences and draw conclusions from them. To prepare for team discussion, complete the following questions and statements during the next few minutes. Allow all team members to finish and then complete the items under *Teamwork*.

1. How clear is it to you "who reports to whom for what?"

1	2	3	4	5	6	7	8	9

   Completely unclear   Completely clear

2. How well do you understand what you are responsible for doing?

1	2	3	4	5	6	7	8	9

   No understanding   Fully understand

3. How effective do you think the organization will be in coordinating the activities to be performed during production?

```
1    2    3    4    5    6    7    8    9
```

Fully ineffective   Fully effective

4. How committed are you to helping this organization work effectively?

```
1    2    3    4    5    6    7    8    9
```

Low commitment   High commitment

5. In your opinion, what is the strongest aspect of the organization plan?

6. In your opinion what is the weakest aspect of the organization plan?

7. What changes in the organization would you recommend in order to make it more effective?

8. Think about what occurred during the last experience on organizing. Focus in on two or three things that affected you or that seemed significant to you. These may be positive or negative elements of the experience. What learnings can you draw from this reflection and what does this mean to you? Don't be concerned about what you ought to have learned, but rather focus on what you did learn and what it means to you.

B. Teamwork.

As a team, complete the following items. The best learning will occur if all team members will share their ideas and feelings in the discussion.

1. Discuss the individual responses to questions 1–8. Explore reasons why people responded as they did.

2. Prepare a brief report to be given to the other teams in your organization that includes the following:

   a. A statement of the strongest aspect of the organization.
   b. A statement of the weakest aspect of the organization.
   c. Any recommended changes the team agrees on.

3. Select a spokesperson to present the brief report during the next step of the activity.

Step 3: Report to the organization   (10 min.)

Each team makes a brief report to the other teams and open discussion follows.

Step 4: Understanding of organization position   (5 min.)

Several sessions from now, your organization will have 15 minutes to make changes and prepare for the two production periods. It is important that you remember your current positions and responsibilities.

To refresh your memory in the later session, answer the following questions based on your current understanding:

1. What are you responsible for doing in the organization?

2. To whom do you report?

3. Who reports to you?

Step 5: Self-evaluation and individual learnings

Spend some "alone" time and think about what occurred during the last experience. Focus in on two or three things that affected you or that seemed significant to you. These may be positive or negative elements of the experience. What learnings can you draw from this reflection and what does this mean to you? Don't be concerned about what you ought to have learned, but rather focus on what you did learn and what it means to you. Based on your reflection of the experience, jot down your responses to the following questions:

1. What were your major learnings from the experience?

2. What implications do your learnings have for you as an individual?

3. What implications do your learnings have for you as a manager?

4. What questions do you have as a result of your experience, reflection, and learnings?

5. What implications will your learnings have on your future experiences?

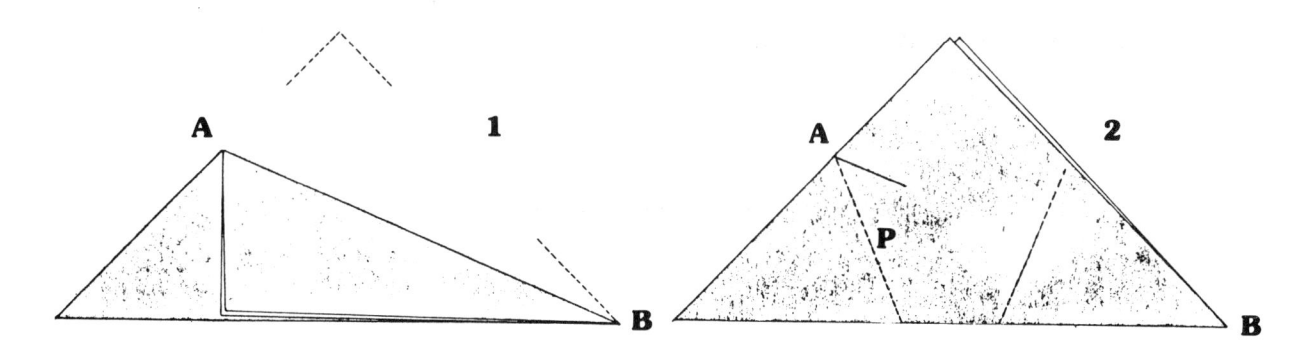

OVAL SHIPPING CONTAINER

1. Establish point A by bringing the top point down so that it forms a perpendicular with the base of the triangle. Return the model to its original shape.
2. Join points A and B to make a valley fold on the dotted line on the right. Turn the model over, and repeat the fold to make a peak fold on the dotted line on the left.
3. Tuck the upper layer only of the top point into the pocket formed on that side.
4. Turn the model over, and tuck the remaining layer into the pocket on that side.
5. The completed oval shipping container.

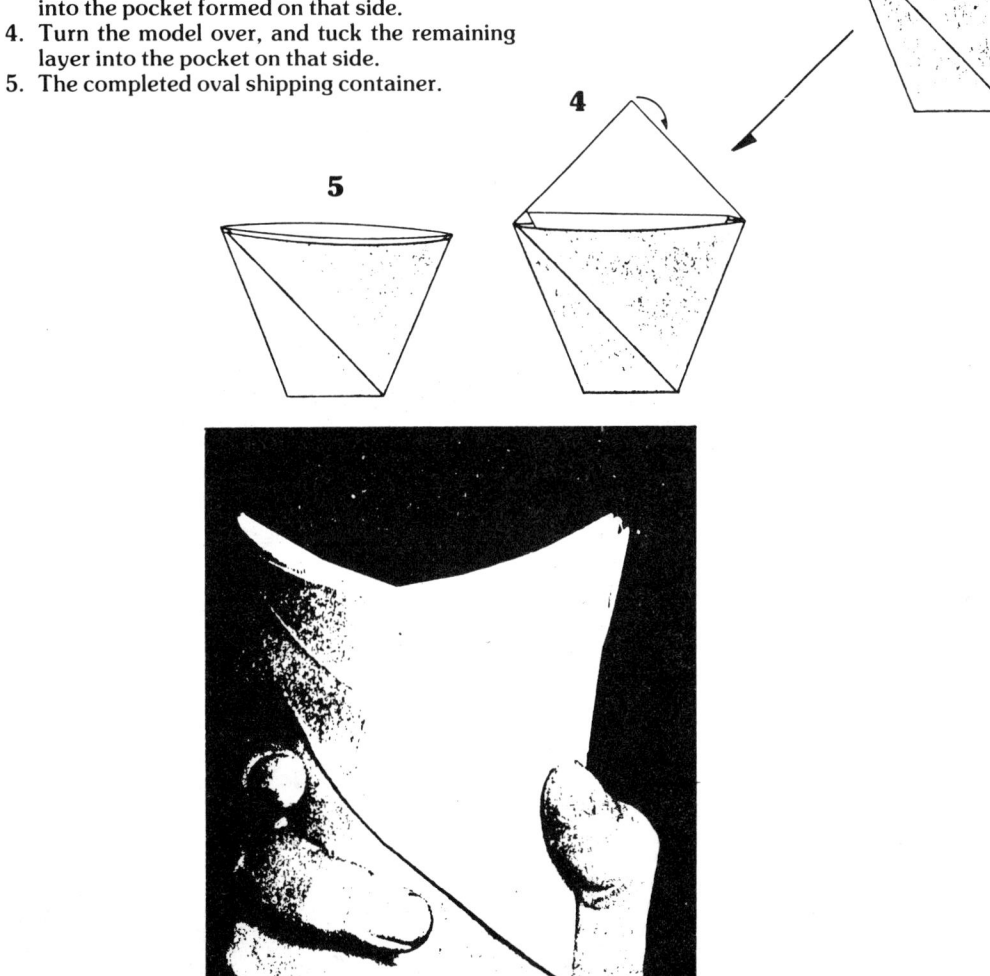

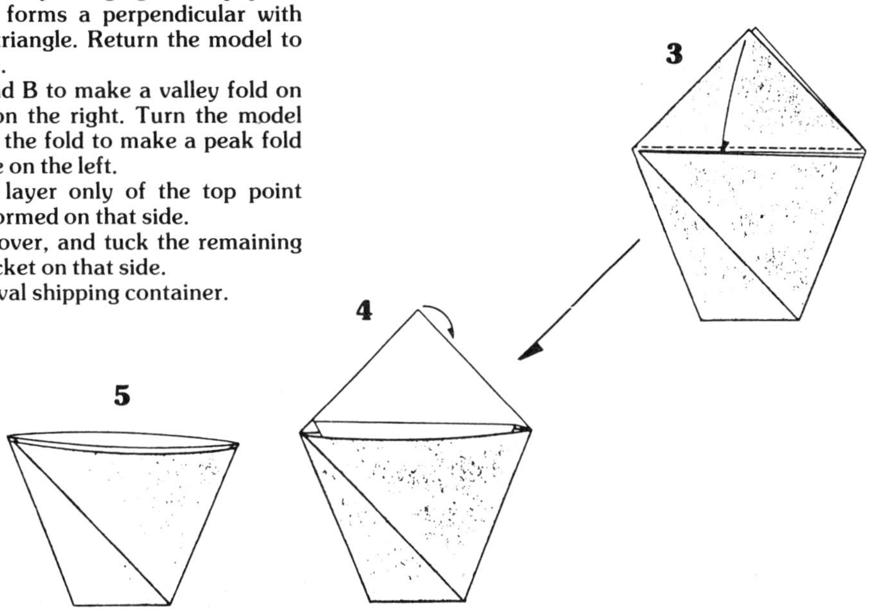

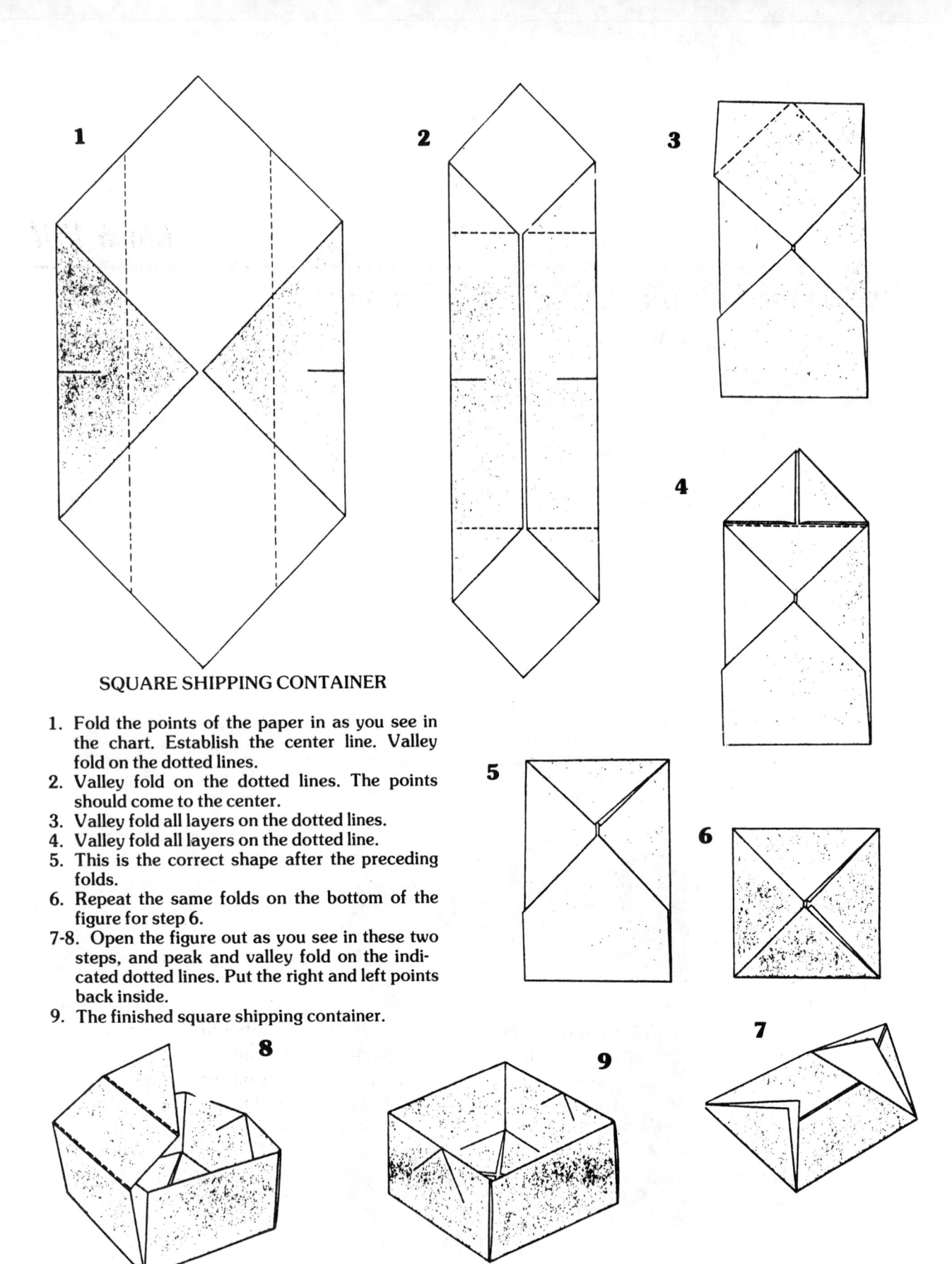

SQUARE SHIPPING CONTAINER

1. Fold the points of the paper in as you see in the chart. Establish the center line. Valley fold on the dotted lines.
2. Valley fold on the dotted lines. The points should come to the center.
3. Valley fold all layers on the dotted lines.
4. Valley fold all layers on the dotted line.
5. This is the correct shape after the preceding folds.
6. Repeat the same folds on the bottom of the figure for step 6.
7-8. Open the figure out as you see in these two steps, and peak and valley fold on the indicated dotted lines. Put the right and left points back inside.
9. The finished square shipping container.

Block VIII

Understanding the organizing function

GOAL

Create an understanding of the organizing function.

PREWORK ASSIGNMENT

Read the following material on "Organizing" for understanding. Answer the ten prework questions at the end of the material.

ORGANIZING

> *Organization design and structure require thinking, analysis, and a systematic approach.*[1]

Organizing is the second function in the performance of the management process. Planning provides a sort of roadmap for performance—a statement of the objectives to be achieved and the activities necessary for achievement of the objectives. The organizing function starts with and builds upon the performance of the planning function to develop an organization structure.

The efficient achievement of almost all organizational objectives requires not only that activities be performed, but that the performance of the activities be coordinated. The organizing function is an attempt to develop a means or tool—an organization structure—to promote the coordinated performance of activities by subordinates. Organizing is a link connecting planning and the means for accomplishing the ideas.

As is the case with planning, organizing is a universal function performed by all managers at all levels. The specifics involved in organizing vary, but the basic process is the same everywhere and the basic concepts are applicable to all management jobs.

The purpose of this reading is to help you understand the organizing function and improve your organizing skill. The information is divided into the following four major sections:

---
[1] Peter Drucker, "New Templates for Today's Organizations," *Harvard Business Review*, vol. 52 (January–February 1974), p. 52.

The nature of organizing.
Basic concepts of organizing.
Grouping activities.
Delegating authority.

THE NATURE OF ORGANIZING

As a managerial function, organizing involves developing a system which helps people cooperate and coordinate their efforts in the performance of activities. The organization structure is a tool for helping coordinate activities.

What organizing really is

Stated quite simply, organizing and the development of an organization structure involve deciding *who* is going to do *what*, and *how* people and activities are going to be related. Thus, organizing involves grouping activities into jobs and establishing superior-subordinate relationships through task assignments and authority delegation. Good organizing results in an organization structure where everyone knows what their job is, to whom they are responsible, and how their job relates to other jobs in the organization.

The importance of organizing

The achievement of most managerial and organizational objectives requires teamwork, and as the quotation at the beginning points out, teamwork is impossible without organization. The importance of the organizing function can be seen clearly in a simple story from Sesame Street,[2] a children's educational television program. The story begins when the King decides that he and all of his subjects will have a picnic. The King calls his subjects together, announces the picnic, and tells them to bring watermelon, potato salad, etc. The subjects leave to prepare the food. On returning to the picnic it is discovered that everybody brought potato salad and nothing else. Needless to say, the King expresses his disappointment at having no watermelon. Lo, and behold! Everyone takes the potato salad home and returns with watermelon. Finally, someone suggests that they divide the task up and assign different things for different people to bring. The story closes with a successful picnic.

While the story is simple (and maybe even foolish to some), it illustrates the importance of organizing—of dividing up the total work to be done, defining everyone's duties and responsibilities, and delegating the authority necessary to perform the duties and responsibilities.

Organization is a tool for making order and system possible in the performance of activities—it makes possible cooperation and coordination. Without organization, chaos is likely because no one knows who is doing what or who is responsible for what. More specifically, without organization there is no effective way to prevent duplication of activities, nor is there any means for assuring that all necessary activities are performed.

Organizing is important from yet another viewpoint. As Figure VIII-1 indicates, organizing links the planning and doing aspects of the management process. Both direction and control are built upon organizing. It is impossible to direct or control subordinate performance in the absence of a structure which defines who is to do what.

[2]"Sesame Street" is a production of the Children's Television Workshop.

FIGURE VIII-1
Organizing place in the management process

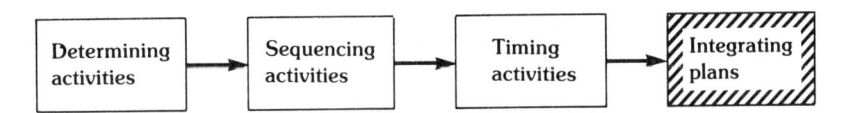

```
Determining   →   Sequencing   →   Timing       →   Integrating
activities        activities       activities       plans
```

The organizing process

The result of organizing is an organization structure—a system of activity-authority relationships. That is, an organization structure is a system of activity groupings tied together with authority. As Figure VIII-2 indicates, organizing or the development of an organization structure is essentially a two-part process consisting of grouping activities into jobs and delegating authority.

FIGURE VIII-2
The organizing process

```
Grouping      +   Delegating   =   Organization
activities        authority        structure
```

The responsibility for organizing

It may seem trite, but it is nevertheless true that all managers at all levels are responsible for organizing that part of the organization they manage. It is every manager's responsibility to create a structure which promotes cooperation and coordination.

Perhaps the nature of a manager's responsibility for organizing can best be seen by considering the entire process by which a relatively large organization is structured initially. The top level of management organizes first. Thus, top management analyzes all of the activities that have to be performed and then groups these activities into jobs. Top management might, for example, decide to group activities on the basis of the functions of production, marketing, and finance as in Figure VIII-3. Each of the three activity groupings is then assigned a position and is a managerial job.

FIGURE VIII-3
Functional grouping of activities

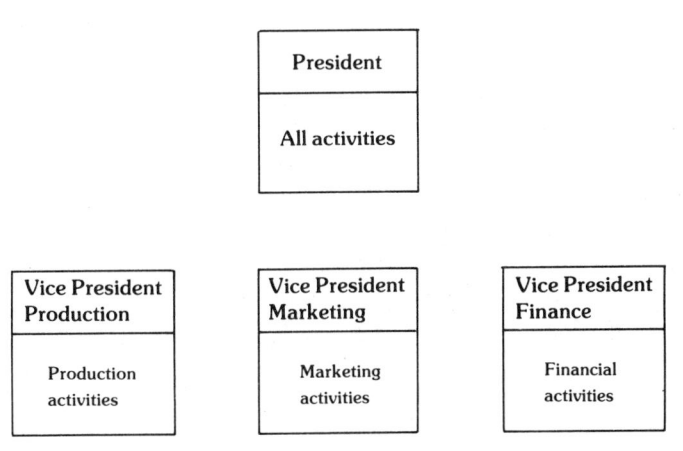

```
                    President
                    All activities

Vice President    Vice President    Vice President
Production        Marketing         Finance

Production        Marketing         Financial
activities        activities        activities
```

It is obvious that for an undertaking of any size, each of these three jobs involves many more activities than one person could ever perform. It is the responsibility of the manager holding the position to further organize the activities for which she or he is responsible. The manager of the marketing department might, for example, decide to group marketing activities into the three groups shown in Figure VIII-4. Each of these three groups would be assigned to a person for performance.

FIGURE VIII-4
Sample marketing department

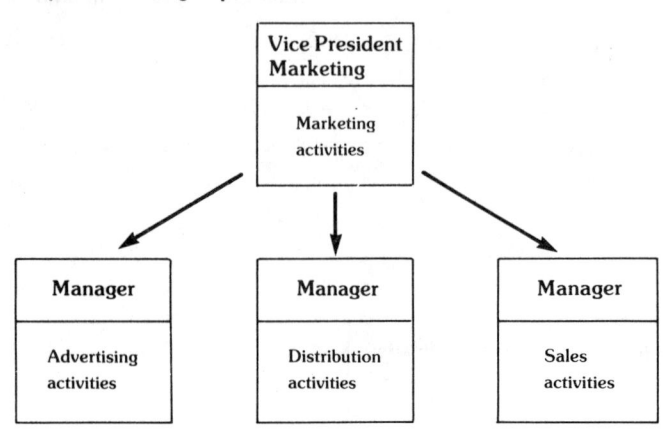

```
                    ┌──────────────┐
                    │Vice President│
                    │  Marketing   │
                    ├──────────────┤
                    │  Marketing   │
                    │  activities  │
                    └──────────────┘
           ↙               ↓               ↘
  ┌───────────┐     ┌───────────┐     ┌───────────┐
  │  Manager  │     │  Manager  │     │  Manager  │
  ├───────────┤     ├───────────┤     ├───────────┤
  │Advertising│     │Distribution│    │   Sales   │
  │ activities│     │ activities │    │ activities│
  └───────────┘     └───────────┘     └───────────┘
```

The organizing process would continue down the organization until the activity groupings are small enough to be performed by the individual to whom they are assigned. Thus, one of the final products of organizing is the creation of jobs. In this manner, the total organization is structured with managers at every level being responsible for organizing the activities and people assigned to them.

Admittedly, this is a rather simple conception of the process by which organization structures are created. Probably no managers at any level are free to organize the activities below them in any way that they choose. All managers operate within guidelines from above which limit their freedom in organizing.

Another point is that organizing is not a one-time process. It is an on-going process, not a function performed only when the organization is established initially. For most managers, organizing is more a matter of changing and reorganizing an existing structure than it is of developing a new structure for the first time. Organization structures are tools with which to implement plans to achieve particular objectives. As objectives and plans change, changes are necessary in the organization structure.

Just as all managers are responsible for planning within given guidelines, they are all responsible for organizing their area of performance. The remainder of this reading is concerned with the performance of the organizing function.

BASIC CONCEPTS OF ORGANIZING

The organizing process takes place in all organizations at all levels, and the basic process is always the same—grouping activities into some logical pattern and tying these activities together with authority relationships. Because the organizing process is universal, there are some basic concepts and principles—specialization of work, unity of command, span of supervision, and authority and responsibility that are described and explained in this section. The application of these concepts in the organizing process is the subject of the next two major sections.

Specialization of work

Perhaps one of the most basic and most widely used concepts in organizing is the economic principle of division of work and specialization. This principle and its use dates back at least to the 1700s.

Basically, the principle of *division of work* and *specialization* states that greater efficiency is achieved when work is divided so that people perform specific types of activities and jobs rather than perform many different types of activities. Thus, the principle of division of work refers to dividing work up into separate tasks so that individuals can specialize in the performance of a relatively limited set of activities.

General benefits of specialization. The general reason for using the principle of division of work and specialization is that it makes tasks that are too large or complex for one person to do, possible. Many jobs (in fact, the overall job of most organizations) are simply too big for one person to physically do. Dividing the job up among many different people makes its performance possible. Closely related to this is the fact that many jobs (again almost all of the overall "jobs" of all organizations) require more knowledge than any one person is likely to possess. Dividing the total job into parts, and according to the knowledge required to do the job, makes performance possible. In this sense, specialization allows humans to overcome their physical and mental limitations and it makes large-scale organization possible.

Specific benefits of specialization. The more specific benefits of division of work and specialization are that it makes higher levels of individual performance possible.

Both research and experience indicate that a person's level of performance on a job is determined by two things—one is the person's level of ability, and the second is the person's motivation to use that ability to do the job. Stated another way:

$$\text{Performance} = \text{Ability} \times \text{Motivation}$$

When work is divided so that a person can specialize in the performance of a limited range of activity, it has the effect of increasing ability. In the equation above, if motivation remains constant and ability is increased, then performance will increase. So division of work and specialization increase performance by increasing peoples' abilities to do the jobs required of them.

Limitations of specialization. While it is believed that the principle of division and specialization is valid, research and experience indicate that extremely high degrees of specialization may decrease, rather than increase, individuals' levels of performance. The evidence suggests that when work activities are divided into extremely small units, people tend to have difficulty relating their performance to meaningful achievement. That is, when people's jobs become highly specialized and very small in scope, they have difficulty seeing the real worth of the job. When this happens, motivation to perform the job is likely to decrease and if there is a large decrease in motivation, performance may not be as high as it otherwise would be. Whether the resulting decrease in motivation actually lowers performance or not depends on whether the decrease caused by less motivation is larger than the increase resulting from a higher level of ability.

It should be pointed out that some degree of division of work and specialization probably increases motivation to perform. Examples of this are work which is entirely too difficult for a single person to do or jobs which are beyond the scope of one person's ability, such as building a dam. It seems reasonable to conclude that some division of work and specialization of these types of jobs would tend to increase people's motivations to perform.

In light of all its effects, it seems that division of work and specialization are a necessity for large organizations to exist and perform efficiently. It also appears that better performance might result from more motivation brought about by less specialization, especially where jobs are very narrow and routine.

Application of the principle. Application of the principle of division of work actually takes place in the organizing process through the grouping of activities into positions and jobs. There is not one but several different bases for grouping activities or dividing work so that specialization results. These different types of specialization are described and explained in the section on grouping activities.

Unity of command

A second fundamental concept of organizing is the principle of *unity of command*. The principle states that coordination of organizational activities is easier when each person has only one superior. Simply stated, everyone in the organization should have only one boss.

Like the principle of division of work and specialization, unity of command is not a recently recognized principle of organization. It dates back to at least biblical times. In the New Testament of the King James version of the Bible, the book of Luke (16:13) states, "No servant can serve two masters: for either he will hate the one, and love the other; or else he will hold to the one and despise the other. . . ."

The application of the principle of unity of command is related to the division of work and specialization. While division of work makes large-scale jobs possible and promotes efficiency through specialization, it also results in some problems. It makes the coordination of organization activities difficult because the activities are divided into relatively small groups performed by different people. The activities of any group of subordinates are easier to coordinate if the subordinates have only one boss.

The reasonableness of this principle is difficult to argue. At some time or another almost everyone has either had two bosses or has tried to share authority over subordinates with another and is familiar with the usual consequences. Confusion, unhappy subordinates and superiors, lack of coordination and generally ineffective performance are not uncommon results.

The real difficulty with the application of unity of command is that it is almost impossible to apply without exception in large complex organizations. The need for consistency of action and the need for expert knowledge in many areas of decision-making cause organizations to divide authority over some things among several people. The result of this is that people have more than one boss, and it seems necessary that this be the case. In actual practice, the application of the principle of unity of command focuses on trying to assure that each person will have only one primary boss and that the authority of secondary bosses be clearly spelled out and understood by all.

The application of the unity of command principle takes place in the organizing process with the delegation of authority. Thus, the degree to which the principle is applied or violated depends on how well task assignments and authority delegations are made. The subject of delegation of authority is covered in more detail in the last section of this reading.

Span of management

Achieving coordination through application of the principle of unity of command and having only one boss for each person is limited by the fact that no one can supervise an unlimited number of people. The term *span of management* refers to the number of people a manager supervises. The concept of span of management refers to the determination of how many people a manager can supervise effectively.

Limitations of the span of management. To supervise and coordinate the activities of a large number of people, the work must be divided up among a number of people (managers) who, in turn, may themselves require a manager above them to supervise and coordinate their activities. Since any one person can supervise only a limited number of people, the effective supervision of large numbers of people and activities may require more than one level of management. Thus, the end result may be that there are managers who supervise managers who supervise workers.

Size of the span affects structure. The number of levels of management and the number of managers needed in an organization depends on the size of undertaking (and therefore the number of activities that must be supervised) and on how many people each manager at each level supervises.

For a particular organization with a given number of people, the number of levels of management and the number of managers needed depends on the span of management for each manager at each level. If broad spans of management (with each manager supervising a relatively large number of people) are used, the organization structure will have fewer levels and fewer managers than if relatively narrow spans of management are used.

Consider the example in Figure VIII-5. If there are 64 workers to be supervised and the span of management is eight at each level, then eight supervisory managers are needed and at least one manager to supervise the eight supervisors. Thus, two levels of manage-

FIGURE VIII-5
Effects of span on structure

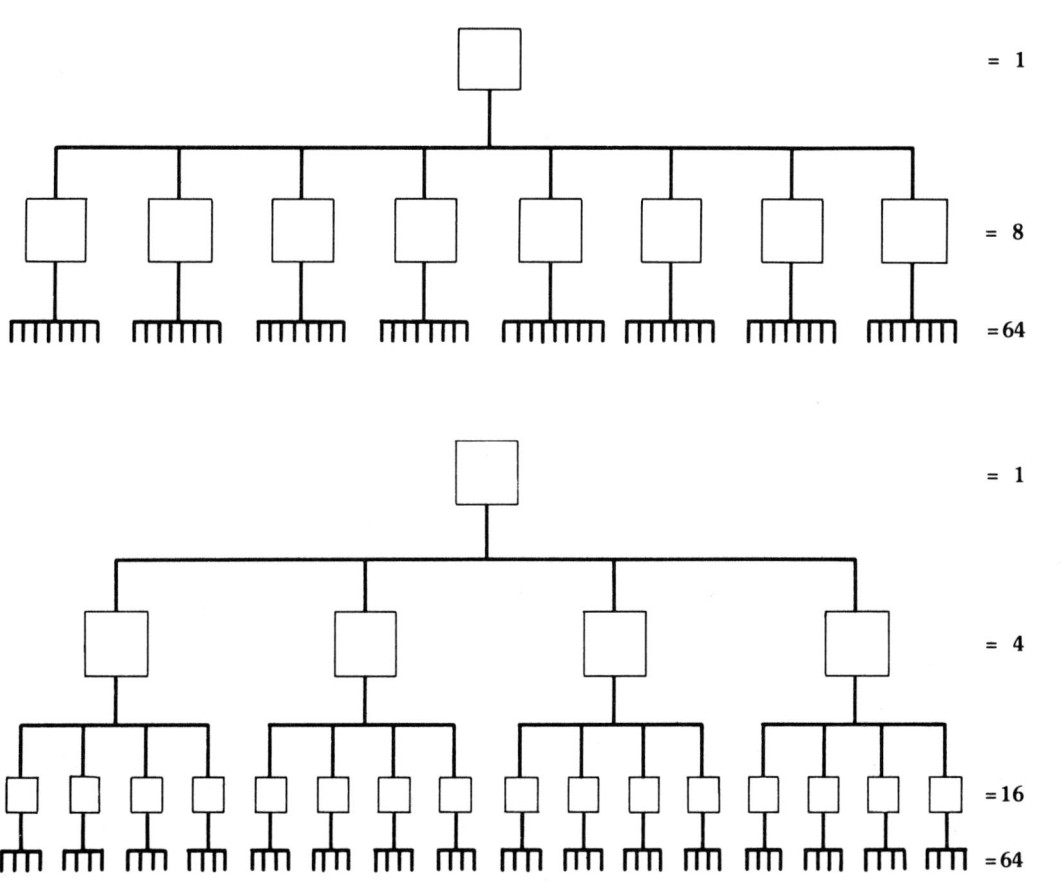

ment and nine managers are needed. In contrast, if the span is four, then three levels of management and twenty-one managers are needed—sixteen supervisors, four managers to supervise the sixteen supervisors and one top manager to supervise the four middle managers.

The number of levels of management and the number of managers have important effects on the organization's effectiveness and efficiency. If there are too few managers and levels, ineffective supervision results. On the other hand, the more levels and managers an organization has, the larger is its salary cost and the more difficult effective communication becomes. So the important question is how wide the span should be, not whether it should be relatively wide or relatively narrow.

Factors affecting the span. There are a number of factors which appear to affect the number of people that a manager can supervise effectively. Among the more important of these factors are: (1) supervisory ability, (2) subordinate ability, (3) complexity of activities supervised, (4) degree to which the activities are interrelated, (5) adequacy of performance standards, (6) amount of authority delegated, and (7) availability of staff assistance.

Certainly the number of people that managers can supervise effectively is influenced by their supervisory ability and by their energy level. Managers have different levels of knowledge and understanding of the management process. Within reasonable limits, the higher the level of supervisory ability, the greater the number of people the manager can supervise. Two important aspects of supervisory ability—performance standards and authority delegation have important effects on the span and are discussed separately below. People also have different energy levels and certainly people with relatively high energy levels can supervise a larger number of subordinates than people with lower energy levels.

The *levels of ability* of the subordinate being supervised also have important effects on the number of people a manager can supervise. The higher the level of subordinates' abilities, the more people the manager can supervise. This is true because their work will require less of the supervisor's time for orientation, instructions, and control.

A third factor affecting the size of the span is the *complexity* and *diversity* of activities supervised. The simpler the activities and the more similar subordinates' activities are, the wider the span can be. When activities are very complex and when subordinates are doing entirely different types of activities, the narrower the span needs to be for effective supervision.

The degree to which the activities of subordinates are *interrelated* also has important effects on the number of people a manager can effectively supervise. Where subordinates' jobs tend to be independent of each other, a greater number of people can be supervised. Where subordinates' jobs are interrelated and the activities of one subordinate affect the activities of other subordinates, more of the manager's time is required to coordinate activities among subordinates. Therefore, fewer people can be supervised where subordinates' jobs dovetail.

The quality and adequacy of the methods used to measure and evaluate subordinate performance are another factor influencing the span of management. The better *performance standards* are, the less time the manger has to spend in direct contact with subordinates. In contrast, if performance standards are poor, more of the manager's time is likely to be needed for direct observation of subordinate performance. So the better the standards of subordinate performance, the wider the span of management can be.

Another factor—*amount of and clarity of authority delegated*—that is related to both subordinate ability and supervisory ability has a significant effect on the number of people a manager can supervise. Generally, the more authority delegated, the wider the span can be because less of the supervisor's time will be needed in decision-making and face-to-face contact. Additionally, the more clear and precise the delegation of authority is, the wider the span can be because there is less room for doubt and less need for the subordinate to check with the supervisor. The amount of authority delegated, however, should be related to the level of ability of the subordinate, so this factor should operate within limits. The clarity and preciseness of the authority delegation depends to a great degree on the supervisor's managerial ability.

Last, the width of the span is affected by the quality and quantity of staff assistance available to the manager. Naturally a manager with good staff assistance in the form of both advice and service can supervise more people than one who must personally do everything related to the job.

Considering how each of the seven factors affects the span of management, several conclusions can be drawn. First, there are no precise rules concerning the appropriate span of management. Second, the appropriate span ultimately depends upon the specific manager, subordinates, and the work supervised. It must be determined for each manager in each situation. So deciding on the appropriate span is a subjective, situational decision.

Spans in practice. While there are and probably never will be any hard and fast rules which state how many people managers at any level can supervise effectively, experience has produced some rather rough conclusions and broad guidelines. It seems generally true that spans need to be narrower the higher the level of one's position in the organization. In practice, spans of 3-11 at the top of organizations are commonly found, while spans from 6-30 are not unusual at lower organization levels. Again, determining the span is a subjective, *situational decision.*

Authority, power, and responsibility

Application of the concepts of specialization, span of management and especially unity of command are closely related to a fourth important set of organizing concepts—authority, power, and responsibility. Limiting the number of people reporting to one person, having people perform a specialized set of tasks, and preserving unity of command is made possible through authority relationships.

Authority is the thread that ties the different groups of activities (jobs) in the organization together. An organization structure is a system of activity—authority relationships. Application of the concepts of specialization and span of management result in an activity system. Through the use of authority, power, and responsibility relationships, the different parts (job activity groupings) of the organization are related to each other and to the total organization in some fashion. The result of the application of all four concepts is a hierarchical organization illustrated in Figure VIII-6. The basic concepts of authority, power, and responsibility are defined and explained below. The application of the concepts is explained in the section on delegating later in the chapter.

Authority is a right. From a management standpoint, authority is the right that a manager has to make decisions and require subordinates to do the things necessary to accomplish the organization's goals. A manager's authority includes such rights as: (1) making decisions within the scope of authority, (2) assigning tasks to subordinates, and (3) expecting and requiring satisfactory performance from subordinates.

Authority is a managerial right delegated from above and has its legal origins in the rights of ownership of private property. In theory, the owners of property (in the case of corporations, stockholders) delegate some of their authority to a Board of Directors, who in turn delegate to top level executives, who further delegate some of their authority

FIGURE VIII-6
A hypothetical organization structure

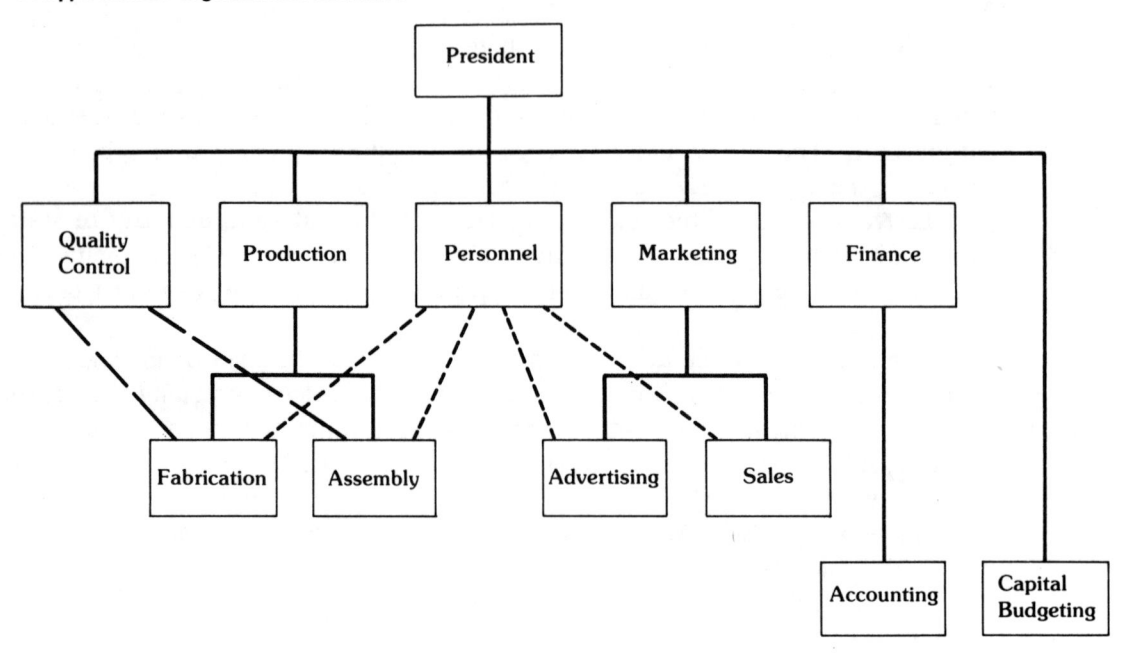

FIGURE VIII-7
Scope of authority

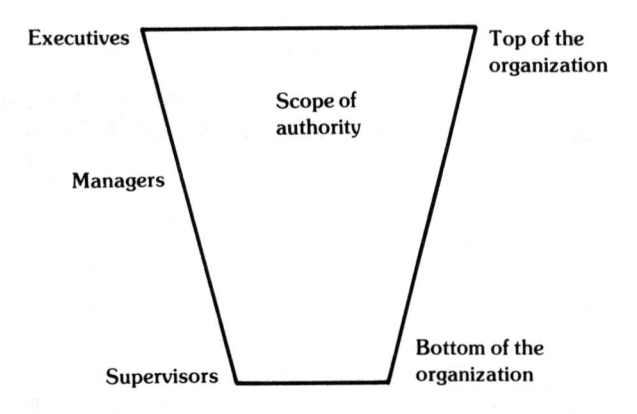

downward. Thus, as Figure VIII-7 illustrates, the scope of authority is broad at the top of the organization and it becomes narrower at lower organizational levels. This results because no one can delegate more authority than one has and because not all of the authority held by a manager is in turn delegated downward to subordinates.

Power is a force. Power and authority are closely related, but they are not the same. Authority is a right: power is a force that backs up the right. Managers may have the right to do something but may not be able to because they lack the power and influence to exercise or enforce the right. On the other hand managers may have the power to do things, but not the right. You probably have seen both these situations.

Power in organizations comes from several sources. It may come from recognized knowledge or competence, from personality, from level in the organization, and from the right to give or withhold rewards and punishments. One of the main sources of power for managers is delegated authority. Delegated authority of managers usually includes the right to provide or withhold rewards and the right to discipline subordinates. Thus, much managerial power is in the form of control or influence over things such as pay, promotions, employment termination, etc.

Responsibility is an obligation. While they are closely associated, responsibility and authority are not the same. Responsibility is a feeling of obligation; it is a sense of duty that a person has to perform one's job. When handled properly, responsibility is created within people when they accept a task or job assignment and are delegated authority.

Unlike authority, responsibility cannot be delegated. A person may delegate authority to you to do a certain thing, but since that person had the authority and the corresponding responsibility initially, that person is still responsible for the use of the authority delegated to you. "Delegating" responsibility in the same sense as authority is delegated is actually abdicating responsibility.

Types of authority. So far we have talked about authority as if there was only one type of authority. When authority is delegated from one person to another person, an authority relationship exists. There are in fact three different types of authority, or more specifically, three different types of authority relationships—line authority, staff authority, and functional authority.

Line authority is decision-making authority that exists between all superiors and all subordinates. If the principle of unity of command (one worker, one boss) is not violated, there is a line authority relationship running from the top of the organization to each person at the bottom of the organization. Line authority and line relationships are the kind generally shown as solid lines as in Figure VIII-6. As can be seen, there is a line relationship (supervisor-subordinate) running from the top to the bottom of the organization.

Staff authority is the authority to serve. It is the right to advise, assist, and help other people; it is not decision-making authority over others. When staff authority is delegated, a staff relationship is created. While line authority flows vertically and creates supervisor-subordinate relationships, staff authority can flow in any direction to create advisory relationships. Staff relationships are most likely to be used to provide managers with expert advice. No manager can be a specialist in all of the areas that he needs to be. The next best thing is to provide expert help and advice to all managers through staff relationships.

Some departments, such as personnel, usually exist primarily in a staff capacity— their relationship to other departments is advisory. For example, a personnel department with staff authority might look like that in Figure VIII-6. Here staff relationships are shown as dotted lines.

A third type of authority relationship is functional. Functional authority is decision-making authority that is limited to an activity or aspect of an activity no matter who performs the activity or where it is performed in the organization. So functional authority results in a superior-subordinate relationship, but it is limited authority that results in a secondary rather than primary superior-subordinate relationship. Functional relationships are usually shown on organization charts as broken lines as in Figure VIII-6.

By now you may have recognized that the use of both line and functional authority relationships result in more than one boss for some people in the organization. If only one manager has functional authority in the organization, a worker has a primary superior to whom one reports for most of one's work and a second boss because of the functional authority. This is a major disadvantage of functional authority. There are situations where this is necessary however. In many cases the need for uniformity of decision-making and action are so great (for example, in safety, accounting practices, etc.) that one person needs to have authority over the activity no matter where it is performed. So while functional relationships are valid and useful they should be used sparingly or else everybody in the organization winds up having several bosses.

Positions or departments are not limited to one type of authority. They may have any or all three types of authority. For example, the Vice President of Finance has line authority over direct subordinates and may have staff authority (advises others) relative to financial analysis, and functional authority (requires action) relative to accounting records. Other departments may only have one type of authority. The delegation process determines the number and type of authority relationships.

Application of authority concepts. The application of the authority concepts and the creation of specific types of authority relationships takes place in the delegation process. This is discussed in the last major section of this reading.

With a basic understanding of the more important fundamental concepts of organization, the discussion turns now to the application of the concepts in the organizing process. Both the activity grouping process and the delegation process are described and explained below.

GROUPING ACTIVITIES

At its most basic level, activity grouping results in jobs. The basic concepts of specialization and span of management are actually applied in the activity grouping part of the organizing process.

Departmentation

The activity grouping process begins at the top of the organization with the grouping of activities into separate units, usually referred to as departments. A department is a distinct area or group of activities that is assigned to a manager along with delegated authority.

Major departments in large organizations are usually broken down into subdepartments by further application of the activity grouping process. For example, managers in charge of all production activities will further group (or divide) their activities into subdepartments to be assigned to subordinates. This subdividing or activity grouping process continues down the organization as long as appropriate. Just how far the subdividing process is necessary depends upon the size of the organization's undertaking and the span of management used.

The process of grouping activities into departments and subdepartments is where the principle of division of work and specialization is applied. There are several different types or bases of departmental specialization found in practice. The most commonly used basis of specialization and departmentation are organizational function, product, territory, customer, process or equipment, and time. Each of these bases of specialization and departmentation tends to be used for different reasons.

Departmentation by function. One of the most widely used bases of specialization and departmentation is by functional activity. All organizations engage in three basic functions no matter what their specific objectives are. All organizations must produce a good or service, market that good or service, and finance the production and marketing of the good or service. Thus, at the top of many organizations, it is not unusual to see production, marketing, and finance departments.

Functional grouping of activities is not limited to the top level of organizations nor to just the three functions mentioned. Each of the three primary functional areas can be further broken down on a subfunctional basis. Additionally, there are other more specific functions for certain types of businesses. Table VIII-1 contains some examples of functional grouping of activities in various types of organizations and some possible subfunctional groupings.

TABLE VIII-1
Functional departments of typical organizational structures

Primary functional departments	Derivative functional departments
In a manufacturing organization	

Production	Manufacturing:
	  Fabrication
	  Assembly
	  Tooling
	Purchasing
	Production control:
	  Scheduling
	  Materials control
	Quality control

Sales	Selling:
	  Selection
	  Training
	  Operation
	Operation
	Advertising
	Sales promotion

Finance	Capital requirements Fund controls Disbursements Credit Accounting
In a department-store organization	

Publicity	Advertising
	Display
	Media public relations
	Buying (organized by product line):
	  Budgeting
	  Merchandising control
	  Sales promotion
	  Sales force

General superintendent	Supplies Customer service Store protection Warehousing Receiving, marking, delivery

Finance	Financial Management:
	  Cash control
	  Credit
	  Accounting

In a wholesale organization	

Sales	Buying (organized by product line):
	  Budgeting
	  Merchandise control
	  Sales promotion
	  Sales force

General superintendent	Warehousing:
	  Receiving
	  Will Call
	  Shipping
	  Stockroom

Finance	Money management Credit and collections Accounting

TABLE VIII-1 (continued)

In a service organization (airline)

Operations	Engineering:
	New equipment
	Modification of equipment
	Communications engineering
	Maintenance
	Line maintenance
	Overhaul
	Ground operations:
	Station management
	Food and commissary
	Flight operations:
	Flying
	Communications
	Dispatching
Traffic or sales	Administration:
	Reservations
	Schedules
	Tariffs
	Sales:
	Passenger sales
	Cargo sales
	Sales promotion
	Advertising:
	Direct mail
	Newspaper and periodical
	Radio and television
Finance	Financial management:
	Gas control
	New financing
	Foreign exchange
	Accounting:
	Revenue
	Disbursements
	General ledger

Source: Koontz and O'Donnell, *Principles of Management*, 5th ed. (New York: McGraw-Hill Book Co., 1972), pp. 269-70.

Functional grouping of activities has both advantages and disadvantages. Foremost among its advantages are that it allows people to specialize in the performance of particular types of activity. It is also a logical method of dividing the work of the organization. Its chief disadvantages are that it separates related activities and makes coordination of all activities associated with a given objective more difficult. It also is not a particularly good form of organization for training executives because of its relatively narrow specialization.

Department by product. A second widely-used basis of departmentation is product. With this basis, the activities associated with a particular product or produce line are grouped into departments.

Product departmentation is used most often near the top of organizations and seems to have only limited use at lower organizational levels, because most product departments cannot be further subdivided on the basis of product. Oftentimes, product departments are subdivided on a functional basis.

Product departmentation, too, has both advantages and disadvantages. It makes the coordination of activities associated with particular products easy, but it may result in duplication of effort in the organization. For example, separate advertising campaigns may be used. And product departmentation may result in overall organizational activity being difficult to coordinate.

Departmentation by territory. Grouping activities on a geographical basis is another basis for departmentation. With this method, all of the activities performed in a certain territory or all of the activities associated with a certain geographic area are grouped into a department. Like product departmentation, territorial departmentation has only limited use because it is impractical to keep subdividing activities on a geographic basis in many cases. Consequently, customer departmentation is often used with some other basis for organization departmentation. In practice, customer departmentation is most often found in connection with sales and marketing activities.

The logic of customer departmentation is to achieve certain marketing advantages. The chief disadvantage of this method is that occupational specialization is lost.

Departmentation by process or equipment. A type of departmentation that is commonly found at lower organizational levels is process or equipment departmentation. Activities are grouped according to the type of process or type of equipment being used. In some respects, process or equipment departmentation is similar to functional departmentation. This type of departmentation does result in occupational specialization, but it also may make it difficult to coordinate activities between departments. Process or equipment departmentation is most commonly found at lower organization levels.

Departmentation by time. Last, one obvious way of grouping activities into departments is by time. This basis of departmentation is usually found at lower organizational levels along with some other basis. For example, activities may be grouped into departments based on process or equipment and then further grouped into time periods such as shift one and shift two.

The big disadvantage of time grouping occurs when the activities of the different shift departments must be closely coordinated. Still, grouping activities on a time basis and operating more than one work shift for departments is often preferable to a larger capacity plant.

Mixed departmentation. The ultimate criterion for grouping activities is the one that will result in the best overall organizational performance. This usually means that different types of departmentation may be appropriate at the same level. Departmentation is not an end in itself; it is a means to the end of achieving organizational objectives. There is no value in a pretty, well balanced (on paper) organizational chart. The real test is how well it works.

In deciding which of the above activities should be grouped in departments and ultimately into jobs, we find asking and answering the following two questions helpful:

1. What will be the positive effects on performance and coordination?
2. What will be the negative effects on performance and coordination?

Answering these questions develops the information needed to decide how activities should be grouped into departments.

Assigning activities

Managers need to understand the basis for departmentation, because at one time or another they will probably be involved in such decisions. However, a much more frequent supervisory problem is where to assign or reassign a specific work activity on either a departmental basis or a job basis. In one sense, any job is just a relatively small department. Jobs, even at the lowest level in the organization, are really one-person departments of activity. So the assignment of new activities or the reassignment of old activities can be done on the same basis as activities are grouped into departments. The same issues and considerations are involved and the same questions are relevant.

One problem in departmentation and the creation of jobs that has not been mentioned is the determination of the amount of work a person can do. Obviously, this affects how many activities are grouped into any department or job. At managerial levels this problem is really one of determining the appropriate span of management and this has already been discussed. At worker or nonmanagerial levels the question is usually answered by research and/or trial and error. With many types of work activity it is possible through various types of work study such as time-and-motion study or Methods Time Measurement to systematically determine the amount of work that a person can do. This is, however, a job for experts in the area. In other cases, systematic study and measurement are impractical and common sense and trial and error must be used.

The organizing process begins at the top of the organization with activities being grouped into major departments and then continues downward as far as necessary. The activities in these major departments may be grouped into subdepartments. This grouping process continues until the final result is jobs at the bottom of the organization. Grouping activities is in reality only the first part of organizing; activities have to be assigned to positions and people, and authority to perform activities has to be delegated.

THE DELEGATION PROCESS

Organizing results in an activity-authority system, so the activity system or structure created by the grouping process must be tied together with authority relationships. Tying activity groupings together with authority takes place through the delegation process.

Delegation of authority is in reality a two-part process involving: (1) the actual assignment of duties and activities and (2) the granting of authority to perform the duties and activities. In practice it is often hard to separate and distinguish between these two steps in delegation because they are so closely related, but managers are more likely to do a better job of delegating if they approach it from this viewpoint.

Assigning job activities

Assigning duties and activities to subordinates is a matter of determining what activities subordinates are supposed to perform, what results they are responsible for and then communicating this to subordinates. Determining what activities are to be performed and what results subordinates are responsible for accomplishing takes place in the grouping process described above. The real issue here is communicating the statement of activities and results to subordinates—the establishment of realistic expectations within subordinates of what is expected of them.

While the assignment of activities is a part of organizing, it is also the point at which the organizing and directing functions mesh. For this reason, assigning job activities is discussed in connection with the directing function in a subsequent reading. This section focuses on the delegation of authority, including issues such as how much authority should be delegated.

Delegating authority

The delegation of authority to perform task assignment involves two questions—what kind of authority and how much authority. The question of what kind of authority (line, staff, or functional) for the most part has already been answered in determining the activities and tasks. For example. if the job is to be in a pure staff relationship to other jobs, the nature of the activities should reflect this. Nevertheless, it is sound delegation practice to spell out as clearly as possible what type of authority the job includes.

Perhaps, the most important issue in delegation is how much authority to delegate. There are no scientific methods of answering this question. It is this question, however, that must be answered for each person performing the job. We believe that the amount of authority delegated depends upon the following situational factors:

1. Nature of the activities.
2. Level of subordinate ability.
3. Results expected.
4. Needs for coordination.

Nature of the activities involved. The amount of authority delegated should depend partly on the nature of the activities performed. Where activities are routine or highly programmed, little authority may be needed for effective performance, but the routine nature of the activities may safely make the delegation of more authority possible. Where activities are not routine or highly programmed, authority delegations may need to be either broad or limited. In some cases the varied nature of the activities may require that people have the authority to make the decisions which arise. In other cases, the varied nature of the activities may require that only limited authority be delegated. The only real guide that can be offered is that activities in a job should be studied to determine how much authority is needed for effective performance.

Level of subordinate ability. A second factor affecting the amount of authority delegated is the level of ability of the person performing the job. No person should be delegated a great deal more authority than they are capable of using effectively for the benefit of the organization. On the other hand, neither should the level of authority delegated be significantly lower than the ability of the person performing the job. This means that delegation of authority should be made in light of both the job to be done and the person doing the job.

Results expected. In most jobs, various levels of performance are possible and the amount of authority that is delegated affects the level of performance. When this is the case, authority should be delegated consistent with the results expected to achieve superior results.

Needs for coordination. The fourth important factor affecting the amount of authority delegated is the need for coordination. Usually, managers do not manage groups of unrelated activities or jobs; many jobs are highly interrelated. Where jobs are related and affect each other, the need for coordination among jobs is greater, and the less authority can be delegated to perform the jobs because coordination is achieved at the level of the superior of the jobs.

In summary, how much authority should be delegated is a question that each manager must answer in light of the job, the performance expected, and the person that will be doing the job.

As a result of each manager at each level performing the organizing process and therefore, delegating authority to those below him or her, the departments and jobs created in the activity grouping process are tied together with authority relationships. The final result then of organizing is an organization structure—a system or structure of activity-authority relationships.

SUMMARY

The organizing function is concerned with deciding who will do what in the achievement of organizational objectives and it is a part of every manager's job. The result of organizing is an organization structure composed of groups of activities tied together by authority relationships. Thus, organizing is a two-part process made up of (1) grouping activities and (2) delegating authority.

Organizing is a universal management process and the basic concepts of organizing are applicable in all organizations at all levels. The more important of these concepts are division of work and specialization, unity of command, span of management, and authority and responsibility. These concepts are implemented in the performance of the two-part organizing process.

Grouping activities begins at the top of organization with departments and ends at the bottom of the organization with workers' jobs. The most widely-used basis for grouping activities into departments are by organization function, by product, by customer, by process or equipment, by territory, by time, and ultimately by various combinations of these bases.

Once activity groupings are established, they must be tied together with authority relationships. This means that authority must be delegated to perform the activity groupings.

The delegation process involves communicating task and job assignments and the granting of line, staff and/or functional authority to perform the assignment.

PREWORK QUESTIONS

Based on the reading in "Organizing," select the best and most complete answer for the following questions. Select only one answer even though others are not wrong. If you are unsure of your choice, it is better to leave it blank. Once you have completed the questions, transfer your individual answers to the Prework Answer Sheet (p. 103) under the column marked *Individual answers*.

Individual answers   *Team answers*

1. The central idea in the principle of "division work" is that:
    a. People would rather be specialists than generalists.
    b. Specialization results in a more effective organization.
    c. Specialization makes people's jobs easier to do.
    d. Jobs and tasks need to be small enough for a person to do well.

2. The principle of "unity of command" assumes that:
    a. Organizations can be structured so that no one has more than one boss.
    b. Organizations operate better when there is a clear level of authority from the top of the organization to the bottom.
    c. People in organizations need a boss.
    d. Managers need almost complete authority over their subordinates.

3. The limitations of the "span of management":
    a. Can be overcome through application of the principles of division of work and unity of command.
    b. Require "tall" organization structures.
    c. Result in communication problems.
    d. Are brought about by lack of managerial ability and can be overcome through managerial development.

4. Authority:
    a. Is an organizational right.
    b. Is the "glue" that ties the parts of the organization together.
    c. Is decision-making power.
    d. And power go hand-in-hand.

5. Line authority:
    a. Is an application of the principle of "unity of command."
    b. Is best used sparingly.
    c. Is somewhat advisory in nature.
    d. Is the power to make decisions.

6. The use of functional authority:
    a. Is seldom justified.
    b. Results in violation of the principle of "unity of command."
    c. Is required by law.

VIII/Understanding the organizing function

d. Should normally be limited to managers who really understand the different types of authority relationships.

7. Staff authority:
    a. Is best described as the right to advise and not to do things.
    b. Is usually delegated only to managers at the top of the organization.
    c. Is not really authority at all.
    d. Is usually used to overcome the limitations resulting from application of the principle of "unity of command."

8. Activities should be grouped:
    a. In light of the job to be done and not in light of the people who will be doing them.
    b. On the same basis at each level in the organization to avoid confusion.
    c. At all levels in the way that promotes coordinated performance.
    d. By staff people specializing in activity grouping.

9. Delegating authority:
    a. And assigning tasks is best done through well developed job descriptions.
    b. Is not necessary if jobs do not require much decision making.
    c. Is a problem that needs to be solved for each person in light of the total situation.
    d. Means that the responsibility for decisions is given to someone else.

10. The overall purpose of organizing is:
    a. To let everyone know what he or she is supposed to do.
    b. To be able to hold people responsible for their performance.
    c. To make some people know when they are accountable.
    d. To make cooperation and coordination possible.

SESSION INTRODUCTION

This session will focus on creating an understanding of the organizing function by drawing on the organizing experience, the text material, and a lecture.

SESSION OVERVIEW

Step 1: Teamwork on prework (25 min.).

Step 2: Scoring individual and team answers, and comparing team effectiveness scores (10 min.).

Step 3: Increasing team effectiveness (30 min.).

Step 4: Cross-team exchange (10 min.).

Step 5: Lecture and discussion (20–40 min.).

Step 6: Self-evaluation and individual learnings.

Step 1: Teamwork on prework (25 min.)

As prework you answered a 10-item multiple-choice test on organizing. Each team is to identify the single best answer for each question. The text is not to be used during the discussion, but you may use your prework answers. Team answers are to be recorded on the Prework Answer Sheet (p. 103) under the column *Team answers*.

You will have 25 minutes to arrive at team answers through discussion and analysis. At that time the individual and team answers will be scored to determine how effectively each team operated. The scoring system reflects the degree of commitment to team answers. Each correct answer receives 10 points. Items unanswered are worth 0 points. An incorrect answer results in –10 points. Thus, the score is calculated by taking the number correct, subtracting the number incorrect, and multiplying by ten.

This step should be completed by _____ .

Step 2: Scoring individual and team answers and comparing team effectiveness scores (10 min.)

Using the Prework Answer Sheet, score your individual and team answers based on the correct responses distributed to you. A simple procedure to follow is to record the correct answers in the column *Correct answers*. Where the given and correct answers match, put +10 in the *Points* column. Where no answer is given, record 0 points and where the given and correct answers do not match, put –10 in the *Points* column. By totaling the points, the individual and team score can be determined.

At least one team member should complete the Team Effectiveness Score Sheet (p. 104) according to the following steps:

a. Determine the average individual score by adding the individual scores and dividing by the number of team members.

b. Subtract the average individual score from the team score to determine a gain or loss. A positive number indicates the team arrived at a higher score than the average of what individuals arrived at working separately. A loss, or negative number, indicates that team discussion and agreement resulted in a lower score than the individuals did working alone.

c. Determine the possible improvement by subtracting the average individual score from the perfect score of 100. This number represents how many points of improvement were possible through team discussion and agreement.

d. Determine team effectiveness by dividing the gain (+) or loss (−) by the possible improvement and multiplying by 100. Once all teams have completed the scoring, the average individual, team, and team effectiveness scores will be collected and posted.

Step 3: **Increasing team effectiveness** (30 min.)

As a team you have now completed several tasks. To get maximum learning and to achieve or to keep obtaining high effectiveness, it is important to review our experiences and draw conclusions from them. Each team is to:

a. Identify barriers in the team preventing full effectiveness.
b. Outline specific steps needed to increase team effectiveness.

Select a spokesperson to present a summary of your barriers and action steps at _____ .

Step 4: **Cross-team exchange** (10 min.)

Step 5: **Lecture and discussion** (20–40 min.)

Step 6: **Self-evaluation and individual learnings**

Spend some "alone" time and think about what occurred during the last experience. Focus in on two or three things that affected you or that seemed significant to you. These may be positive or negative elements of the experience. What learnings can you draw from this reflection and what does this mean to you? Don't be concerned about what you ought to have learned, but rather focus on what you did learn and what it means to you. Based on your reflection of the experience, jot down your responses to the following questions:

1. What were your major learnings from the experience?

2. What implications do your learnings have for you as an individual?

3. What implications do your learnings have for you as a manager?

4. What questions do you have as a result of your experience, reflection, and learnings?

5. What implications will your learnings have on your future experiences?

PREWORK ANSWER SHEET

Questions	Individual answer	Individual points*	Correct	Team points*	Team answer
1					
2					
3					
4					
5					
6					
7					
8					
9					
10					
	Individual score		Team score		

*Blanks—(no answer given)—receive 0 points; where correct and given answers match +10 points; where correct answer and given answers do not match −10 points.

TEAM EFFECTIVENESS SCORE SHEET

Individual scores

1. _____
2. _____
3. _____
4. _____
5. _____
6. _____
7. _____
8. _____

Average individual score

(A) (_____) ÷ (_____) = [_____]
     Total individual scores   No. members

Team score
Less average individual score

(B) [_____]

Perfect score (C) [100]
Less average individual score

Team effectiveness

(D) (_____) ÷ (_____) = (_____) × 100 = _____ %
    Gain (+) or loss (−)   Possible improvement

Block IX

Directing experience—Pattern assembly

GOALS

1. Increase awareness of planning and directing the accomplishment of a task which is performed by others.
2. Increase the awareness of performing a task based on the instructions of others.
3. Increase the awareness of the role of communication in directing.

PREWORK ASSIGNMENT

None.

SESSION INTRODUCTION

Directing is a function of management that involves leading and motivating subordinates through the communication process. This exercise gives you the opportunity to engage in a directing experience as a manager or working member.

SESSION OVERVIEW

Step 1: Determining managers and workers and preparing for task (5 min.).
Step 2: Directing and assembly phase (15 min.).
Step 3: Reviewing the experience (15 min.).
Step 4: Reverse roles and repeat assembly using a new pattern (15 min.).
Step 5: Review the experience and prepare for a cross-team exchange (15 min.).
Step 6: Cross-team exchange and discussion (10 min.).
Step 7: Self-evaluation and individual learnings.

Step 1: Determining managers and workers and preparing for task (5 min.)

Each team is to divide into two groups. One group will be the managers and direct the completion of the task. The other group will be the workers who will perform the task.

As soon as you are divided into workers and managers, punch out one page of the construction panels contained at the end of the book. All of the panels can be used in the pattern assembly.

Step 2: Directing and assembly phase   (15 min.)

The managers are to instruct the workers in assembling exact replicas of the pattern assembly which will be on display. The managers and workers may go about the task in any way they see fit as long as they do not violate the following ground rules imposed to help focus on directing:

1. The managers may go out and look at the pattern assembly as often as they wish.
2. The managers may give any type instructions that they think will be helpful to the workers in assembling the pattern.
3. The managers may not touch any of the construction panels.
4. The workers may not see the pattern assembly which is displayed.

So basically, the managers are to go look at the pattern assembly and direct the workers in completing the task. The workers are to assembly the replicas. The winning team will be the one which completes exact replicas of the pattern assembly that equals the number of *workers* in the team plus one in the shortest time. Thus, where there are three workers, that team must complete four exact replicas of the pattern assembly (3 + 1 = 4).

As soon as you have completed the pattern assemblies required of your team, notify your observer who will record the time and inspect your assembly work for accuracy. The times will be posted as each team completes its required number of replicas.

Step 3: Reviewing the experience   (15 min.)

A. Individual work.

To get maximum learning from our experience we must review our experiences and draw conclusions from them. To prepare for a team discussion, complete the following questions or statements as an individual during the next minutes. Allow all team members to finish before moving to the teamwork.

1. How effectively did the managers and workers communicate during the assembly phase?

1	2	3	4	5	6	7	8	9
Fully ineffective								Fully effective

2. Identify the things that were done that were helpful in accomplishing the task.

3. Identify something that could have been done that would have increased your motivation to complete the task.

4. Identify something that you would like to see done differently by your team members during the next directing and assembly phase.

B. Teamwork.

As a team, discuss the individual responses to the above questions. Explore reasons for why people responded as they did. Examining the reasons for responses and giving specific examples of behavior can serve as the basis of team-wide understanding and agreement.

Step 4: Reverse roles and repeat assembly using a new pattern (15 min.)

You are to now reverse roles so that the managers become the workers and the workers become the managers. In this phase, the workers will be assembling exact replicas of a new pattern assembly which will be displayed. Again, the same ground rules must be observed to help focus on the directing function of management:

1. The managers may go out and look at the pattern assembly as many times as they wish.
2. The managers may give any type instructions that they think will be helpful to the workers in assembling the pattern.
3. The managers may not touch any of the construction panels.
4. The workers may not see the pattern assembly which is displayed.

Again, the winning team is the team that produces exact replicas of the new pattern assembly equal to the number of workers plus one in the shortest time. Notify your observer when you have finished the required number of pattern assemblies.

Step 5: Review the experience and prepare for a cross-team exchange (15 min.)

A. Individual work.

To get maximum learning from our experience we must review our experiences and draw conclusions from them. To prepare for a team discussion, complete the following questions or statements as an individual during the next minutes. Allow all team members to finish before moving to the teamwork.

1. How effectively did the managers and workers communicate during the assembly phase?

1	2	3	4	5	6	7	8	9
Fully ineffective							Fully effective	

2. Identify the things that were done that were helpful in accomplishing the task.

3. Identify something that could have been done that would have increased your motivation to complete the task.

B. Teamwork.

As a team, discuss and complete the following items. The best learning will occur if all team members will share their ideas and feelings in the discussion.

1. Discuss the individual responses to the above questions. Explore reasons for why people responded as they did. Examining the reasons for responses and giving specific examples of behavior can serve as a basis for team-wide understanding and agreement.

2. The team is to discuss and come to a team-wide agreement and understanding on two things they learned from the experience.

Select a spokesperson to present (in the next step) the team's learnings.

Step 6: **Cross-team exchange and discussion**   (10 min.)

Each team makes a report to the other teams and open discussion follows.

Step 7: **Self-evaluation and individual learnings**

Spend some "alone" time and think about what occurred during the last experience. Focus in on two or three things that affected you or that seemed significant to you. These may be positive or negative elements of the experience. What learnings can you draw from this reflection and what does this mean to you? Don't be concerned about what you ought to have learned, but rather focus on what you did learn and what it means to you. Based on your reflection of the experience, jot down your responses to the following questions:

1. What were your major learnings from the experience?

2. What implications do your learnings have for you as an individual?

3. What implications do your learnings have for you as a manager?

4. What questions do you have as a result of your experience, reflection, and learnings?

5. What implications will your learnings have on your future experiences?

Block X

Understanding the directing function

GOAL

1. Create an understanding of the directing function.
2. Improve skills in assigning job activities.

PREWORK ASSIGNMENT

Read the following material on "Directing" for understanding. Answer the ten prework questions at the end of the material.

DIRECTING

> *I define power as the capacity to modify the conduct of other employees in a desired manner, together with the capacity to avoid having one's own behavior modified in undesired ways by other employees.*[1]

We have stated several times that managers plan, organize, direct, and control in order to achieve organizational objectives with and through others. In one sense the planning and organizing functions are preparation for achievement. It is through the directing function that the action needed to actually reach objectives is started and maintained. So directing is the action link between planned objectives and their achievement. It is then a function performed by all managers.

While the performance of the entire management process involves interpersonal interaction, the directing function is usually considered the interpersonal aspect of managing. It involves influencing subordinates to do the things necessary to achieve organizational objectives. Thus, directing involves communicating job assignments and leading and motivating subordinates to do the things that have been planned and organized.

The directing function is not an easy one to perform well. How to achieve organizational objectives and at the same time satisfy the needs of employees is a question that has been asked in one form or another, time and time again. And as yet, there are no "pat" answers to the question. This does not mean that little is known about the direct-

---

[1] Robert N. McMurry, "Power and the Ambitious Executive," *Harvard Business Review* (November–December 1973), p. 140.

ing function. In fact, just the opposite is true; during the relatively recent past, a lot has been learned about leadership and motivation. As is usually the case, the knowledge that is available is useful and helpful, but it does not provide a "cut-and-dried" solution for effective performance of the directing function.

The objective of this reading (Block X) and the next two readings (Blocks XII and XIV) is to help you understand the directing function better. In this reading we introduce the directing process and discuss the important issues in actually assigning jobs to people. The material is organized into the following four sections:

The nature of directing.

Assigning job activities.

Job-well-done conference.

Developing understanding and agreement.

Motivation is discussed in Block XII and leadership is discussed in Block XIV.

For the ideas and information which follow to be most useful in improving your directing skill, you should try to relate what you read to your own experience and most important, try to apply the ideas and learn from your experiences in application.

THE NATURE OF DIRECTING

Directing is essentially an attempt to influence other people to achieve particular objectives. It is important because it is the part of the management process that deals with converting objectives into realities. Since it is an essential part of management, all managers are responsible for effective performance of the directing process. The directing function can be better understood by looking more closely at what directing is, its importance, the responsibility for it and the directing process itself.

What directing is

The directing function is an attempt to influence subordinates to do their jobs so that organizational objectives are achieved efficiently. The directing function has two related but distinct influence objectives. First, directing attempts to influence employees in the right direction—that is, to accomplish the desired objectives. Second, directing attempts to influence peoples' levels of motivation to perform in pursuit of these objectives.

Directing has been defined as an attempt at influencing employees, but it should be pointed out that all managers direct. It is untrue that only some managers direct and influence employees; all managers do in fact influence employees in some ways. Everything managers do probably has some influence on employee behavior, so it is not a matter of whether managers do or do not direct; it is more a matter of whether their directing efforts have the intended influence and effect. Later readings describe various approaches to directing.

The importance of directing

The directing function is an important part of the management process because it is through the performance of this function that work toward organizational objectives actually begins. Planning and organizing are necessary prerequisites for effective achievement, but until things are set in motion, objectives will not be achieved. As Figure X-1 shows, directing is the vital actuating link in the management process.

FIGURE X-1
Directing in the management process

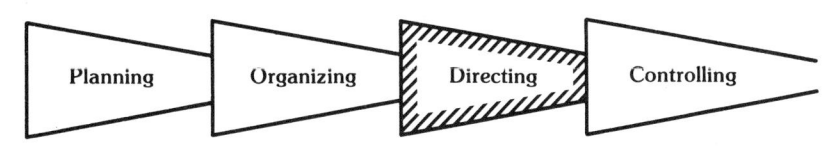

Planning → Organizing → Directing → Controlling

It is through the directing process that managers try to keep employee performance aimed in the right direction. Thus, performance of the directing function provides the leadership and guidance necessary for achievement. Without such guidance it is likely that little would be accomplished.

The responsibility for directing

Directing is a fundamental part of the management process performed by all managers at all levels in all organizations. A manager may provide a great deal of direction or only minimal direction. His directing may be effective or ineffective; but the nature of the superior-subordinate relationship requires that all managers direct. Because directing is inherent and inevitable in managing, all managers have a responsibility to perform the directing function effectively. This responsibility is created through acceptance of the managerial job.

The directing process

While quite a lot is known about directing, the directing process is more difficult to meaningfully describe than is the planning or organizing process. Directing is basically a process of influencing, and the influencing process is extremely complex.

The purpose of directing is to influence subordinates in the right direction and to influence them to certain levels of activity. Directing is then essentially communicating assignments, and leading and motivating subordinates. Both leadership and motivation are attempted through communication. So explanation of the directing process is in terms of leadership and motivation.

The directing process is illustrated in Figure X-2 and takes place in the following way. Whether they are aware of it or not, managers make certain assumptions about the nature of the people they manage and particularly about their work behavior. Based on these assumptions, they perform their leadership role in a certain way (adopt and use particular leadership styles). The leadership style used affects subordinates' motivations to perform and, therefore, the achievement of both organizational objectives and employees' personal objectives.

FIGURE X-2
The process of directing

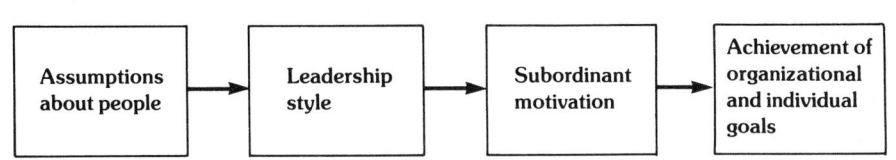

Assumptions about people → Leadership style → Subordinant motivation → Achievement of organizational and individual goals

ASSIGNING JOB ACTIVITIES

While the actual assignment of job activities and results may seem simple, both research and practical experience indicate that it is a difficult thing to do well. Studies investigating the degree to which managers and employees agree on what employees' jobs involve rarely indicate substantial agreement. Apparently, managers and employees have different ideas about employees' jobs. This is probably not a surprising result to most subordinates.

Certainly employees have a responsibility for establishing a clear understanding of what is expected of them, but superiors have at least as much and possibly more responsibility here. After all, it is the manager's job to achieve organizational objectives with and through employees and this requires that subordinates know what they are expected to accomplish.

In practice several methods of communicating job assignments are found. One of the most widely used is simply oral assignments. Another widely-used method is written job descriptions. Oral face-to-face job and task assignments have the potential for being the most effective method of assignment available, but observation indicates that most oral job assignments result in much misunderstanding. The objective in job assignment is for subordinates to understand exactly what is expected of them. This is essentially a communication task and potentially the most effective type of communication is verbal face-to-face. The reason this method results in ineffective job assignments is that we tend to take communication for granted. The tendency is to assume that when something is said, it means exactly the same things to the other person as it does to the person saying it. Job and task assignments would probably be much more effective if managers would simply "check out" employees' understandings of what is expected of them. At least then lack of mutual understanding might be uncovered and cleared up.

Along with oral assignments, written job descriptions are also commonly used to inform subordinates of what is expected of them. These types of descriptions generally include one or more of the following types of information about a particular job:

1. Duties and activities.
2. Responsibilities.
3. Tools and equipment.
4. Skills and qualifications necessary.
5. Performance results expected.

Good job descriptions can be a valuable aid in making face-to-face communication. It is our experience that job descriptions tend to be used poorly in many cases. Some managers rely solely on written descriptions to assign tasks. No matter how good a job description is, it can never be complete. Another serious problem is that many job descriptions are poorly developed and written. A good job description should contain accurate information on the activities and responsibilities involved in the job and most importantly a clear statement of the level of performance required on the job. Many job descriptions are so general and vague that they are either meaningless and worthless or even worse, they may *cause* misunderstanding about the job.

Developing good job descriptions is not an easy task. Managers without expertise in this area should seek the help of qualified staff when possible. Most large organizations have staff qualified in the area who actually do most of the work involved in writing job descriptions. The managers' responsibility is to see that descriptions of the jobs are accurate and as complete as possible.

Whatever method is used to communicate job assignments to subordinates, the real objective is to help subordinates understand what is expected of them. In doing this, good job descriptions are helpful, but they can never take the place of good face-to-face communication.

JOB-WELL-DONE CONFERENCE

An approach that we find especially helpful in communicating job assignments and in performing the directing process in general is the job-well-done conference.[2] Essentially the job-well-done conference is an attempt to develop mutual understanding and agreement between managers and employees concerning subordinate performance. It is then a problem-solving conference where both parties' ideas, information and expectations are explored to create better mutual understanding and expectations.

Job-well-done conferences focus on three important related aspects of employee performance—the contribution of the job, task or activity; the methods used; and the results expected. One logical approach is to explore each of these topics in the order listed and try to reach understanding on each aspect before moving to the next topic. Thus, the general agenda for such a conference would take the following form:

I. Contribution of job:

  A. Share your ideas about the contribution of subordinate's jobs.
  B. Find out subordinate's ideas about the contribution of her or his job.
  C. Try to reach agreement on the contribution of the job.

II. Job methods:

  A. Inform subordinate about your ideas concerning job methods.
  B. Try to understand subordinate's ideas about job methods.
  C. Try to reach agreement on job methods.

III. Results expected:

  A. Explain the job results you expect.
  B. Find out what subordinate thinks her or his results should be.
  C. Try to reach agreement on results.

The idea behind this approach is that it is easier to develop understanding and agreement in sequential steps on each important aspect of the job than on the total job. The three aspects of performance are used to help focus discussion.

The objective is mutual agreement, but job-well-done conferences will never completely eliminate disagreement. They do, however, bring such disagreement to light and in this manner almost always improve understanding. Naturally, if true agreement is not possible, the boss *is* still the boss.

DEVELOPING UNDERSTANDING AND AGREEMENT

Basically the idea in the job-well-done conference is development of mutual understanding of problem solutions. The truth is that mutual understanding and agreement are difficult things to develop. There are, however, some techniques which are helpful in creating this understanding. Some of the more important techniques are described below.

[2] We are indebted to Practical Management Associates for the concept of the Job-Well-Done Conference.

The first technique is the use of the open-ended question. An open-ended question cannot be answered with yes or no. They usually start as follows:

How do you feel about . . .?
What do you think of . . .?
What is your opinion of . . .?
What's your ideas on . . .?

This type question allows the employee to get into the open that which is important and is on their mind. Also, since you have asked the question, there is a better chance of listening and trying to understand their point of view.

The second technique that is helpful is to use directives for understanding. These statements usually start with:

Please talk more about . . .
I'm not sure what you meant by . . .
Please talk a little more about that . . .
Talk about your opinions of . . .
Talk about your ideas on . . .

These types of directives free employees to reveal their viewpoint. These statements offer a much wider range of opportunities for discussion and are likely to bring up issues which would otherwise not come out.

The third technique is listening checks. It may be very helpful during any problem-solving session to rephrase in your own words what you have heard your subordinates say, or how they seem to feel. This will insure that you are understanding what has been said. Often this is helpful to the subordinate in understanding their own ideas. Listening checks can start with:

I hear you saying . . .
It seems you're saying . . .
I understand your position . . .
So you're saying . . .
So your position is . . .

The fourth technique is called summarizing. When you have reached a point where there is mutual understanding or conclusion, it may be helpful to summarize what has happened by starting the statement with:

In summary, it seems that . . .
Well, let's see if we have the same understanding. It seems that we are saying . . .
Here's my understanding of the points we have touched on . . .
Looking back over our discussion it seems that . . .

The use of summarizing statements should be interspersed in the conversation when appropriate. But certainly they should be used a least a minimum of one time at the end or conclusion of the session.

Developing skill in the use of these techniques is one important way of improving your performance of the directing function, especially that part dealing with job assignments and solving job-related problems.

SUMMARY

Directing is the process of helping and influencing employees to do their job so that organizational objectives are achieved effectively and efficiently. Thus, directing involves communicating job assignments and then motivating and leading people to do their jobs.

Assigning job activities is a difficult task. It is probably best done with good written job descriptions supplemented with generous use of good two-way communication.

Job-well-done conferences are one approach to creating mutual understanding and clear expectations between managers and employees. The job-well-done conference focuses on the development of understanding and agreement of the contribution of the job, the job methods used, and the job results expected.

Understanding and agreement are not easily created. The use of such techniques as open-ended questions, directives, listening checks, and summaries can help make job-well-done conferences more productive.

PREWORK QUESTIONS

Based on the reading in "Directing," select the best and most complete answer for the following questions. Select only one answer, even though others are not wrong. If you are unsure of your choice, it is better to leave it blank. Once you have completed the questions, transfer your individual answers to the Prework Answer Sheet (p. 120) under the column marked *Individual answers*.

Individual answers			*Team answers*
_____	1.	As a part of the management process directing is primarily concerned with:	_____
		a. Giving instructions and orders.	
		b. Supervising the work of subordinates.	
		c. Influencing people to do their job well.	
		d. Communication.	
_____	2.	Because of the nature of directing:	_____
		a. All managers do in fact direct.	
		b. It is best done in an impersonal fashion so that personality conflicts are minimized.	
		c. It is best left to true behavioral experts.	
		d. Managers should try to always play the role of the manager.	
_____	3.	The objective in assigning job activities is to:	_____
		a. Make sure people understand what needs to be done and how.	
		b. Develop mutual understanding of what is expected of the subordinate.	
		c. Leave subordinates with only a general idea of what the job involves so that they have the opportunity to show some initiative.	
		d. Detail the job so thoroughly that subordinates have absolutely no way of misunderstanding.	
_____	4.	Written job descriptions:	_____
		a. Are better than oral assignments becuase they provide a concrete record of what people are supposed to be doing.	
		b. Should be general so that job assignments can be changed easily.	
		c. Should focus primarily on how jobs should be done.	
		d. Should be used as a basis for discussion between superiors and subordinates to help make good job assignments.	
_____	5.	Job-well-done conferences are:	_____
		a. A problem-solving technizue.	
		b. Are most useful mainly with "problem" employees.	
		c. Are really a sly way of getting employees to accept your own idea and think that it was their idea.	
		d. Are not very useful in assigning job activities.	

6. The job-well-done conference focuses on:
    a. The development of understanding between superiors and subordinates.
    b. The creation of mutual understanding and agreement concerning subordinate performance.
    c. The idea that bosses know more about what subordinates should do than do the subordinates.
    d. The idea that mutual agreement is more important than understanding.

7. In the job-well-done conference, the most important topic is:
    a. What is being done wrong.
    b. What is being done well.
    c. The methods of the job.
    d. The nature of the job and the results expected.

8. The most basic assumption of the job-well-done conference is that people:
    a. Are committed to ideas that they understand and accept.
    b. Must originate ideas themselves before they truly accept them.
    c. Can be persuaded to accept the ideas of others.
    d. Must be led.

9. The techniques for creating mutual understanding and agreement focus primarily on:
    a. Helping people hear both sides of the question.
    b. Helping people see their mistakes.
    c. Helping people understand.
    d. Personal problems.

10. Directing is:
    a. A clear-cut step-by-step procedure of management.
    b. A process of leading and motivating through communication.
    c. Primarily negative in nature.
    d. Almost always done best on a highly formal basis.

SESSION INTRODUCTION

This session will focus on creating an understanding of the directing function by drawing on the directing experience, the text material, and a lecture.

SESSION OVERVIEW

Step 1: Teamwork on prework (25 min.).

Step 2: Scoring individual and team answers, and comparing team effectiveness scores (10 min.).

Step 3: Increasing team effectiveness (30 min.).

Step 4: Lecture and discussion (20–40 min.).

Step 5: Self-evaluation and individual learnings.

Step 1: Teamwork on prework (25 min.)

As prework you answered a 10-item multiple-choice test on "Directing." Each team is to identify the single best answer for each question. The text is not to be used during the discussion, but you may use your prework answers. Team answers are to be recorded on the Prework Answer Sheet (p. 121) under the column *Team Answers*.

You will have 25 minutes to arrive at team answers through discussion and analysis. At that time the individual and team answers will be scored to determine how effectively each team operated. The scoring system reflects the degree of commitment to team answers. Each correct answer receives 10 points. Items unanswered are worth 0 points. An incorrect answer results in −10 points. Thus, the score is calculated by taking the number correct, subtracting the number incorrect, and multiplying by 10.

This step should be completed by _____ .

Step 2: Scoring individual and team answers and comparing team effectiveness scores (10 min.)

Using the Prework Answer Sheet, score your individual and team answers based on the correct responses distributed to you. A simple procedure to follow is to record the correct answers in the column *Correct answers*. Where the given and correct answers match, put +10 in the *Points* column. Where no answer is given, record 0 points and where the given and correct answers do not match, put −10 in the *Points* column. By totaling the points, the individual and team score can be determined.

Individuals and teams can be compared based on their scores. However, individuals come to teams with varying degrees of preparation and knowledge. As a result the final score may not reflect how information was shared and how decisions were made during the team discussion. To take this into account, a Team Effectiveness Score can be determined.

At least one team member should complete the Team Effectiveness Score Sheet (p. 122), according to the following steps:

a. Determine the average individual score by adding the individual scores and dividing by the number of team members.
b. Subtract the average individual score from the team score to determine a gain or loss. A positive number indicates the team arrived at a higher score than the average of what individuals arrived at working separately. A loss, or negative number, indi-

cates that team discussion and agreement resulted in a lower score than the individuals did working alone.

c. Determine the possible improvement by subtracting the average individual score from the perfect score of 100. This number represents how many points of improvement were possible through team discussion and agreement.

d. Determine team effectiveness by dividing the gain (+) or loss (−) by the possible improvement and multiplying by 100. Once all teams have completed the scoring the average individual, team, and team effectiveness scores will be collected and posted.

Step 3: **Increasing team effectiveness** (30 min.)

In the teamwork and review of teamwork on "Organizing," your team developed barriers preventing full effectiveness and specific steps were needed to increase team effectiveness. Your team is to discuss:

a. Did you implement the steps to increase effectiveness?
b. Did the implementation improve the way the team operated?
c. Does your score support your conclusion for (b)?
d. What are some further steps needed to increase team effectiveness?

Select a spokesperson to present a summary of your discussion at _____ .

Step 4: **Lecture and discussion** (20–40 min.)

Step 5: **Self-evaluation and individual learnings**

Spend some "alone" time and think about what occurred during the last experience. Focus in on two or three things that affected you or that seemed significant to you. These may be positive or negative elements of the experience. What learnings can you draw from this reflection and what does this mean to you? Don't be concerned about what you ought to have learned, but rather focus on what you did learn and what it means to you. Based on your reflection of the experience, jot down your responses to the following questions:

1. What were your major learnings from the experience?

2. What implications do your learnings have for you as an individual?

3. What implications do your learnings have for you as a manager?

4. What questions do you have as a result of your experience, reflection, and learnings?

5. What implications will your learnings have on your future experiences?

PREWORK ANSWER SHEET

Questions	Individual answer	Individual points*	Correct	Team points*	Team answer
1					
2					
3					
4					
5					
6					
7					
8					
9					
10					
Individual score			Team score		

*Blanks—(no answer given)—receive 0 points; where correct and given answers match +10 points; where correct answer and given answers do not match −10 points.

TEAM EFFECTIVENESS SCORE SHEET

Individual scores

1. _____
2. _____
3. _____
4. _____
5. _____
6. _____
7. _____
8. _____

Average individual score

(A) (_____) ÷ (_____) = _____
     Total individual scores   No. members

Team score
Less average individual score

(B) _____   (C) Perfect score 100
                      Less average individual score

Team effectiveness

(D) (_____) ÷ (_____) = (_____) × 100 = _____ %
    Gain (+) or loss (−)   Possible improvement

122 Basic management: An experience-based approach

Block XI

Directing experience—Problem solving

GOALS

1. Increase one's awareness of the value of effective problem solving.
2. Gain practical skills in assisting others in solving job-related or personal problems through interviewing and counseling.

PREWORK ASSIGNMENT

Read the following material on "Techniques for problem solving."

TECHNIQUES FOR PROBLEM SOLVING

Directing is the function of management we are studying. As managers, you often have or will have employees come to you with some job-related or personal problem, or you call an employee in to solve a job-related problem. When you do this, you are trying to assure that the final result is in line with the performance desired. Hopefully, the result is that the subordinate will develop or accept an idea or plan that will lead to the results you are striving for, but, as we all know, we only accept an idea or plan when we believe in it and it makes sense to us. So, it is important that both the superior and subordinate see the problem from the same viewpoint and each have a clear understanding of the appropriate solution. There are some techniques which may be helpful to you in creating this understanding.

The next work session activity is going to focus on the use of four techniques for gaining and creating understanding. You will have the opportunity to practice and build skills in utilizing these four techniques.

The first technique is the use of the open-ended question. An open-ended question cannot be answered with yes or no. They usually start as follows:

How do you feel about . . .?
What do you think of . . .?
What is your opinion of . . .?
What are your ideas on . . .?

This type question allows subordinates to get ideas out that are important to them and on their mind. Also, since you have asked the question there is a better chance of you listening and trying to understand their point of view.

The second technique that may be helpful to you is using directives for understanding. These statements usually start with:

Please talk more about . . .
I'm not sure what you meant by . . .
Please talk a little more about . . .
Talk about your opinions of . . .
Talk about your ideas on . . .

These types of directives free participants to reveal their viewpoint. These statements offer a much wider range of opportunities for discussion and are likely to bring up issues which would otherwise not come out.

The third technique is listening checks. It may be very helpful during an interview or problem-solving session to rephrase in your own words what you have heard your subordinates say, or how they seem to feel. This will insure that you are understanding what has been said. Often this is helpful to subordinates in understanding their own ideas.

Listening checks can start with:

I hear you saying . . .
It seems you're saying . . .
I understand your position is . . .
So you're saying . . .
So your position is . . .

The fourth technique is called summarizing. When you have reached a point where there is mutual understanding or conclusion it may be helpful to summarize what has happened by starting the statement with:

In summary, it seems that . . .
Well, let's see if we have the same understanding. It seems that we are saying . . .
Here is my understanding of the points we have touched on . . .
Looking back over our discussion it seems that . . .

The use of summarizing statements should be interspersed in the conversation when appropriate. But certainly they should be used at least a minimum of one time at the conclusion of the session.

During the next session, you and others are going to have the opportunity to gain skills in utilizing the above techniques. You also will have the opportunity to get some help on some personal or job-related problem. To prepare for the next session, jot down *two* real personal and/or job-related problems that you would like help on and would be willing to discuss with someone else.

SESSION INTRODUCTION

This activity will give you an opportunity to gain skills in utilizing the techniques discussed in the prework materials for solving job related or personal problems.

SESSION OVERVIEW

Step 1: Triad role playing (30 min.).
Step 2: General discussion (15 min.).
Step 3: Self-evaluation and individual learnings.

Step 1: Triad role playing (30 min.)

The participants are to join others to form triads. Each member of the triad is to assume the role of a helper (superior or friend), helpee (friend or subordinate), or observer. The helper is to talk with the helpee about a real job-related or personal problem that he or she is currently encountering. They are to spend 6 minutes on the discussion. If you are the helper, really push yourself to utilize one or two of the helping techniques. Also, refrain from giving advice unless it is really clear that this is what is wanted. Even then, try not to give advice unless you have made a listening check and have gotten no new information.

If you are the observer, sit back and observe the conversation. Don't get involved in the conversation until time is up *even though* they may say they are through. Just observe and see what happens.

At the end of the discussion, all three parties are to spend 3 minutes reviewing the experience by using the following:

1. The helper and observer express how they feel about the interview and what they feel was helpful.
2. The superior shares her or his ideas and feelings about the techniques.
3. The observer and subordinate give the helper (friend or superior) feedback on how to improve on using the techniques, etc. After that round, they are to switch roles so that the observer becomes the helper, the helper becomes the helpee, and the helpee becomes the observer. Go through the same process until all three have performed all three roles. It should take a total of 30 minutes for the three rounds.

Step 2: General discussion (15 min.)

Participants discuss learning, applications, etc.

Step 3: Self-evaluation and individual learnings

Spend some "alone" time and think about what occurred during the last experience. Focus in on two or three things that affected you or that seemed significant to you. These may be positive or negative elements of the experience. What learnings can you draw from this reflection and what does this mean to you? Don't be concerned about what you ought to have learned, but rather focus on what you did learn and what it means to you. Based on your reflection of the experience, jot down your responses to the following questions:

1. What were your major learnings from the experience?

2. What implications do your learnings have for you as an individual?

3. What implications do your learnings have for you as a manager?

4. What questions do you have as a result of your experience, reflection, and learnings?

5. What implications will your learnings have on your future experiences?

Block XII

Understanding motivation and behavior

GOALS

1. Create an understanding of motivation and behavior in organizations.
2. Improve motivation skills.

PREWORK ASSIGNMENT

Read the following material on "Motivation" for understanding. Answer the ten prework questions at the end of the reading.

MOTIVATION

An employee will work because the work interests and challenges him and when he performs effectively will reward himself for doing well.[1]

Motivation is a central concept in directing, and in all of managing, for that matter. Most managers are aware that a person's ability determines what one *can* do, but motivation ultimately determines what *is* done. The age-old question is, "how can employees be motivated to do their jobs well." As yet, there are no simple answers to this question. Employee motivations at work are complex and diverse. Behavioral science and empirical research have, however, shed some light on the motivation question. The purpose of this reading is to explain the more basic concepts of motivation and behavior at work.

Assumptions about work behavior

Behind all managers' approaches to directing (and their entire approach to management for that matter) is a set of assumptions about the basic nature of people and more specifically about the work behavior of people. These assumptions cause managers to consciously or unconsciously choose and use a particular approach to performing the directing function.

The assumptions behind managers' approaches to directing are learned from their past experience. The assumptions may, or may not, however, fit reality very well.

---

[1] J. Richard Hackman, "Is Job Enrichment Just a Fad?" *Harvard Business Review*, vol. 53 (September–October 1975), p. 137.

Generally, false assumptions may still be held because the approach which results from them has at least allowed the manager to perform well enough to survive.

There are probably as many different assumptions about people's work behavior as there are managers, but research indicates that there are many similarities among the assumptions held by different managers. Perhaps the most meaningful statement of the possible range of assumptions upon which managers base their behavior was made by Douglas McGregor. McGregor described two opposing and somewhat extreme sets of assumptions about human behavior in organizations which he called "Theory X" and "Theory Y." As Figure XII-1 indicates, these two sets of assumptions tend to exist at opposite ends of a continuum.

FIGURE XII-1
Theory X and Theory Y

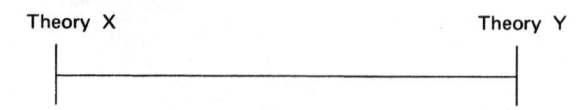

Theory X   Theory Y

|—————————————————|

Theory X represents a set of assumptions which contain a rather negative view of the work behavior of most people. The most important of these assumptions are:

1. *The average human being has an inherent dislike of work and will avoid it if he can.*
2. *Because of this characteristic dislike of work, most people must be coerced, controlled, directed, and threatened with punishment to get them to put forth adequate effort toward the achievement of organizational objectives.*
3. *The average human being prefers to be directed, wishes to avoid responsibility, has relatively little ambition, and wants security above all.*[2]

Certainly these assumptions view peoples' work behavior in an unfavorable light.

Theory X assumptions seem to be based primarily upon the belief that most people see little satisfaction in work and view it more as a necessary evil. The approach to direction which tends to result from the assumptions is more or less obvious.

At the other extreme are Theory Y assumptions. The more important of these are:

1. *The expenditure of physical and mental effort in work is as natural as play or rest. The average human being does not inherently dislike work. Depending upon controllable conditions, work may be a source of satisfaction (and will be voluntarily performed) or a source of punishment (and will be avoided if possible).*
2. *External control and the threat of punishment are not the only means for bringing about effort toward organizational objectives. Man will exercise self-direction and self-control in the service of objectives to which he is committed.*
3. *Commitment to objectives is a function of the rewards associated with their achievement.* The most significant of such rewards . . . can be direct products of efforts directed toward organizational objectives.
4. *The average human being learns under proper conditions, not only to accept, but to seek responsibility.* Avoidance of responsibility, lack of ambition, and emphasis on security are generally consequences of experience, not inherent human characteristics.
5. *The capacity to exercise a relatively high degree of imagination, ingenuity, and creativity in the solution of organizational problems is widely, not narrowly, distributed in the population.*

---

[2] Douglas McGregor, *The Human Side of Enterprise* (New York: McGraw-Hill Book Co., 1964), pp. 33-34. (Italics in original.)

6. *Under conditions of modern industrial life, the intellectual potentialities of the average human being are only partially utilized.*[3]

These assumptions present a more positive view of the average person's work behavior.

Theory Y assumptions seem to imply that not only is work not undesirable to most people but that it can be very satisfying. Certainly an approach to directing based on Y assumptions would be different than one based on X assumptions.

It was McGregor's belief that most managers used an approach based primarily on assumptions similar to those described in Theory X. Today behavioral science indicates that Theory Y assumptions are probably more realistic and accurate assumptions about most people. Because of this, McGregor believed that many managers were less effective than they could be because they used an approach based on the inaccurate assumptions of Theory X.

We agree with McGregor, but we also know that assumptions are hard to change and that managers are more effective at any given time when they are aware of their assumptions and when they use the best approach they can that is consistent with their assumptions, no matter whether the assumptions tend to be like X or Y. The lesson to be learned from Theory X and Y is:

1. Consciously examine your assumptions to see what they really are.
2. Consciously examine your approach to see if it fits your assumptions.
3. Analyze and try to improve whatever approach fits your assumptions.
4. Consciously and continuously test your assumptions to see if they fit the situations in which you find yourself.

While we believe a good approach to directing based on Theory Y assumptions is more effective than a good approach based on Theory X assumptions, we recognize that people have a right to whatever assumptions they hold at any particular time. Additionally, we believe that the most effective approach managers can use is one that is consistent with their assumptions. Neither X nor Y is bad. If you truly believe X assumptions fit most people, try to be the best "X" manager you can, but constantly test your assumptions and approach. The same thing holds true for "Y" assumptions.

UNDERSTANDING HUMAN BEHAVIOR AT WORK

In the last 10 to 15 years, the behavioral sciences have made significant contributions to explaining how people behave and to understanding why they behave as they do. The more important concepts and ideas about work behavior are explained in this section.

A model of behavior

The simplest and probably most widely-held explanation of human behavior is illustrated in Figure XII-2. The most important assumption in the model is that behavior is not random or chance. People do not just do things—behavior is caused and has a specific purpose whether that purpose is recognized or not. The model indicates that behavior is caused by needs within the individual and that it has satisfaction of needs as its objective. Behavioral scientists generally agree that all people have needs within them which cause behavior. When these needs are unsatisfied, they cause tension within the individual and this tension results in behavior that the individual perceives will satisfy the need and relieve the tension. So behavior is caused by internal needs.

[3] Ibid., pp. 47-48. (Italics in original.)

FIGURE XII-2
Model of behavior

Needs → Wants → Behavior → Goals

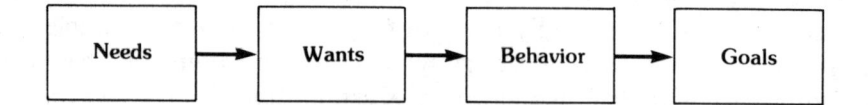

Needs cause behavior in the first place, but needs are most often expressed as wants and desires. Needs and wants and desires are closely related—wants and desires stem from needs—but they are not the same thing. Needs are more basic and general, while wants and desires are more specific. For example, an employee may feel a *need* for more status on the job and to satisfy this need, may *want* a more prestigious sounding title. Certainly not all wants and desires lead to behavior; but the stronger wants and desires do and, ultimately, all behavior is caused by wants and desires which result from unsatisfied needs.

The third part of the model is behavior. Behavior is action—mental or physical—that people take to satisfy their needs. What behavior are we referring to? Almost all of the behavior that each of us sees every day. From another standpoint, behavior is an expression and use of an individual's abilities. Individuals have abilities as well as needs, and they use their abilities (through behavior) to try to satisfy their needs. Behavior is then the means through which individuals use their abilities to try to satisfy their needs.

Goals—the fourth and last element in the model—are the things that behavior is directed toward. Goals are the specific things that individuals believe will satisfy their needs and that they seek through behavior. Goals may be objects, conditions, or activities. For example, the goal of a particular person's behavior might be stated as food (an object), a feeling of satisfaction (a set of conditions), or as eating (an activity). Goals, obviously, are closely related to wants and desires and needs. But goals are usually outside of the person while needs and wants and desires are inside the person. Goals also tend to be more specific than either needs or wants. People may have several goals associated with the same want or desire.

Several comments about the above model need to be made. First, the model is a general explanation of all behavior, but people may or may not be aware of why they behave as they do or even that their behavior at a particular time is aimed at satisfying their needs. In fact, people exhibit much behavior without ever being consciously aware of a need or a want or desire or even a goal; nevertheless, this is what causes behavior. Second, needs can never be observed; they can only be inferred from behavior. And this is extremely difficult, even for well-trained psychologists.

The above model has two important implications. The first is that all behavior is caused—there is a reason for it. The second implication is that all behavior is rational and selfish. It is rational behavior because, consciously or unconsciously, it is designed to satisfy needs with the person. Behavior is selfish for the very same reason. What a person does may help or harm other people, but the basic reason that it is done is to satisfy needs. This does not make people good or bad, it just makes them people trying to satisfy their needs.

While the model and explanation above provide some insight into behavior, the model is even more useful in understanding behavior when you know more about human needs.

Common human needs

The most widely known and used classification and description of common needs was developed by the prominent psychologist, Abraham Maslow. In its simplest form, Maslow's explanation of motivation and behavior is made up of three statements.[4] Each of these statements is explained below.

Unsatisfied needs. A human is a wanting being—one always wants, and one wants more. The idea here is that all human needs are never satisfied. If a particular need becomes satisfied, a new one arises to take its place. Moreover, the "new" need or want will probably be of a higher level of aspiration than the satisfied one. This means that individuals never satisfy all of their needs. All people are constantly seeking need satisfaction.

Motivating needs. A satisfied need does not cause behavior. The second idea advanced by Maslow is that not all needs lead to behavior at any one time. Individuals are not motivated by needs which are relatively well satisfied. At any one time, it is the unsatisfied needs which motivate individuals and cause them to act. Once a need is relatively well satisfied, a person's behavior will no longer be aimed primarily at satisfying that particular need; behavior will be directed toward the satisfaction of some other relatively unsatisfied need. It is the unsatisfied needs which are the primary cause of a person's behavior at any given time.

Hierarchy of needs. Human needs are arranged in a series of levels—a hierarchy of importance. The third idea about human behavior is really a combination of two related ideas. The first is that people's needs tend to be grouped into a particular pattern, and the second idea is that people tend to try to satisfy their needs in a predetermined order. As shown in Figure XII-3, people have five identifiable categories of needs which they try to satisfy in ascending order. The most basic needs are physiological needs.

The lowest level of needs on the hierarchy and the ones which people try to satisfy first are those which must be satisfied to sustain life. They include the needs for food,

FIGURE XII-3
Hierarchy of needs

- Self-realization
- Esteem
- Social
- Security
- Physiological

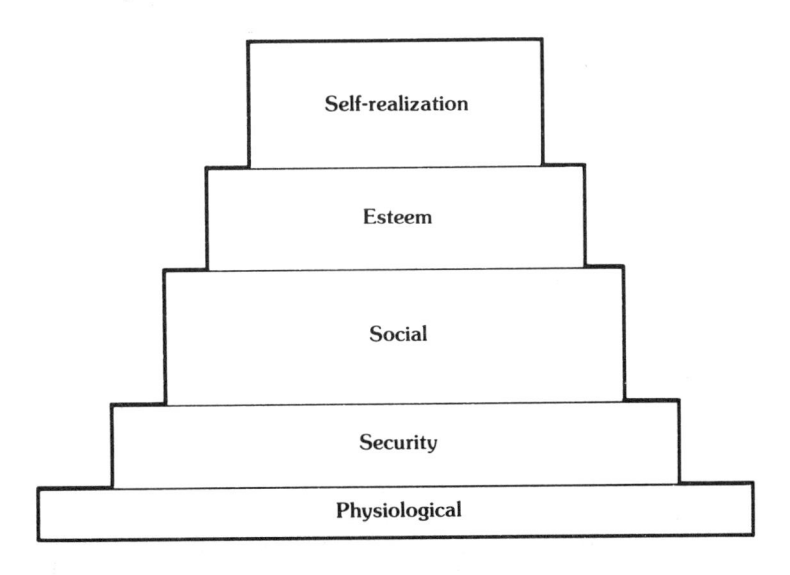

[4] A. H. Maslow, *Motivation and Personality* (New York: Harper and Row, Pub., Inc., 1954). The discussion of the need hierarchy draws heavily on this source.

oxygen, protection from the elements, and rest. These are needs of the body, and they are present in all people. Until these needs are at least partially satisfied, most of a person's behavior will be aimed at this level of needs.

Safety needs are the next set of needs which arise to have a dominant influence on people, and these include the need for protection from physical harm and the need for economic security. As one writer states, "When individuals have satisfied their physiological needs fairly well, they seek some assurance that these needs will continue to be satisfied in the future and with less effort and worry if possible."[5]

Social needs are the next highest level on the hierarchy. They do not arise to be a very significant cause of behavior until safety needs are relatively well satisfied. This category includes the needs for both giving and receiving love and affection, the need to accept, associate with and be accepted by others, and the need to belong or to feel a part of social groups. Social needs can never be fully satisfied. They are needs of the mind (as are the next two higher classes of needs), not of the body. Since they can never be fully satisfied, they continue to influence behavior once they are activated. However, when some level of satisfaction is reached, the esteem needs arise and more of the individual's behavior is directed toward satisfying these needs.

Most experts in the area agree that the majority of people in our society have fairly well satisfied the bottom three levels of needs in the hierarchy, and that the behavior of most people is aimed at satisfying the esteem and self-realization needs.

The fourth level of needs in the hierarchy are the needs for esteem, both self-esteem and esteem for others. The need for self-esteem includes the needs for self-respect, achievement, recognition, appreciation, independence, freedom, status, and to respect other people. Thus, people have needs for dignity and to respect the dignity of others.

The highest level of needs in the hierarchy are the needs for self-realization and fulfillment. They influence behavior at all times, but they tend to dominate it only after esteem needs are at least partially satisfied. Self-realization needs include needs for realizing one's potential and for self-fulfillment by the greatest possible utilization of one's abilities. Included here also is the need for creative expression. The highest level of needs are those that people have for *becoming* and *being* all that they are capable of as a person.

Although almost all people are believed to have the need hierarchy described, they are not necessarily aware of the hierarchy or of the specific needs that influence their behavior. A great deal of the influence of needs on behavior is unconscious, but it is still there.

Movement up the hierarchy. The idea that the five classes of needs influence people's behavior in the particular order described is not as simple as it might seem. The two highest levels of needs—esteem and self-realization—generally do not have a big effect on most people's behavior until later in their lifetimes, but this does not mean that people spend one part of their lives satisfying one level of needs and another part of their lives satisfying another level of needs. Some of the categories (especially physiological needs) must continue to be satisfied fairly often. During the course of a lifetime or even a day, for that matter, people move up and down the hierarchy trying to satisfy the lowest level needs that are relatively unsatisfied at the particular time.

Threatened needs. The behavior of any person *can* be highly influenced by a need that is presently well-satisfied. For example, when the continued satisfaction of a presently well-satisfied lower-level need is *threatened*, the individual's behavior is likely to be

---

[5] Keith Davis, *Human Behavior at Work: Human Relations and Organizational Behavior*, 4th ed. (New York: McGraw-Hill Book Co., 1972), pp. 46–47.

directed toward making sure that the threatened need will continue to be satisfied as it has been in the past. With this in mind, it can be said that any particular time an individual's behavior tends to be aimed at satisfying the lowest-level, relatively unsatisfied needs or the lowest-level needs whose continued satisfaction is threatened.

Assumptions and needs. It seems clear that there is a definite relationship between McGregor's Theory X and Theory Y and Maslow's Hierarchy. Theory X assumptions focus heavily on the lower-level needs, while Theory Y assumptions emphasize the higher-level needs. The Theory X approach to motivation concentrates on providing extrinsic satisfactions, such as money and benefits, for work performed, i.e., the familiar "carrot and stick" approach. In contrast, the Theory Y approach emphasizes the intrinsic satisfaction associated with work; that is, it focuses on creating conditions where people are motivated from within to satisfy ego needs through work.

Work as a source of need satisfaction. Maslow's hierarchy of needs is a general statement of the needs that people have and the order in which they go about trying to satisfy their needs. From a management standpoint, however, the question is: Does this explanation apply to work behavior on the job. It seems fairly safe to say that work is probably the most important source of satisfaction for all of the needs in the hierarchy. These are the needs that cause the behavior that managers see and deal with every day.

When trying to lead and motivate subordinates, it is one thing to know what needs people are trying to satisfy; but knowing what will actually satisfy the needs is an entirely different matter. This is, however, precisely what all managers need to know to direct people effectively. Understanding what people really want from their work is the next order of business.

Need satisfiers at work

As pointed out at the beginning of the chapter, the real problem in directing is to make it possible for employees to achieve their own goals and satisfy their own needs through doing their best to achieve organizational goals. To lead and motivate employees, managers need to know what employees really want from their work.

Certainly, different people are motivated by different things, but both research and experience indicate that most people tend to be motivated to work by similar things. The research of Frederick Herzberg[6] was aimed specifically at trying to determine what affected employees' motivations to perform at work. From this research, Herzberg developed the Satisfier-Dissatisfier Theory. The research on which the theory is based includes literally thousands of people at all levels in all types of organizations. It seems that the ideas and concepts seem to fit most of the people in our society.

The basic assumption of the Satisfier-Dissatisfier Theory is that people are motivated to do their jobs well to the degree that they achieve their own goals and satisfy their own needs from doing their job. The theory indicates that satisfaction (and motivation to perform at high levels) and dissatisfaction are two entirely different things. Job satisfaction and high levels of motivation tend to be influenced by the work and jobs that people do, while dissatisfaction and poor performance tend to be highly influenced by the conditions under which the job is done.

Satisfaction and dissatisfaction. According to this explanation, job satisfaction (and high levels of motivation) and dissatisfaction are not opposites. The opposite of job satisfaction is not dissatisfaction, but just no satisfaction. The opposite of dissatisfaction is not satisfaction, but just not dissatisfaction. Figure XII-4 indicates there is a neutral or

---

[6]Frederick Herzberg and others, *The Motivation to Work* (New York: John Wiley and Sons, Inc., 1959). The discussion in this section draws heavily on this source.

FIGURE XII-4
Satisfaction, dissatisfaction and performance

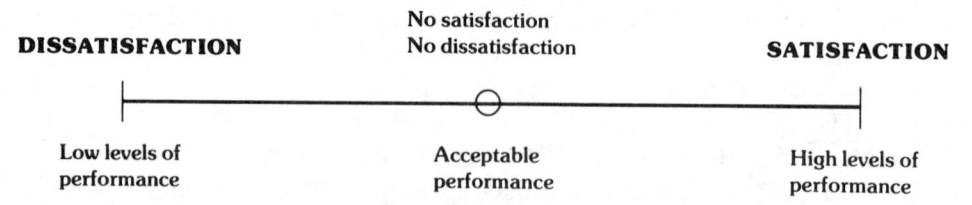

DISSATISFACTION	No satisfaction / No dissatisfaction	SATISFACTION
Low levels of performance	Acceptable performance	High levels of performance

zero point at which employees are neither satisfied nor dissatisfied, and at that point they work simply at a satisfactory level.

The significance of the distinction between satisfaction and dissatisfaction is that each of the two things tend to be caused by different sets of factors in the work situation. One set of factors—satisfiers—tends to affect satisfaction, motivation, and performance above satisfactory levels, while a second set of factors—dissatisfiers—tends to affect dissatisfaction, motivation, and performance below and up to satisfactory levels.

Satisfiers. The things which have the greatest effect on satisfaction, motivation, and performance above satisfactory levels are achievement, recognition, work itself, responsibility, and growth and advancement.

1. Achievement refers to doing something well. It means such things as completing a job successfully, solving problems, seeing the outcome of one's work, and generally the outcomes of situations which can be thought of as being good or bad. Whether these types of situations result in job satisfaction or not depends on whether they provide a feeling of achievement or opportunity for achievement.
2. Recognition refers to valid feedback on performance—praise or blame for the outcome of achievement situations. Recognition can be positive or negative, but to be motivating it must be deserved recognition.
3. Work itself refers to the nature of the work being done and whether or not it is interesting to the person doing it. Work can be routine or varied, interesting or uninteresting, easy or difficult, challenging or dull. Work which people see as interesting, varied, and challenging tends to be motivating, whereas, work which is seen as dull, routine, and uninteresting produces little satisfaction and motivation to perform at high levels.
4. Responsibility refers to employees' accountability for their own work, the work of others or to increase in such accountability. Responsibility and increases in responsibility tend to have a motivating effect on most people.
5. Growth and advancement refer to movement up in the organization and to opportunities to grow in terms of ability. Growth and advancement and opportunities for growth and advancement provide satisfaction and motivation to perform at higher than just satisfactory levels.

The important point about all of the satisfiers is that their greatest effect on employee motivation and performance is from satisfactory levels of motivation and performance to high levels of motivation and performance. If the motivators are present, employees are likely to be highly motivated and performing at better then merely satisfactory levels; but if the satisfiers are not present, employees are not necessarily highly dissatisfied. They are just not satisfied; and as a result, they do not necessarily restrict their performance below satisfactory levels; they are more likely to perform at a satisfactory level.

Dissatisfiers. The factors which have the greatest effect on dissatisfaction and motivation to perform below and up to satisfactory levels are salary, company policy and administration, supervision, interpersonal relations, and working conditions.

1. Salary refers to the pay that employees receive for doing their job and to expectations about pay increases. If pay is perceived as being good, it does not necessarily motivate employees to perform higher than satisfactory levels. If, however, pay is considered inadequate, it can cause dissatisfaction and may result in people doing as little as they can possibly get by with. It should be kept in mind that when pay and pay increases are seen as achievement and as recognition for achievement, it can result in satisfaction and motivation.

2. Company policy and administration refer to the adequacy of the organization's policies including such things as authority delegation, personnel policy, and fringe benefits. When these things are good, they do not cause much motivation to perform at high levels; but when they are bad, they can cause a lot of dissatisfaction that can result in performance reduction.

3. Supervision refers to how technically competent the employee's boss is. Technical incompetence results in dissatisfaction, but technically competent supervision does not result in high levels of motivation. Normally, technically competent supervision simply eliminates dissatisfaction and results in satisfactory performance.

4. Interpersonal relations refers to how well employees get along with their boss and co-workers. If interpersonal relations are poor, dissatisfaction is likely; if interpersonal relations are good, dissatisfaction disappears, but high levels of motivation to perform do not necessarily result.

5. Working conditions refer to the actual physical conditions under which the job is done. When working conditions are undesirable, dissatisfaction results. When working conditions are desirable, there is little dissatisfaction with working conditions but also little real satisfaction and motivation to perform at higher than required levels. Dissatisfiers do affect employee motivation and performance, but they tend to have little power to produce satisfaction and motivation to perform at higher than acceptable or required levels.

Importance of satisfiers and dissatisfiers. Both the satisfier factors and dissatisfier factors influence performance and therefore, both are important to employee motivation. Generally, the satisfiers do not work well if the dissatisfiers aren't also good and producing little dissatisfaction. The moral for managers seems clear. Make the dissatisfiers good to eliminate dissatisfaction and make the satisfiers available to provide the motivation to perform at high levels.

McGregor, Maslow, and Herzberg

Earlier the discussion pointed out that Theory X and Theory Y were related to the Need Hierarchy. It also seems that Herzberg's theory is related to both Theory X and Theory Y and to the Need Hierarchy. Figure XII-5 illustrates the relationship. Theory X and the lower level needs match up well with the Dissatisfiers. Theory Y assumptions are consistent with the higher level needs and with the Motivators. Thus, there is a definite pattern and consistency in the three theories.

MOTIVATION IN PRACTICE

In the final analysis, much of directing is motivating subordinates to achieve organizational objectives. In the previous section, some of the more useful explanations of work

FIGURE XII-5
Relationship between X and Y, the Need Hierarchy and Motivator-Dissatisfier Theories

McGregor assumptions	Maslow needs	Herzberg satisfiers
Theory X	Physiological Safety and security Social	Salary Interpersonal relations Working conditions Company policy and administration Supervision
Theory Y	Esteem Self-actualization	Work itself Achievement Recognition Responsibility Growth and advancement

behavior were presented, but these ideas and concepts are of little practical value to managers until they are actually put to use. This section describes some of the more significant attempts at practical application of motivation theory.

During the late 1960s, efforts at practical application of motivation increased significantly. The major theme in most of the application efforts was to enrich jobs to make them more meaningful and motivating and/or to motivate performance by reinforcing it with positive feedback.

Job enrichment

Job enrichment is the term used most often to describe attempts to systematically implement the motivators of Herzberg's Theory. The basic approach is to "enrich" jobs by changing the nature of what people do so that more of the motivators are inherent in the work and jobs done. Herzberg advocates enriching jobs by (1) removing some of the day-to-day controls, (2) granting more authority, (3) providing employees more information directly, (4) providing more complete natural units of work, (5) holding people personally accountable for performance, (6) allowing people to become specialists in some meaningful task, and (7) introducing more challenging tasks in jobs.[7]

Application of these principles has shown good results in many cases. In one experiment with shareholder correspondents in a large corporation, job performance increased approximately 40 percent, job satisfaction increased, and turnover and absenteeism decreased after the job changes.[8] In another experiment involving salespeople, performance sales increased 19 percent and job satisfaction measures improved.[9]

M. Scott Meyers describes an entirely different approach with the same enrichment objectives. The approach was developed at Texas Instruments and is referred as the problem-solving goal-setting approach. Unlike Herzberg's approach of changing individual jobs, the procedure here involves adding planning and control responsibility to "natural" work groups.[10]

[7] Frederick Herzberh, "one More Time: How Do You Motivate Employees?" *Harvard Business Review*, vol. 46 (January–February 1968), pp. 53–62.
[8] Ibid.
[9] William J. Paul, et al., "Job Enrichment Pays Off," *Harvard Business Review*, vol. 46 (January–February 1969), pp. 61–78.
[10] M. Scott Meyers, *Every Employee a Manager* (New York: McGraw-Hill Book Co., 1970), pp. 81–95.

Procedurally, the approach is for the manager to present the employee work group with a "customer" problem. Employees brainstorm solutions and then pick the best solutions to be implemented. The employee work group then sets performance goals based on the changes that they recommended. The work changes are made and the work group is kept informed of its progress toward the goals set.[11] This approach has also shown some rather remarkable results. In one of the reported examples, assembly time for a complex navigational instrument was reduced from 138 hours to 32 hours.[12] Other examples report less spectacular, but significant, results.

A somewhat different approach from either of the two above is that reported by Sirota.[13] This approach combines usage of some of Herzberg's enrichment principles with the concept of work territories. Essentially, the approach is to provide employees with a work territory (such as a particular machine) that produces some identifiable output. In one example, employees were assigned to particular machines rather than being rotated among machines, and were granted more authority over decisions concerning machine maintenance. Product quality and job satisfaction increased, while machine down-time decreased.

Reinforcement theory

Based on the work of B. F. Skinner, an approach to increased motivation that is conceptually different from job enrichment was evolved. It is variously referred to as behaviorism, positive reinforcement, and reinforcement theory. It is based on the psychological principle that people tend to repeat behavior that is rewarded and tend to decrease behavior that is not rewarded or that is negatively rewarded.

In practice, the approach is quite simple. The first step is to establish some sort of meaningful performance measure for people so that the desired behavior (higher levels of performance) can be recognized by both managers and employees. The second part of the approach is to reinforce good performance with generous amounts of recognition and praise. Negative recognition is used sparingly.

This approach has also produced good results. Using these techniques, Emery Air Freight reported that increased motivation almost doubled usage of containers in shipping where previous efforts had failed to produce appreciable results.[14] Thus, it seems that entirely different approaches are capable of producing higher levels of motivation, performance, and satisfaction.

Vroom's Expectancy Model

Vroom's Expectancy Model of motivation sheds some light on how such different approaches might produce the same results. Rather than focusing on internal needs, this model focuses on goals. As indicated in Figure XII-6, the model postulates that motivation is a function of the strength of the goal and that the strength of the goal for an individual is determined by one's beliefs about one's ability to exhibit the behavior necessary and one's beliefs about the probability that the behavior will actually result in the goal. Thus, this model explains how some goals might motivate higher performance in some pople but not in others.

[11] Ibid.
[12] Fred K. Foulkes, *Creating More Meaningful Work* (New York: American Management Association, 1969), pp. 97–151.
[13] David Sirota, "Job Enrichment: Is It for Real?" *SAM Advanced Management Journal*, vol. 38 (April 1973), p. 25.
[14] "Where Skinner's Theories Work," *Business Week* (December 2, 1972), pp. 64–65.

FIGURE XII-6
Vroom's Expectancy Model

```
Beliefs about ability to
exhibit required behavior ──┐
                            ↓
                    Strength of goal ──→ Motivation
                            ↑
Beliefs that the behavior ──┘
will result in the goal
```

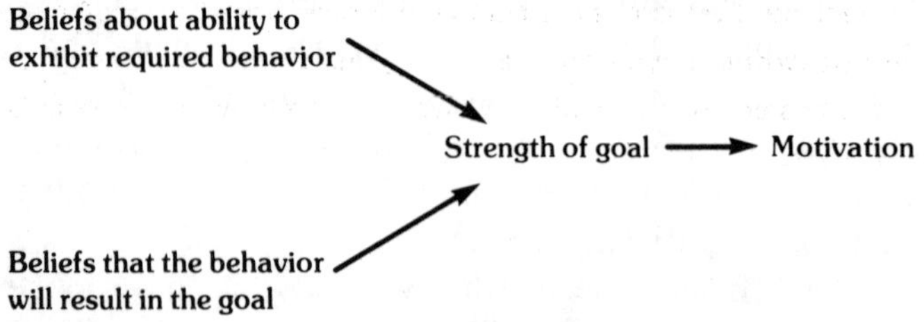

Source: Based on Victor H. Vroom, *Work and Motivation* (New York: John Wiley and Sons, Inc., 1964).

An example helps understand the model. Suppose a person is offered a pay increase for a higher level of performance. Whether the individual really tries to reach the level of required performance depends on beliefs about one's *ability* to reach the level of performance required and beliefs about whether one will actually get the pay increase if the required level of performance is reached.

SUMMARY

Motivation is a central theme in all of management because it is one of the critical elements affecting individual performance and, ultimately, organizational effectiveness. Behind every manager's approach to management and motivation are assumptions about the behavior of people. McGregor set forth two somewhat extreme sets of assumptions about employee behavior. Theory X assumptions hold that most people seek only extrinsic satisfaction from work. Theory Y assumptions are based on the belief that work can be and is intrinsically satisfying.

Maslow theorized that all behavior is aimed at satisfying one or more of five common internal needs—physiological needs, safety needs, social needs, esteem needs, and self-realization needs. Additionally, these needs are believed to influence behavior in a particular order of importance beginning with physiological and continuing through self-realization.

Herzberg's research shows that two sets of factors tend to influence work behavior in different ways. Motivators such as work itself, achievement, recognition, responsibility, and growth and advancement tend to cause people to perform at higher than acceptable levels. Dissatisfiers such as pay, company policy, supervision, working conditions, and interpersonal relations tend to affect performance from low levels up to satisfactory levels.

Practical application of motivation theory has taken place through the techniques of job enrichment and positive reinforcement. Job enrichment is an attempt to enrich jobs to make them more meaningful by providing more of the motivators in Herzberg's theory. Positive reinforcement attempts to increase higher performance through feedback and praise.

Vroom's Expectancy Model of motivation indicates that different goals have different motivational strengths for different individuals. This happens because people differ in their beliefs about their abilities and their beliefs about the probability that their behavior will result in the attainment of the goal.

PREWORK QUESTIONS

Based on the material in "Motivation," select the best and most complete answer for the following questions. Select only one answer even though others are not wrong. If you are unsure of your choice, it is better to leave it blank. Once you have completed the questions, transfer your individual answers to the Prework Answer Sheet (p. 144) under the column marked *Individual answers*.

Individual answers   *Team answers*

1. The main idea in McGregor's Theory X and Theory Y is:

    a. That manager's approaches are based on their assumptions about people.
    b. That people are different.
    c. That people can be good or bad.
    d. That most managers hold the wrong assumptions about people.

2. Theory X assumptions:

    a. Can produce an effective approach to management.
    b. Should never be used.
    c. Can produce fairly effective or ineffective approaches to management.
    d. Are not too widely held.

3. Theory Y assumptions:

    a. Are always more effective than X assumptions.
    b. Do not fit all people.
    c. Are more realistic assumptions about most people.
    d. Are the direct opposite of X assumptions.

4. The most important implication of Maslow's Need Hierarchy concept is that:

    a. Motivation is a responsibility of the manager.
    b. There is a reason for the way people behave; behavior is caused.
    c. People do different things to satisfy their needs.
    d. Everybody should realize their potential as a human being.

5. Maslow's Need Hierarchy implies that:

    a. Everybody is self-actualizing.
    b. Barring blockages, people grow to self-actualization.
    c. Lower order needs are not too important.
    d. People motivated by higher order needs are happier.

6. The most significant thing about the motivators in the Satisfier-Dissatisfiers Theory is that:

    a. They are different from the dissatisfiers.
    b. They are concerned more with the work that people do than with job conditions.
    c. They tend to result from the achievement of organizational objectives.
    d. They do not affect dissatisfaction.

_____ 7. The dissatisfiers in the Satisfier-Dissatisfier Theory:

    a. Do not affect motivation to perform at all.
    b. Are less important than the motivators.
    c. Are more improtant than the motivators.
    d. Affect performance in a different way than the motivators.

_____ 8. Job enrichment attempts to:

    a. Manipulate people.
    b. Make work more interesting.
    c. Take the drudgery out of work.
    d. Make work more intrinsically satisfying.

_____ 9. Positive reinforcement means:

    a. Never criticizing employee behavior.
    b. That employees are praised for whatever they do.
    c. That desirable behaviors are rewarded.
    d. That employees are given good feedback.

_____ 10. Vroom's model of motivation:

    a. Emphasizes goals and differences in perceptions.
    b. Contradicts Maslow's Need Hierarchy.
    c. Provides a practically useful guide to motivating employees.
    d. Is inconsistent with Herzberg's Theory.

SESSION INTRODUCTION

This session will focus on creating an understanding of motivation and behavior drawing on the directing experience, the text material, and a lecture.

SESSION OVERVIEW

Step 1: Teamwork on prework (30 min.).
Step 2: Scoring individual and team answers, and comparing team effectiveness scores (10 min.).
Step 3: Increasing team effectiveness (30 min.).
Step 4: Lecture and discussion (20–40 min.).
Step 5: Self-evaluation and individual learnings.

Step 1: Teamwork on prework (30 min.)

As prework you answered a 10-item multiple-choice test on "Motivation." Each team is to identify the single best answer for each question. The text is not to be used during the discussion, but you may use your prework answers. Team answers are to be recorded on the Prework Answer Sheet (p. 144) under the column *Team answers.*

You will have 30 minutes to arrive at team answers through discussion and analysis. At that time the individual and team answers will be scored to determine how effectively each team operated. The scoring system reflects the degree of commitment to team answers. Each correct answer receives 10 points. Items unanswered are worth 0 points. An incorrect answer results in −10 points. Thus, the score is calculated by taking the number correct, subtracting the number incorrect, and multiplying by 10.

This step should be completed by _____ .

Step 2: Scoring individual and team answers and comparing team effectiveness scores (10 min.)

Using the Prework Answer Sheet, score your individual and team answers based on the correct responses distributed to you. A simple procedure to follow is to record the correct answers in the column *Correct answers.* Where the given and correct answers do not match, put −10 in the *Points* column. By totaling the points the individual and team score can be determined.

Individuals and teams can be compared based on their scores. However, individuals come to teams with varying degrees of preparation and knowledge. As a result, the final score may not reflect how information was shared and how decisions were made during the team discussion. To take this into account a *Team effectiveness score* can be determined.

At least one team member should complete the Team Effectiveness Score Sheet (p. 145), according to the following steps:

a. Determine the average individual score by adding the individual scores and dividing by the number of team members.
b. Subtract the average individual score from the team score to determine a gain or loss. A positive number indicates the team arrived at a higher score than the average of what individuals arrived at working separately. A loss, or negative number, indicates that team discussion and agreement resulted in a lower score than the individuals did working alone.

c. Determine what the possible improvement was by subtracting the average individual score from the perfect score of 100. This number represents how many points of improvement were possible through team discussion and agreement.

d. Determine team effectiveness by dividing the gain (+) or loss (−) by the possible improvement and multiplying by 100. Once all teams have completed the scoring, the average individual, team, and team effectiveness scores will be collected and posted.

Step 3: Increasing team effectiveness (30 min.)

In the teamwork and review of teamwork on "Directing," your team developed barriers preventing full effectiveness and specific steps are needed to increase team effectiveness. Your team is to discuss:

a. Did we implement the steps to increase effectiveness?
b. Did the implementation improve the way the team operated?
c. Does your score support your conclusion for (b)?
d. What are some further steps needed to increase team effectiveness?

Select a spokesperson to present a summary of your discussion at _____ .

Step 4: Lecture and discussion (20–40 min.)

Step 5: Self-evaluation and individual learnings

Spend some "alone" time and think about what occurred during the last experience. Focus in on two or three things that affected you or that seemed significant to you. These may be positive or negative elements of the experience. What learnings can you draw from this reflection and what does this mean to you? Don't be concerned about what you ought to have learned, but rather focus on what you did learn and what it means to you. Based on your reflection of the experience, jot down your responses to the following questions:

1. What were your major learnings from the experience?

2. What implications do your learnings have for you as an individual?

3. What implications do your learnings have for you as a manager?

4. What questions do you have as a result of your experience, reflection, and learnings?

5. What implications will your learnings have on your future experiences?

PREWORK ANSWER SHEET

Questions	Individual answer	Individual points*	Correct	Team points*	Team answer
1					
2					
3					
4					
5					
6					
7					
8					
9					
10					
	Individual score		Team score		

*Blanks—(no answer given)—receive 0 points; where correct and given answers match +10 points; where correct answer and given answers do not match −10 points.

TEAM EFFECTIVENESS SCORE SHEET

Individual scores

1. _____

2. _____

3. _____

4. _____

5. _____

6. _____

7. _____

8. _____

Average individual score

(A) (_____) ÷ (_____) = _____
    Total individual scores No. members

Team score Less average individual score

(B) _____

Perfect score (C) 100 Less average individual score

Team effectiveness

(D) (_____) ÷ (_____) = (_____) x 100 = _____ %
    Gain (+) or loss (−) Possible improvement

XII/Understanding motivation and behavior

Block XIII

Production organization simulation—Shipping containers (continued)

GOALS

1. Assess the effectiveness of the production organization previously formed.
2. Determine variables that influence motivation and commitment to job and organization.

PREWORK ASSIGNMENT

In a previous session (Block VII) you were part of creating a production organization. In this Block, you will have the opportunity to make needed changes and operate the organization. To prepare for this Block, you need to review your notes in Block VII, paying particular attention to the notes you made in Step 4 relative to understanding your organizational position.

SESSION INTRODUCTION

During a previous session (Block VII), you created an organization to produce four different shipping containers. During this session the organization will operate so that you can see the outcomes of the organizing process and assess variables that influence motivation and commitment to job and organization.

SESSION OVERVIEW:

Step 1: Preparing to manufacture (15 min.).
Step 2: Manufacturing (30 min; two 15-minute production periods back-to-back).
Step 3: Determining and reporting results. (5 min.).
Step 4: Optional (where more than one organization exists).
Step 5: Reviewing and assessing the organization operation (20 min.).
Step 6: Cross-team exchange and discussion (10 min.).
Step 7: Self-evaluation and individual learnings.

Step 1: Preparing to manufacture (15 min.)

During the next 15 minutes your organization is to get ready to produce. At the end of the 15 minutes, you will receive your first 15-minute market bulletin from Brasan Brokerage Company. You will get two 15-minute bulletins during the next step back-to-back.

Step 2: **Manufacturing** (30 min.)

Utilizing the materials contained at the end of the book, your organization is to produce shipping containers according to the market requirements of Brasan Brokerage Company.

You will get a 15-minute marketing bulletin from Brasan. At the end of the first 15 minutes, you will receive a second 15-minute marketing bulletin.

Time is called 15 minutes after the second marketing bulletin is handed out.

Step 3: **Determining and reporting results** (5 min.)

The production data is assembled and gross profit is determined by completing the Gross Profit Statement in Session VII (p. 74). The results are reported to all members.

Step 4: **Optional** (where more than one organization exists)

Each organization selects a spokesperson to make a brief report to other organizations on:

a. How your organization is structured.
b. How it operates.
c. The results of operation.

Each spokesperson presents a report (maximum 10 min.).

Step 5: **Reviewing and assessing the organization operation** (20 min.)

To extract the learning from the previous experience return to your original teams and complete the following individual work and teamwork.

This step should be completed in _____ .

A. Individual work.

To get maximum learning from our experience we must review our experiences and draw conclusions from them. To prepare for a team discussion, complete the following questions or statements as an individual during the next few minutes. Allow all team members to finish and then complete the items under Teamwork.

1. How committed were you to doing your job?

   1   2   3   4   5   6   7   8   9
   ─────────────────────────────────
   Fully   Fully
   uncommitted   committed

2. How committed were you to helping the organization achieve its objectives?

   1   2   3   4   5   6   7   8   9
   ─────────────────────────────────
   Fully   Fully
   uncommitted   committed

3. Identify some things that contributed to your commitment to your job. Be as specific as possible.

4. Identify some things that interferred with your commitment to the organization. Be specific.

5. What are some things that would have improved your commitment to job and/or organization?

6. Think about what occurred during the last experience. Focus in on two or three things that affected you or that seemed significant to you. These may be positive or negative elements of the experience. What learnings can you draw from this reflection and what does this mean to you? Don't be concerned about what you ought to have learned, but rather focus on what you did learn and what it means to you.

B. Teamwork

As a team, discuss and complete the following items. The best learning will occur if all team members will share their ideas and feelings in the discussion.

1. Discuss the individual responses to the above questions. Explore reasons for why people responded as they did.

2. a. The team is to discuss and come to team-wide understanding and agreement on two things they learned from the experience.
   b. Select a spokesperson to present the team's learning in the next step.

Step 6: Cross-team exchange and discussion (10 min.)

Each team presents their brief report developed in the previous step.

Step 7: **Self-evaluation and individual learnings**

Spend some "alone" time and think about what occurred during the last experience. Focus in on two or three things that affected you or that seemed significant to you. These may be positive or negative elements of the experience. What learnings can you draw from this reflection and what does this mean to you? Don't be concerned about what you ought to have learned, but rather focus on what you did learn and what it means to you. Based on your reflection of the experience, jot down your responses to the following questions:

1. What were your major learnings from the experience?

2. What implications do your learnings have for you as an individual?

3. What implications do your learnings have for you as a manager?

4. What questions do you have as a result of your experience, reflection, and learnings?

5. What implications will your learnings have on your future experiences?

Block XIV

Understanding leadership

GOALS

1. Create an understanding of managerial leadership and leadership styles.
2. Improve leadership skills.

PREWORK ASSIGNMENT

Read the following material on "Leadership" for understanding. Answer the ten prework questions at the end of the reading.

LEADERSHIP

The proper blend of authoritarian and democratic leadership knowingly applied is best.[1]

The directing process is one of helping, influencing, and motivating subordinates. *Managerial leadership* is a term that is often used to refer to the totality of this process. Based on the behavioral concepts presented in the last reading (Block XII), our purpose here is to describe the nature of managerial leadership, identify common leadership styles, and present some of the more important research on leadership effectiveness. The material is organized into the following major sections:

1. The nature of leadership
2. Leadership styles
3. Leadership effectiveness

THE NATURE OF LEADERSHIP

Leadership has been variously defined and described. Traditional and more modern approaches to explaining leadership tend to differ sharply. We present both views below.

Traditional view of leadership

Traditionally, leadership has been viewed in a rather simple light. Jack Gibb summarizes the traditional, extreme view of leadership in a rather dramatic fashion.

[1] Louis A. Allen, *The Management Process* (New York: McGraw-Hill Book Co., 1964), p. 264.

151

People must be led. People perform best under leaders who are creative, imaginative, and aggressive—under leaders who lead. It is the responsibility of the leader to marshall the forces of the organization, to stimulate effort, to capture the imagination, to inspire people, to coordinate efforts, and to serve as a model of sustained effort.

The leader should keep an appropriate social distance, show no favorites, control his emotions, command respect, and be objective and fair. He must know what he is doing and where he wants to go. He must set clear goals for himself and for the group or institution, and then communicate these goals well to all members of the organization. He must listen for advice and counsel before making decisions. But it is his responsibility to make decisions and to set up mechanisms for seeing that the decisions are implemented. After weighing the facts and seeking expert counsel, he must make policy and rules, set reasonable boundaries, and see that these are administered with justice and wisdom, even compassion.

The leader should reward good performance and learn effective ways of showing appreciation. He must be equally ready to give negative criticism where warranted and to appraise performance frequently, fairly, and unequivocally. He must command strong discipline, not only because people respect a strong leader, but because strength and firmness communicate care and concern. Good leadership requires good followship. People tend to follow good leaders. Leaders are born. Methods of election and selection are thus very important. Finding the right chairman or president is the critical variable in the success of a program or an institution. The quality of an organization is often judged by the perceived quality of the leadership.[2]

What leadership is

Based on behavioral science, beliefs about leadership are now changing. Today, leadership is viewed as a complex process influenced by many variables in addition to those of leaders themselves. More recent views approach leadership as a function or process and focus their definitions around interpersonal influence. Today, leadership is defined as interpersonal influence towards the attainment of specific goals in specific situations.[3] As one authority states, "The essence of leadership is interpersonal influence, involving the influencer in an attempt to affect the behavior of the influencee."[4] Thus, leadership is defined as attempts to influence other people in particular directions in specific situations.

This definition of leadership includes three important implications. The first is that leadership is attempted influence and can then be effective or ineffective in varying degrees. Influence is attempted and exercised through communication and more generally through behavior. Leaders influence the behavior of others through exhibiting behavior that communicates.

The second important element in the definition is that of specific goals. The ultimate objective of leadership and leader behavior is the achievement of specific goals.

The third important element in the definition is the specific situation. Leaders do not try to lead people in general; they try to lead particular people toward particular goals in particular situations. Since leadership is attempted influence, the situations in which the influence is attempted are important determinants of leadership effectiveness. A given leadership act may have one effect in one situation and an entirely different effect in another situation.

[2] Jack R. Gibb, "Dynamics of Leadership and Communication," in *In Search of Leaders* from the series *Current Issues in Higher Education, 1967*, p. 55.

[3] Robert Tannerbaum and Fred Massarik, "Leadership: A Frame of Reference," in Donald E. Porter and Phillip B. Applewhite, eds.; *Organizational Behavior and Management* (Scranton, Pa.: International Textbook Co., 1968), p. 413.

[4] Ibid., p. 414.

Leadership functions

As the above definition implies, we believe that it is more meaningful to look at leadership as a set of functions rather than as a prescribed role to be played. Modern-day descriptions of leadership functions vary, but it is generally believed that managerial leadership involves two important functions: task functions and group maintenance functions. Thus, as one authority points out, "A good football team must be skilled in blocking and tackling and in performing the complex offensive and defensive play patterns (task functions), but team "spirit," cooperation, interdependence, and member satisfaction (maintenance functions) must also exist at a high level if the team is to be successful."[5]

Task functions. Task functions refer to those things relating directly to the effective completion of the task. From a managerial leadership standpoint, some of the more important of these functions are: (1) initiating activity—suggesting ideas, defining problems, proposing approaches and/or solutions to problems; (2) seeking information—asking for ideas, suggestions, information, or facts; (3) giving information—offering facts, generalizations, and personal experiences relative to the problem; (4) stating opinions—stating opinions about problems, suggestions, and proposed solutions; (5) elaborating—classifying, explaining, and developing meanings and understanding of concepts and consequences; (6) coordinating—pointing out relationships and drawing activities together; (7) summarizing—pulling together related ideas and suggestions; (8) testing—studying the practical applicability of ideas and suggestions; (9) evaluating—measuring accomplishments and comparing them to some measure of effectiveness; and (10) diagnosing—predicting and identifying problems and determining following steps.[6] Thus, task functions center around activities directly related to task accomplishment.

Maintenance functions. The group maintenance functions of leadership focus on the activities essential for the group to remain together and continue to work together to achieve goals. The more important of these functions are: (1) encouraging—respecting, supporting, and encouraging the contribution of others; (2) gatekeeping—regulating one's own and others' contributions so that all can contribute; (3) setting standards—developing standards for group use in evaluating procedures and problem solutions; (4) following—agreeing with and following the ideas of others and serving as an audience for ideas and suggestions; (5) expressing group feeling—describing and expressing group feeling; (6) evaluating—testing group decisions by comparison with group standards and goals; (7) consensus testing—asking for identifying the degree of group agreement on proposals and problem solutions; (8) harmonizing—mediating and conciliating conflicts of opinion; and (9) reducing tension—draining off negative or unconstructive feelings with humor or putting the situation in context.[7] Thus, task functions focus on the elements that influence togetherness, cooperation, and teamwork.

All leaders perform these two sets of functions in some manner with some degree of effectiveness. Leadership styles refer to the manner in which these functions are handled.

LEADERSHIP STYLES

Leadership is a function or process in which individuals exhibit behavior designed to influence other people; so descriptions of leadership are descriptions of behavior. Any attempt to describe all of the acts in which people engage in the performance of leadership functions would be futile. Additionally, different people do similar things with

---

[5] William R. Lassey, "Dimensions and Leadership," in William R. Lassey ed.; *Leadership and Social Change* (Iowa City, Iowa: University Associates, 1971), p. 5.

[6] Ibid., pp. 5–6.

[7] Ibid.

different effects. We need a way of categorizing general leadership styles—that is, the characteristic way in which the leaders go about performing their leadership functions.

In this section, two of the more popular and, in our opinion, more meaningful ways of describing general leadership styles are explained.

The leadership style continuum

One of the first comprehensive attempts to describe alternative leadership styles is the continuum developed by Tannerbaum and Schmidt.[8] The continuum shown in Figure XIV-1 illustrates the possible range of leadership styles based primarily on the way the manager uses authority. In all, eight specific styles are identified.

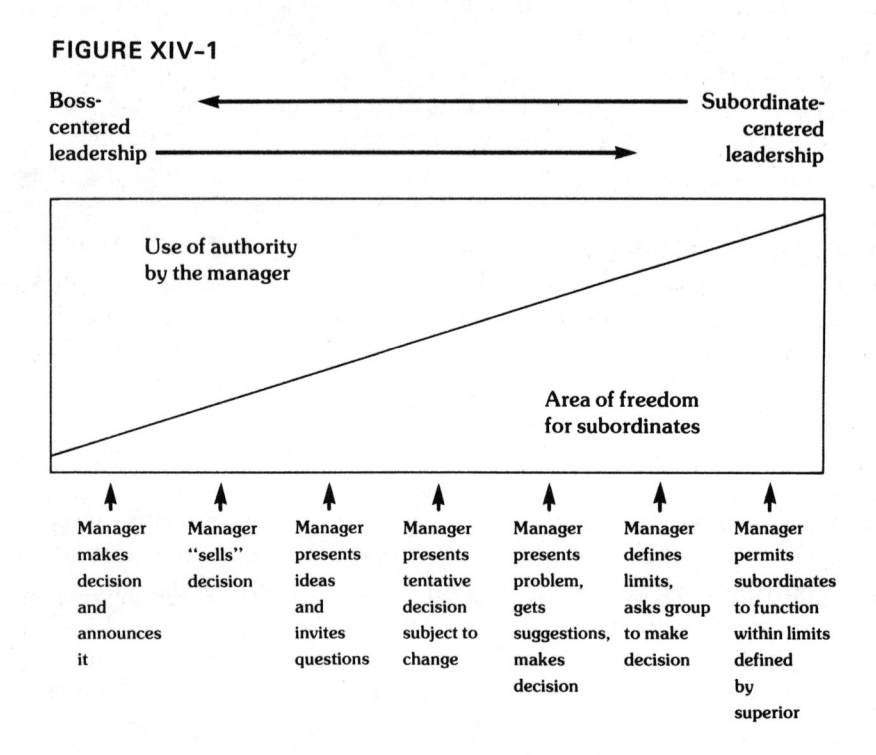

FIGURE XIV-1

Boss-centered leadership ←————————————→ Subordinate-centered leadership

Use of authority by the manager

Area of freedom for subordinates

| Manager makes decision and announces it | Manager "sells" decision | Manager presents ideas and invites questions | Manager presents tentative decision subject to change | Manager presents problem, gets suggestions, makes decision | Manager defines limits, asks group to make decision | Manager permits subordinates to function within limits defined by superior |

Use of authority. In this scheme, the way in which authority is used is the main dimension of the leadership style. That is, in Figure XIV-1 the vertical distance from the bottom of the rectangle to the top of the rectangle represents the total authority of the manager and/or the amount of influence on decisions the manager has. The diagonal line, then, represents the way authority is used to make decisions or the division of influence on decisions between the manager and subordinates. Moving from left to right on the continuum, the leadership style changes as less and less authority is used to make decisions; and as more and more authority is shared with subordinates. On the extreme left are styles characterized by extensive use of authority to maintain a high degree of control resulting in relatively little freedom of action and influence on decisions by subordinates. On the extreme right are styles characterized by extensive sharing of authority and influence on decisions.

[8] Robert Tannerbaum and Warren Schmidt, "How to Choose A Leadership Pattern," *Harvard Business Review* (May–June 1973), pp. 162–80. This discussion of the continuum draws heavily on this source.

Specific styles

In terms of day-to-day behavior, and general styles, 8 styles are identified on the continuum.

Managers make and announce decision. A specific instance of managerial leadership behavior on the extreme left might resemble the following: the manager is aware of a problem to be solved or a decision that needs to be made. She considers the alternatives, makes a decision, announces it, and enforces it. Employees are given little or no opportunity to influence the decision made or its implementation, and the manager probably does not allow her ideas concerning what employees think to have much influence on her decision.

Managers sell decision. A little further to the left is a similar but slightly different style. Here, the manager still might identify the problem and make the decision, but he tries to convince employees that it is the best decision instead of simply announcing and enforcing it. The fact that the manager tries to sell his decision indicates that he recognizes the possibility of resistance on the part of employees and tries to overcome it. Selling the decision forces the manager to consider what he believes the reactions of his subordinates will be; consequently, with this style, employees have more influence on the decision and there is less use of authority than in the previous style.

Sale and Inquiry. The next style to the right on the continuum is easily recognizable in practice and is one where the manager goes yet a step further. He still makes his own decisions and tries to sell the decision to employees; but he now invites their questions and gives them a chance to see and understand the basis upon which his decision is being made. Knowing that he will give people the opportunity to ask questions, he thinks they are likely to ask; and, as a result, employees are given the opportunity to have a greater indirect effect upon the decision. This example characterizes a style that has even less use of authority and more freedom for employees than either of the previous two.

Tentative decisions. The next easily identifiable style to the right is one in which subordinates have the potential for at least some direct influence on decisions affecting them. Using this style, a manager might present to her employees her decisions for problems she perceives and asks for their opinions. In effect, the manager says, "This is the decision I want to make, but I want to know what you think about it." Employees are not given veto powers, but they are given not only the opportunity to question, but to criticize as well. The manager still reserves the final decision for herself and she may or may not make the decision with which employees agree; nevertheless, the fact that the decision has been presented to them with the opportunity to criticize and change offers them a greater influence on the decision and reduces her use of authority.

Survey of ideas. Still further to the right on the continuum is a style with even more freedom for employees and even less use of authority. An attempt at leadership using this style would be one in which the supervisor presents a problem to employees and asks for their ideas and opinions before making a decision. The manager still identifies the problem and makes the decision, but it is made in consideration of what the subordinates think. Using this approach, the manager has given employees more influence on the decision and, consequently, probably makes a decision which will be accepted without extensive use of authority.

Bounded group decision. Approaching the right end of the continuum is a style in which employees have a significant, direct effect upon decisions. Under this style, a manager defines the problem and the boundaries within which the decision has to be made. Then, the manager turns the right to make the bounded decision over to the group. The manager may or may not join the subordinates as a member of the group which is making the decision. It is clear that this leadership style involves relatively large areas of freedom and influence for subordinates, although it employs only a slight use of authority by the manager.

Limited group autonomy. At the extreme right end of the continuum is a style resulting in nominal usage of authority and great amounts of freedom and influence for subordinates. Using a style such as this, a manager simply might impose the same limitations on employees as are imposed upon him or her. Within these limits, employees are allowed as a group (probably democratically) to identify problems and make decisions. The manager may or may not join the group in making the decisions; but if one does, one uses no more authority and has no more influence on the decision than has any other member of the group.

Before leaving the descriptions of managerial leadership styles, some comments are in order. First of all, the discussion has pointed out and described briefly only a few easily recognizable general leadership styles. In reality, there are an infinite number of different styles and readers, with discriminating observation, can identify styles slightly different from any of those described above. Second, it should be pointed out that the styles at both ends of the continuum are extreme cases. In reality, there probably is no such thing as absolute use of authority to the extent that subordinates have no freedom and influence on decisions; on the other hand, it is also true that rarely are subordinates given almost complete autonomy—even as a group. Readers should recognize that the leadership styles represented at both extreme ends of the continuum are not used extensively by many managers.

It should be remembered also that the descriptions of the preceding styles are not complete, explicit descriptions of all the important variables influencing the effectiveness of leadership behavior. For example, the following discussion points out that leader orientation has a significant effect upon leadership effectiveness, yet the continuum and style descriptions do not mention specifically this element of leader behavior. Other important elements or dimensions of leader behavior covered in the discussion of effectiveness are more easily related to the style descriptions. The fact that the descriptions of leader behavior do not mention explicitly all the important variables affecting leadership is a result of the exisiting fragmented state of leadership theory in general. The fact that leadership and its effectiveness are not fully understood by anyone is not sufficient reason to discard them altogether, especially since practical experience indicates that the practice of what is known can improve managerial leadership significantly.

Three general leadership styles. Having identified and described briefly several different leadership styles, and with the understanding that there is an infinite number of such styles, it probably would be more meaningful if all the different styles were grouped into one of three broad categories for the sake of discussion. All the styles on the continuum will be classified as autocratic, participative, or democratic, as indicated in Figure XIV-2. Each of these three broad general styles will be described briefly now.

Autocratic leadership. Autocratic managerial leaders centralize power and decision-making in themselves. Autocratic leaders make extensive use of authority to structure the work environment and actions of their subordinates. Consequently, subordinates have relatively little freedom or influence on decisions; but, by the same token, they are responsible only for obeying orders and doing what they are told. Communication and influence flow in only one direction—from superiors to the subordinates.

Participative leadership. Participative leadership shares managerial authority and

FIGURE XIV-2

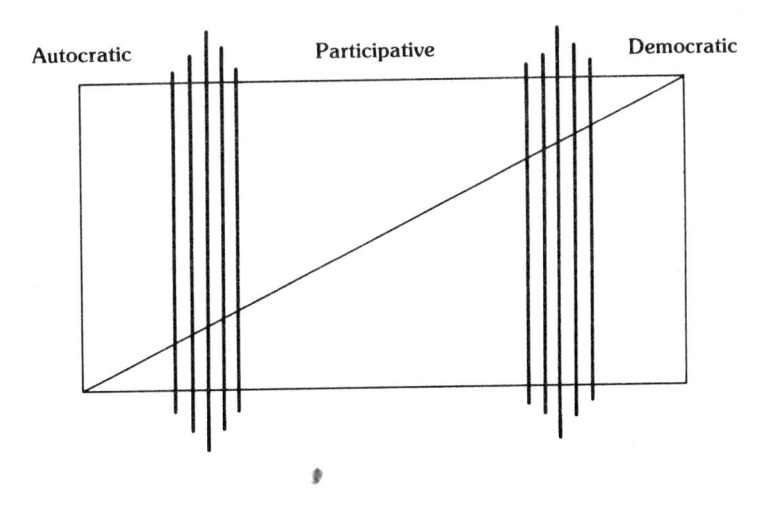

responsibility almost equally with subordinates as a group. Since authority is decentralized, both superiors and subordinates exert significant influence on decisions which the superiors feel are needed. There is two-way communication and influence between superiors and individual group members, and also between members of the subordinate group.

Democratic leadership. Democratic managers use authority sparingly and delegate to the individuals in the group as a whole large amounts of authority and the freedom and decision-making associated with them. Authority and influence are centered in the group instead of being divided among individuals. Naturally, managerial leaders operate under the restrictions of their own superiors and they cannot delegate more authority than has been delegated to them; therefore, the authority of the employee group is not unlimited. Generally, however, the employee group (within limits) sets its own goals and makes its own decisions. The manager is no longer the central force in decision-making and the authority and influence are centered in the group.

The Managerial Grid®

Another popular way of describing leadership behavior and general styles is the approach of Blake and Mouton.[9] The *grid* identifies five common leadership styles based on three key variables—concern for production, concern for people, and how the two concerns are put together or integrated.

Dimensions of leadership style. According to this approach, all leadership styles are determined primarily by three related factors—the degree of concern shown for people, the degree of concern shown for production, and the way that these two degrees of concern are linked together.

Obviously, managers can show different degrees of concern for both people and production and can link these two concerns together in different ways. The different combinations of the two degrees of concern and the resulting leadership styles are illustrated on the grid shown in Figure XIV-3. In reality, there are 81 different combinations of the two concerns and, therefore, 81 different leadership styles; but only five general styles are illustrated on the grid. Each of these five styles is described below in terms of the approach to decision-making, directing, and communication.

[9]Robert R. Blake and Jane S. Mouton, *The Managerial Grid* (Houston: Gulf Publishing Co. 1964). This explanation of the "grid" is based primarily on this source.

The 9,1 style. The style illustrated in the lower right-hand corner of the grid is the 9,1 style which represents a *high* degree of concern for production and a *low* degree of concern for people. A basic belief in this style is that there is a conflict between the needs of the organization and the needs of employees—both cannot be achieved so employees' goals must be sacrificed in order that organizational goals can be achieved.

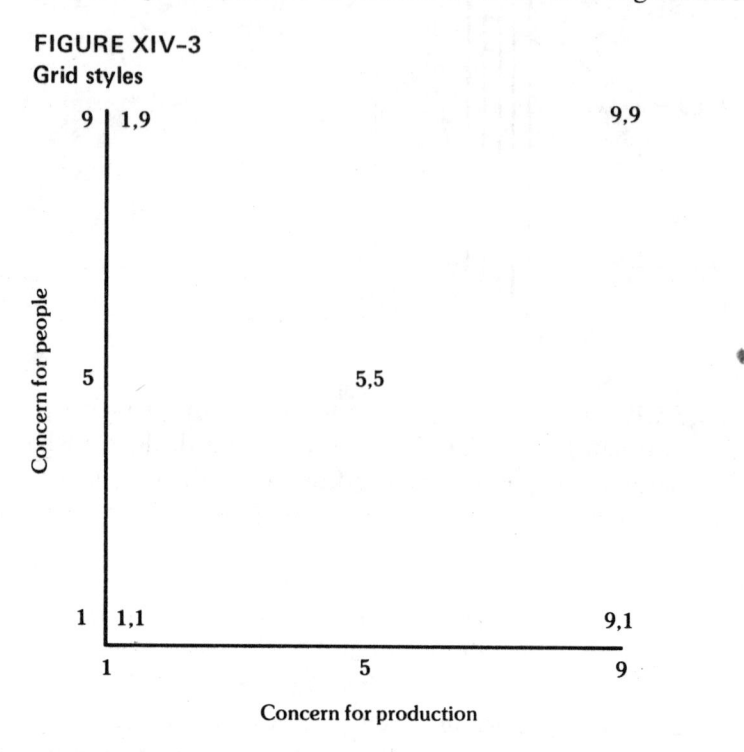

FIGURE XIV-3
Grid styles

```
Concern for people
9 | 1,9                              9,9


5 |         5,5


1 | 1,1                              9,1
    1        5        9
       Concern for production
```

Using the 9,1 style a manager basically tries to create a situation in which employees cannot interfere too much with the achievement of organizational goals. Decision-making is reserved for the manager. The manager may listen to or even seek out employee opinions; may only announce or may "sell" decisions; but the manager makes and ultimately enforces almost all of the significant decisions, such as what will be done and how it will be done.

Directing is exercised by the manager over the employee on a one-to-one basis. The 9,1 style relies heavily on the use of authority and control over rewards and punishment to direct people. Directing is basically in the form of orders and subordinates are expected to obey. Much directing is in the form of continual checking on subordinates to see that they are doing as they have been told. Communication is, for the most part, formal, and follows strictly formal channels. The information communicated is likely to be limited primarily to only that which the superior feels is essential for subordinates to do their job. In summary, a manager using a 9,1 style tries to spell out exactly what one wants and to make sure that what one says is what is done; one expects subordinates to do exactly what one says, no more and no less.

The 1,9 style. The style illustrated in the upper left-hand corner of the grid is the 1,9 style which represents a *high* degree of concern for people and a *low* degree of concern for production. A basic feature of this style is that people must be kept happy. As with the 9,1 style, underlying this belief is that there is a basic conflict between the needs of the organization and the needs of the employees. Both cannot be achieved, but the 1,9 manager believes that the organization's goals must be sacrificed so that the employees' can be met and employees can be kept happy. The belief is that this is the only way any work toward achieving organizational goals will ever result.

Using the 1,9 style, a manager basically tries to create a work situation where people can work together with comfort, ease, and security. In short, a situation where people can be happy. Decision-making with a 1,9 style is aimed also at keeping people happy or at least not making people too unhappy. The 1,9 decision-making strategy is likely to be to find out what people want and then let that happen. The criteria for decisions, then, is that which won't make too many people unhappy or that which will keep most people happy. Little real direction is exercised by the superior with a 1,9 style. When people get too far out of line, the 1,9 manager is likely to use gentle persuasion. People are rarely held accountable for their performance; and there is likely to be a general looseness of enforcement of any type of rules, regulations, or policies. In almost all matters of direction, a manager using a 1,9 style is likely to focus on the group as the unit and deal with the group as a whole rather than dealing with individuals. Communication in the 1,9 style is most informal. There is little use made of formal channels and the content of communication is likely to be aimed at keeping people happy rather than achieving organizational objectives. Communication is used as one of the vehicles for keeping people from becoming too dissatisfied. The content of much communication focuses on "the things that are good around here." In summary, the manager using a 1,9 style seeks most of all to be accepted and to create a trouble-free, secure situation in which people can be happy and work.

The 1,1 style. The style illustrated in the lower left-hand corner of the grid is the 1,1 style which represents a *low* degree of concern for production and a *low* degree of concern for people. A basic belief in this style also is that there is a conflict between the needs of the organization and the needs of employees. Both cannot be achieved. In contrast to either the 9,1 or 1,9 manager, however, the 1,1 style basically abandons both the organization's goals and the individual's goals.

Using the 1,1 style, managers usually try to create a situation in which they isolate themselves from their superior and from their employees in order to be more secure. The 1,1 style is not a natural managerial style. It is most often created by environmental conditions. The 1,1 style is one in which the manager has basically given up. The main objective is to maintain the position. In a 1,1 style, decision-making is almost nonexistent. The 1,1 style avoids making decisions because it makes a manager conspicuous. Rather than make decisions, the superior generally passes along to employees what is passed down to her or him or passes up to superiors what is passed upward from employees. Direction using a 1,1 style is almost nonexistent. Little direction of any sort is given except in extreme emergencies. Communication under the 1,1 style is minimal. It includes generally formal communication and, in many cases, written communication about what has been communicated down from above. A manager using the 1,1 style tends to be a communication relay between the organization above and subordinates below. In summary, managers using the 1,1 style try to create a situation in which they are inconspicuous to their superior and also conspicuous to their subordinates. They try to avoid anything that will make them noticeable.

The 5,5 style. The style indicated in the middle of the grid is the 5,5 style which represents a moderate degree of concern for production and a moderate degree of concern for people. A basic belief in this style also is that there is a conflict between the needs of the organization and the needs of the employees. Both cannot be satisfied at the same time. In contrast to the other styles illustrated, however, the 5,5 style is based upon the belief that both organizational goals and employee's goals can be sacrificed to some extent so that both can be achieved to some degree.

Using the 5,5 style, a manager basically tries to create a situation in which production can be achieved, but a situation which will not unduly disturb employees. Using the 5,5 style, a manager relies heavily on persuasion and logic to get employees to accept doing things in the name of the organization. In making decisions, 5,5 managers are likely to make the decisions themselves; but their decisions must be, in the final analysis, acceptable to employees. If not, they will modify their decisions so that they are acceptable. So the difference between 5,5 managers and 9,1 managers with respect to making decisions is that 9,1 managers make and enforce their decisions; 5,5 managers make to enforce. In directing employees, managers using the 5,5 style are likely to use a lot of persuasion and logic and deal with subordinates on a one-to-one basis rather than as a group or as a team. Most direction under the 5,5 style is likely to be positive rather than negative and to emphasize rewards rather than punishment. Communication using the 5,5 style is likely to be a combination of both formal and informal communication. The formal channels are used to relay information upward and downward. Informal channels are used to "take the pulse" of what's really going on in the organization. The content of the communication using the 5,5 style is likely to focus in on positive information rather than on problem-solving information, whatever its nature. In summary, managers using the 5,5 style are likely to try to be very benevolent autocrats.

The 9,9 style. The style illustrated in the upper right-hand corner of the grid is the 9,9 style which represents a high degree of concern for production and a high degree of concern for people. A basic belief in this style is that there is absolutely no conflict between the needs of the organization and the needs of the employees. Both can and must be satisfied at the same time for either the employees or the organization to effectively achieve their goals. Using the 9,9 style a manager basically tries to create a set of conditions which will allow and encourage people to use their abilities to develop the best solutions to organizational problems. The 9,9 style of making decisions is to try to get the decision made in the way that will be the best for the organization. This means not only making the best decision but making the best decision that people will be committed to carrying out. Much decision making under the 9,9 approach is by consensus of the manager and subordinates. Overt directing and control are also likely to be minimal under the 9,9 approach because directing and control result from subordinates understanding what they are doing, why, and from being committed to helping achieve organizational objectives because they have a personal stake in achieving them. In other words, employees exercise self-direction and self-control because they realize and understand they are satisfying or will satisfy their own needs by doing their best to achieve organizational objectives. The focus in directing is on the team rather than on the relationships between the superior and individuals. Using the 9,9 style, communication is likely to be open, frank, candid, and oriented toward solving problems which interfere with the achievement or organizational objectives.

As yet we have said little regarding leadership effectiveness and specifically the effectiveness of particular leadership styles. We now turn our attention to that topic.

LEADERSHIP EFFECTIVENESS

While there has been quite a lot of empirical research on leadership effectiveness, not all of it has been done based on the style descriptions presented above. We will, in this section, however, summarize the most important research on leadership effectiveness.

The University of Michigan studies

Based on a relatively large amount of research, Likert and his colleagues at the Institute for Social Research succeeded in differentiating between more- and less-productive managers on two related bases.[10]

Based on the way they led, managers were classified as either job-centered or employee-centered. The job-centered managers tended to structure the jobs of subordinates highly, supervise closely, and use incentives to stimulate effort. The employee-centered managers tended to focus on the human aspects and on teamwork. They provided considerable freedom to subordinates to do their tasks once goals were specified. Figure XIV-4 shows the results of one of the studies. Clearly, the employee-centered leaders tended to be more effective.

FIGURE XIV-4

Number of supervisors who are:

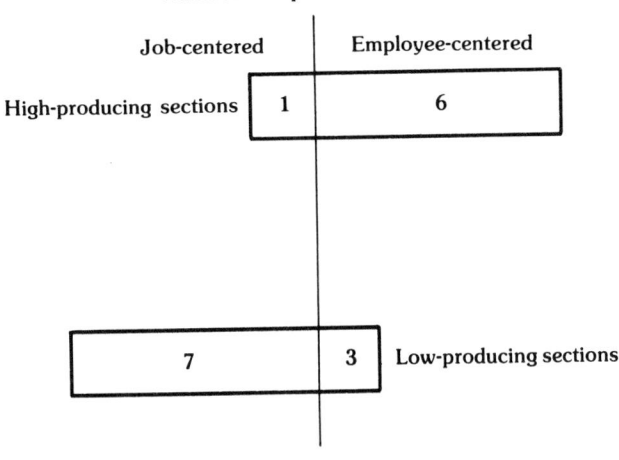

	Job-centered	Employee-centered
High-producing sections	1	6
	7	3	Low-producing sections

Another of the studies classified leaders as either close supervisors or general supervisors. Figure XIV-5 shows the results of this study. Again, general supervision tended to be more effective than close supervision.

FIGURE XIV-5

Number of supervisors who are:

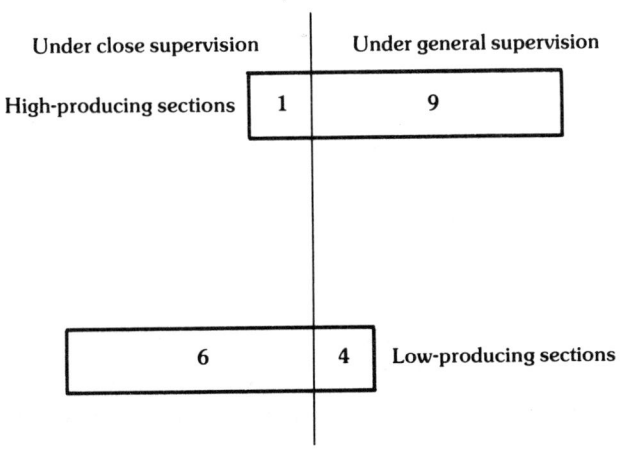

	Under close supervision	Under general supervision
High-producing sections	1	9
	6	4	Low-producing sections

[10] Rensis Likert, *New Patterns of Management* (New York: McGraw-Hill Book Co., 1961). This section draws heavily on this source, and Figures XIV-4 and XIV-5 are based on this source.

The Ohio State studies

A team of researchers at Ohio State University, after extensive research, have added some more information to the data on leadership effectiveness. They were successful in isolating two dimensions of leadership—initiating structure and consideration—which seemed to be related to effectiveness.[11]

The two dimensions of initiating structure and consideration are somewhat similar to those identified in the University of Michigan studies. The initiating structure dimension refers to the degree to which managerial leaders structured their own and subordinates' roles. The consideration dimension refers to the degree to which leaders developed work situation atmospheres where there was mutual trust and respect for subordinates' ideas and feelings and good two-way communication. Those low in consideration tended to be more impersonal in their dealings with subordinates.

The results of the Ohio State studies are somewhat confusing. Based on performance ratings by superiors, production managers high in initiating structure and low in consideration were more productive. The reverse was true for managers in non-production areas. In both types of situation, however, managers high in initiating structure and low in consideration had higher rates of such things as absenteeism, tensions, and grievances. So, while their bosses saw them as better, other variables did not *support* the superiors' ratings.

While neither the Michigan nor Ohio State studies investigated the specific styles described by Tannerbaum and Schmidt's continuum or Blake and Mouton's grid theory, two conclusions can be drawn. The first is that close supervision, job-centered and initiating structure seem to be related to the boss-centered (or autocratic) end of the style continuum and to the 9,1 style described by Blake and Mouton, while employee-centered and consideration seem to correspond to the subordinate-centered end of the continuum and to the concern for people dimension of the grid and to the 1,9 style. The second conclusion is that both of these studies ignored everything but leaders' behaviors—aspects of the situation and subordinates were not investigated.

Possible independence of leadership dimensions

In fairness to Blake and Mouton, we think it should be pointed out that the grid theory is also based on research and that it contends that the employee-centered and job- or production-centered dimensions are independent of each other.[12] Thus, a manager could be high or low or some combination of both. The implication is that a style made up of a high degree of concern for production (job-centered, initiating structure) and a high degree of concern for people (employee-centered, consideration) is the most effective of all styles.

Contingency theory

The research of Fiedler and his associates[13] is more easily related to the style continuum of Tannerbaum and Schmidt in that it includes styles similar to the two ends of the continuum and does include the situational elements of subordinates and task situations.

The results of these studies indicate that effectiveness of a particular leadership style is contingent on the three broad situational factors of leader-subordinate relations, task

---

[11] R. M. Stogdill and A. E. Coons, *Leader Behavior: Its Description and Measurement*, Monograph 88 (Columbus: Bureau of Educational Research, Ohio State University, 1957).

[12] See Blake and Mouton, *Grid*, pp. 5-9.

[13] Fred E. Fiedler, *A Theory of Leadership Effectiveness* (New York: McGraw-Hill Book Co., 1967).

structure, and power position. Leader-subordinate relations refer to the degree to which subordinates accept, like, and have confidence in the leader, and can be good or bad. Task structure refers to the degree to which jobs or routine are defined and can be highly- or lowly-structured. Power position refers to the degree to which leaders have the authority (power) to give or withhold rewards and punishment, and it can be strong or weak.

After exhaustive study of varying combinations of these three variables, Fiedler concluded that different styles were more effective with different combinations of the three situational factors. Table XIV-1 summarizes the results. Fiedler's conclusion is that we might have more success engineering jobs to fit managers than in trying to change managers to fit jobs.[14]

TABLE XIV-1
Summary of Fiedler investigations of leadership

Condition	Group situation			Leadership style correlating with productivity
	Leader-member relations	Task structure	Position power	
1	Good	Structured	Strong	Directive
2	Good	Structured	Weak	Directive
3	Good	Unstructured	Strong	Directive
4	Good	Unstructured	Weak	Permissive
5	Moderately poor	Structured	Strong	Permissive
6	Moderately poor	Structured	Weak	No Data
7	Moderately poor	Unstructured	Strong	No relationship found
8	Moderately poor	Unstructured	Weak	Directive

Some conclusions

While all of the evidence is, hopefully, not yet in, we think some conclusions can be drawn. First of all, we think there is no such thing as the most effective style for any particular leader. The most effective style for any manager is the one that is most natural for that person. Styles that ignore the personality of the leader seem sure to fail. So the moral is, be yourself in your leadership style.

In view of this, however, we do feel strongly about two things. One is that leaders should continually experiment (in relatively low-risk situations) with different styles to test their effectiveness. The second is that the effectiveness of any style can be enhanced through improving certain basic skills—communication and interpersonal, conceptual, and analytical skills such as planning and problem-solving. So, leaders with any style can improve the effectiveness of their style. In short, try to develop skills to be the best leader you can with the style that is natural to you, and constantly experiment with different styles.

SUMMARY

Leadership is attempted interpersonal influence toward the attainment of specific objectives. It is a process or function invoking tasked-related activities and group-maintenance activities.

[14] Fred E. Fiedler, "Engineer the Job to Fit the Manager," *Harvard Business Review*, vol. 43 (September–October 1965), pp. 115–22.

The general approach taken to this influence process is called the leadership style. One scheme of leadership styles ranges from boss-centered to subordinate-centered depending on how authority is used to make decisions. A second framework of leadership descriptions uses the dimensions of concern for employees, concern for production, and integration of the two concerns to describe five common leadership styles.

Much research on leadership style effectiveness still has not produced definite answers. Some research indicates that employee-centered versus job-centered leaders are more productive. Other research shows mixed evidence concerning whether styles high in initiating structure or high in consideration are more effective. Still other research indicates that the dimensions—concern of employers and concern for product—are independent of each other. And, yet, still other research indicates that the most effective leadership style depends on particular situational factors. We think no one style is most effective for all leaders.

PREWORK QUESTIONS

Based on the material in "Leadership," select the best and most complete answer for the following questions. Select only one answer, even though others are not wrong. If you are unsure of your choice, it is better to leave it blank. Once you have completed the questions, transfer your individual answers to the Prework Answer Sheet (p. 170) under the column marked *Individual answers*.

Individual answers   *Team answers*

1. Leadership is:

    a. A formal position in the organization.
    b. A quality some have and some do not have.
    c. Influence.
    d. A process of performing particular functions.

2. Using a 9,1 leadership style, a manager would be most likely to emphasize:

    a. The motivator factor of the satisfier-dissatisfier theory.
    b. Both the motivators and dissatisfiers of the satisfier-dissatisfier theory.
    c. The dissatisfiers of the satisfier-dissatisfier theory.
    d. Maslow's need hierarchy.

3. Using the 9,9 leadership style, a manager would be most likely to concentrate motivational efforts on:

    a. Higher-level needs.
    b. The motivators in satisfier-dissatisfier theory.
    c. The dissatisfiers in the satisfier-dissatisfier theory
    d. All levels of needs and both the motivators and dissatisfiers.

4. Using a 1,9 leadership style, managers would be most likely to emphasize:

    a. Lower-level needs.
    b. Higher-level needs.
    c. Dissatisfiers.
    d. Satisfiers.

5. Using a 5,5 leadership style, managers would be most likely to:

    a. Use their authority to force people to produce.
    b. Try to persuade employees that they have to take some bad with the good.
    c. Emphasize the motivators.
    d. Emphasize lower-level needs.

6. The styles in the grid correspond to the styles in the style continuum in the following way:

    a. (9,9–democratic), (5,5–participative), (9,1–autocratic)
    b. (9,1–autocratic), (1,9–democratic), (1,1–participative)
    c. (9,1–autocratic), (9,9–no corresponding style), (5,5–democratic)
    d. (5,5–participative), (1,9–democratic), (9,1–autocratic)

_____ 7. The Michigan leadership studies indicated that:

   a. Job-centered leaders are more productive.
   b. Employee-centered leaders are more productive.
   c. A combination of job-centered and employee-centered leaders are more productive.
   d. No relationship between job-centered and employee-centered leaders and productiveness was found.

_____ 8. The Ohio State leadership studies indicated that:

   a. Initiating structure made leaders more productive.
   b. Consideration was positively related to production.
   c. Initiating structure was viewed favorable by superiors.
   d. Consideration increased laxness in adherence to work rules.

_____ 9. The contingency theory indicates leadership effectiveness:

   a. Depends on the situational factors of leader-subordinate relations, personality, and task structure.
   b. Depends on structuring the leadership situation.
   c. Depends on leader-member relations, task structure, and power position.
   d. is not influenced by the variables considered in the University of Michigan and Ohio State studies.

_____ 10. The most effective leadership style for a manager is:

   a. The style one really believes in.
   b. 9,9.
   c. 5,5.
   d. 9,1.

SESSION INTRODUCTION

This session will focus on creating an understanding of leadership by drawing on the directing experience, the text material, and a lecture.

SESSION OVERVIEW

Step 1: Teamwork on prework (30 min.).

Step 2: Scoring individual and team answers, and comparing team effectiveness scores (10 min.).

Step 3: Increasing team effectiveness (30 min.).

Step 4: Lecture and discussion (20–40 min.).

Step 5: Self-evaluation and individual learnings.

Step 1: Teamwork on prework (30 min.)

As prework you answered a 10-item multiple-choice test on "Leadership." Each team is to identify the single best answer for each question. The text is not to be used during the discussion, but you may use your prework answers. Team answers are to be recorded on the Prework Answer Sheet (p. 170) under the column *Team answers.*

You will have 30 minutes to arrive at team answers through discussion and analysis. At that time, the individual and team answers will be scored to determine how effectively each team operated. The scoring system reflects the degree of commitment to team answers. Each correct answer receives 10 points. Items unanswered are worth 0 points. An incorrect answer results in −10 points. Thus, the score is calculated by taking the number correct, subtracting the number incorrect, and multiplying by 10.

This step should be completed by _____ .

Step 2: Scoring individual and team answers and comparing team effectiveness scores (10 min.)

Using the Prework Answer Sheet, score your individual and team answers based on the correct responses distributed to you. A simple procedure to follow is to record the correct answers in the column *Correct answers.* Where the given and correct answers match, put +10 in the *Points* column. Where no answer is given, record 0 points and where the given and correct answers do not match, put −10 in the points column. By totaling the points, the individual and team score can be determined.

Individuals and teams can be compared based on their scores. However, individuals come to teams with varying degrees of preparation and knowledge. As a result the final score may not reflect how information was shared and how decisions were made during the team discussion. To take this into account a *Team effectiveness score* can be determined.

At least one team member should complete the Team Effectiveness Score Sheet (p. 171), according to the following steps:

a. Determine the average individual score by adding the individual scores and dividing by the number of team members.

b. Subtract the average individual score from the team score to determine a gain or loss. A positive number indicates the team arrived at a higher score than the average of what individuals arrived at working separately. A loss, or negative number, indicates that team discussion and agreement resulted in a lower score than the individuals did working alone.

c. Determine what the possible improvement was by subtracting the average individual score from the perfect score of 100. This number represents how many points of improvement were possible through team discussion and agreement.

d. Determine team effectiveness by dividing the gain (+) or loss (−) by the possible improvement and multiplying by 100. Once all teams have completed the scoring, the average individual, team, and team effectiveness scores will be collected and posted.

Step 3: Increasing team effectiveness (30 min.)

To improve team effectiveness and to help others become more effective team members, complete the following:

A. Individual work.

1. The way we operate as team members is:

1	2	3	4	5	6	7	8	9
Fully ineffective								Fully effective

2. Identify specific behaviors in the team that are helpful for team effectiveness—be specific.

3. Identify specific behaviors in the team that hinder team effectiveness—be specific.

B. Teamwork.

Discuss the individual responses to the above questions. Identifying specific behaviors with specific team-members can make for a more enriching and meaningful discussion. Also, the discussion will be more open and useful if you will let others know that you desire the feedback (if you do).

Step 4: Lecture and discussion (20–40 min.)

Step 5: Self-evaluation and individual learnings

Spend some "alone" time and think about what occurred during the last experience. Focus in on two or three things that affected you or that seemed significant to you. These may be positive or negative elements of the experience. What learnings can you draw from this reflection and what does this mean to you? Don't be concerned about what you ought to have learned, but rather focus on what you did learn and what it means to you. Based on your reflection of the experience, jot down your responses to the following questions:

1. What were your major learnings from the experience?

2. What implications do your learnings have for you as an individual?

3. What implications do your learnings have for you as a manager?

4. What questions do you have as a result of your experience, reflection, and learnings?

5. What implications will your learnings have on your future experiences?

PREWORK ANSWER SHEET

Questions	Individual answer	Individual points*	Correct	Team points*	Team answer
1					
2					
3					
4					
5					
6					
7					
8					
9					
10					
	Individual score	_____	Team score	_____	

*Blanks—(no answer given)—receive 0 points; where correct and given answers match +10 points; where correct answer and given answers do not match −10 points.

TEAM EFFECTIVENESS SCORE SHEET

Individual scores

1. _____
2. _____
3. _____
4. _____
5. _____
6. _____
7. _____
8.

(A) (   ) ÷ (   ) =   Average individual score
Total individual scores   No. members

(B) Team score Less average individual score

(C) Perfect score 100 Less average individual score

Team effectiveness

(D) (   ) ÷ (   ) = (   ) x 100 =   %
Gain (+) or loss (−)   Possible improvement

Block XV

Feedback on leadership style

GOALS

1. To gain more insight into one's own leadership style.
2. To provide participants the opportunity to get personal feedback on their leadership style.

PREWORK ASSIGNMENT

Awareness of our own leadership style is important for managerial effectiveness. The next activity will provide you the opportunity to learn about your leadership style by completing and scoring a questionnaire and by discussing your leadership style with one or more of your team members.

To prepare for the next session, complete the following questionnaire. Don't answer it in terms of how you would like to be, but rather answer it in terms of how you actually are.

You will score your own questionnaire and the accuracy of the feedback is dependent on how honestly you answer the questions. So complete the questionnaire as you really are prior to the next session.

Directions.[1]   The following are various types of behavior which a supervisor (manager, leader) may engage in in relation to subordinates. Read each item carefully and then put a check mark in one of the columns to indicate what you would do.

If I were the supervisor, I would:	*Make a great effort to do this*	*Tend to do this*	*Tend to avoid doing this*	*Make a great effort to avoid this*
1. Closely supervise my subordinates in order to get better work from them.	_____	_____	_____	_____

---

[1] "Supervisory Attitudes: The X-Y Scale." Reprinted from J. William Pfeiffer and John E. Jones, eds., *The 1972 Annual Handbook for Group Facilitators* (La Jolla, Calif.: University Associates, 1972), p. 67. Used with permission.

	Make a great effort to do this	Tend to do this	Tend to avoid doing this	Make a great effort to avoid this
If I were the supervisor, I would:				
2. Set the goals and objectives for my subordinates and sell them on the merits of my plans.	_____	_____	_____	_____
3. Set up controls to assure that my subordinates are getting the job done.	_____	_____	_____	_____
4. Encourage my subordinates to set their own goals and objectives.	_____	_____	_____	_____
5. Make sure that my subordinates' work is planned out for them.	_____	_____	_____	_____
6. Check with my subordinates daily to see if they need any help.	_____	_____	_____	_____
7. Step in as soon as reports indicate that the job is slipping.	_____	_____	_____	_____
8. Push my people to meet schedules if necessary.	_____	_____	_____	_____
9. Have frequent meetings to keep in touch with what is going on.	_____	_____	_____	_____
10. Allow subordinates to make important decisions.	_____	_____	_____	_____

SESSION OVERVIEW

Step 1: Lecture and score predictions (10 min.).
Step 2: Scoring (10 min.).
Step 3: Score interpretation (20 min.).
Step 4: Discussion (10–20 min.).
Step 5: Self-evaluation and individual learnings.

Step 1: **Lecture and score predictions** (10 min.)

Based on the lecture, think about your own attitudes toward subordinates, and locate on the scale below where you think you are, in reference to Theory X–Theory Y assumptions. Write "Me-1" where you think you are.

```
Theory X                                              Theory Y
   |10          20          30          40|
```

Step 2: **Scoring** (10 min.)

Participants score their own questionnaire and enter their score based on instructions given orally.

Step 3: **Score interpretation** (20 min.)

Join one or two other team members. Each of you are to:

1. Show and give your interpretation of your prediction and score.
2. Share your reaction to your scores.
3. Ask "What things do I do that make you think my score fits?"
4. Ask "What things do I do that make you think my score does not fit?"

Step 4: **Discussion** (10–20 min.)

Step 5: **Self-evaluation and individual learnings**

Spend some "alone" time and think about what occurred during the last experience. Focus in on two or three things that affected you or that seemed significant to you. These may be positive or negative elements of the experience. What learnings can you draw from this reflection and what does this mean to you? Don't be concerned about what you ought to have learned, but rather focus on what you did learn and what it means to you. Based on your reflection of the experience, jot down your responses to the following questions:

1. What were your major learnings from the experience?

2. What implications do your learnings have for you as an individual?

3. What implications do your learnings have for you as a manager?

4. What questions do you have as a result of your experience, reflection, and learnings?

5. What implications will your learnings have on your future experiences?

Block XVI

Control experience—The branch office

GOALS

1. To experience the control function of management.
2. To improve skills in controlling.

PREWORK ASSIGNMENT

Read the following case, "The Branch Office," for understanding. Answer the questions at the end of the case.

THE BRANCH OFFICE

The XYZ is a large national organization selling one product to business and consumers. All business is conducted through branch offices located throughout the country. Branch offices are located so that each branch has the same market potential. That is, each branch office serves a particular territory and territories have been set up so that both sales and profit potential are approximately the same in all territories.

Branch offices are managed by a branch manager who has three subordinate managers reporting to him or her—a sales supervisor, an operations supervisor, and an office supervisor. Thus, the organization chart for a branch is as shown in Figure XVI-1.

FIGURE XVI-1

```
                    Branch Manager
                          |
        ------------------+------------------
        |                 |                 |
      Sales            Office          Operations
    Supervisor       Supervisor        Supervisor
        |                 |                 |
   Salespeople      Office Workers    Operations Workers
```

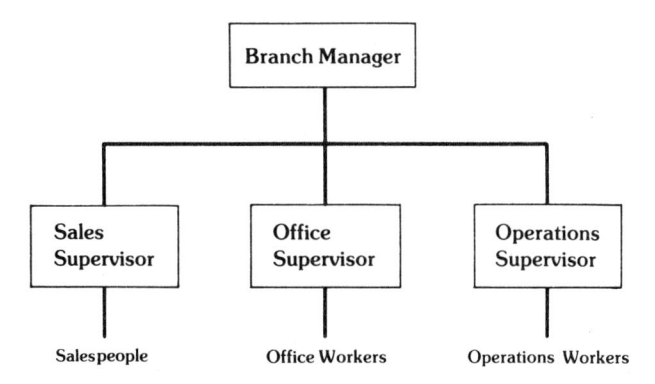

The company is highly decentralized and within broad policy, branch managers operate their branches almost as small independent companies. Company-wide control of branches is exercised through broad policy and financial controls dealing mainly with return on investment.

A summary of the responsibilities of a branch manager are as follows:

Branch managers are responsible for the conduct of all company operations in their territory and, therefore, for the profitability of their branch. More specifically, they are responsible for the recruitment, training, supervision, and evaluation of the sales supervisor, the operations supervisor, and the office supervisor, and they are responsible for coordinating all branch activities. Branch managers are evaluated based on the profitability of their branch.

At the end of the company's last fiscal year (six months ago) this particular branch was producing below-average results. Average sales for all company branches was $1,120,000 and the average profit as a percent of sales for all branches was 14 percent. In contrast, sales at this branch were $1,000,000 and profits were 9 percent of sales.

Based on this information, both the branch manager and his boss agreed that the branch could be brought up to at least the average in one year.

In light of this, they agreed on and set two goals for the branch—sales of $1,120,000 and profit as a percent of sales of 14 percent.

Six months has now passed and the branch manager just received the following statement of results for the first six months of the year:

Results of Operations
for
First Half of Fiscal Year

	This branch	Average of all branches
Sales	$540,000	$560,000
Profit as percent of sales	11%	14%
Expense as percent of sales	14%	12%
Number of salespeople	6	8
Average sales/salesperson	$ 90,000	$ 70,000
Number of customers	1,200	1,100
Average sales/customer	$ 450	$ 509

Questions

1. How does actual performance of the branch compare with planned performance? Be as specific as possible in your answer.

2. Based on the information you have, determine what changes need to be made to

correct for any deviations you find between actual and planned performance. Again be as specific as you can.

SESSION INTRODUCTION

Controlling involves making sure that what is actually being achieved is what was planned or intended. Specifically, control involves (1) measuring actual performance, (2) comparing actual performance to planned performance (goals and standards), and (3) correcting for any deviations. This task provides you the opportunity to actually engage in the performance of the control function.

SESSION OVERVIEW

Step 1: Teamwork on case (30 min.).
Step 2: Cross-team reports (15 min.).
Step 3: Lecture on case (10 min.).
Step 4: Self-evaluation and individual learnings.

Step 1: Teamwork on case (30 min.)

As prework, you read "The Branch Office" case and answered two questions about control of the branches' performance. Each team is to discuss and agree on the best answer to each of the two questions. Team answers are to be recorded below. You will have 30 minutes to arrive at your team answers through discussion, analysis, and agreement. Identify some person in the team to report your results to other teams.

Team answers

1. How does actual performance of the branch compare with planned performance? Be as specific as possible in your answer.

2. Based on the information you have, determine what changes need to be made to

correct for any deviations you find between actual and planned performance. Again, be as specific as possible.

Step 2: **Cross-team report** (15 min.)

Each team reports its answers to the two questions.

Step 3: **Lecture on case** (10 min.)

Step 4: **Self-evaluation and individual learnings**

Spend some "alone" time and think about what occurred during the last experience. Focus in on two or three things that affected you or that seemed significant to you. These may be positive or negative elements of the experience. What learnings can you draw from this reflection and what does this mean to you? Don't be concerned about what you ought to have learned, but rather focus on what you did learn and what it means to you. Based on your reflection of the experience, jot down your responses to the following questions:

1. What were your major learnings from the experience?

2. What implications do your learnings have for you as an individual?

3. What implications do your learnings have for you as a manager?

4. What questions do you have as a result of your experience, reflection, and learnings?

5. What implications will your learnings have on your future experiences?

Block XVII

Understanding the control function

GOAL

Create an understanding of the control function.

PREWORK ASSIGNMENT

Read the following material on "Controlling" for understanding. Answer the ten prework questions at the end of the material.

CONTROLLING

> *A control system and the way that it is used constitutes a potentially powerful tool for influencing the behavior of individuals in organizations.*[1]

So far, we have seen that managing involves planning (deciding what is to be achieved and how), organizing (grouping activities and delegating authority to achieve coordinated performance), and directing (influencing, helping, and guiding subordinates in their tasks); but this is not all there is to managing. Managers need to make sure that what is being achieved is what was actually intended. This is what the managerial function of control is all about—making sure that results actually turn out to be what they are supposed to be. Thus, as Figure XVII-1 shows, controlling is the fourth and the last function in the management process.

FIGURE XVII-1
Controlling in management

| Planning | Organizing | Directing | Controlling |

---

[1] Cortlandt Cammann and David A. Nadler, "Fit Control Systems to Your Managerial Style," *Harvard Business Review*, vol. 54 (January–February 1976), p. 72.

The objective of this reading is to help you understand the control part of management better, so that you can improve your controlling skills. The discussion is organized into four parts:

The nature of control.
The basic control process.
Characteristics of good control.
Managerial control in practice.

The first part of the reading defines controlling as a management function, points out its importance, and identifies responsibility for its performance. The second part explains the basic control process and how it is implemented. The third part describes the characteristics of good control systems. Last, the fourth part of the reading focuses on the everyday practice of control in managerial situations.

THE NATURE OF CONTROL

Control is, in our opinion, one of the most misunderstood functions in the management process. It is often viewed as a "negative" function because it deals with evaluation of performance. It seems that many people see controlling as restrictive rules and regulations, as "looking over people's shoulders" and checking on them, and disciplining and punishing subordinates. While controlling does involve many of these things, it is not necessarily negative in nature. In fact, the purpose of control is positive in that it focuses on achieving organization objectives. From another standpoint, even the so-called negative aspects of controlling produce the best results when handled in a positive, problem-solving way. So we do not see control in a "negative" light—rather we see control as an integral part of the management process.

The remainder of the first part of this reading is devoted to defining more specifically what control really is, to explaining the importance of control, and to discussing the responsibility for controlling.

What control really is

Controlling is a part of the basic management process. It is defined as that part of managing which involves making sure that the results achieved are in line with the planned results. As Figure XVII-2 indicates, controlling involves checking on actual performance, comparing actual performance to planned performance, and correcting for any deviations.

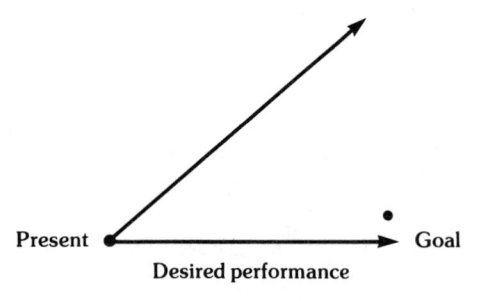

FIGURE XVII-2
Controlling

While controlling is an important function that involves several steps, its primary focus is change in people's behavior. As the quote at the beginning of the reading states, the main feature of control is action to correct performance deviations and/or to insure that expected results are forthcoming. What this statement points out is that people determine performance and control of performance winds up being control of behavior—control in the sense of influencing people to make the changes and do the things necessary to correct for deviations.

The importance of control

Managers can plan, organize, and direct; but what is ultimately important is what is actually achieved. Even the best attempts at planning, organizing, and directing do not always produce the anticipated results. So there is a definite need for monitoring what does happen and controlling serves this important purpose.

Control is important for another reason—it is the function which links the end of the management process to the beginning (planning) of the process. "Correction of deviation in performance is the point at which control coalesces with the other managerial functions; the manager may correct by redrawing his plans or by modifying his goal."[2] Figure XVII-3 indicates the control function is what makes the planning process circular. So control is important because it is the foundation on which future planning rests.

FIGURE XVII-3
Control completes management process

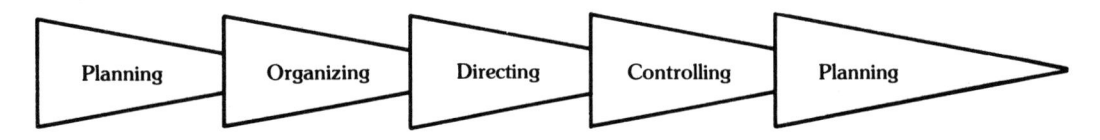

Planning → Organizing → Directing → Controlling → Planning

The responsibility for control

Control is a fundamental part of the management process all managers practice and it is therefore the responsibility of all managers. In light of the presence of sophisticated control techniques and the emphasis placed on the control of overall organizational performance, it is easy to get the idea that the major responsibility for control rests with top management or at least with high organizational levels. Nothing could be further from the truth. The responsibility for actual control is with the manager who executes the plans. And that is every manager.

From another standpoint, controlling is something that *every* manager does with some degree of effectiveness. It is not a matter of whether managers do or do not control—all managers control—it is more a matter of whether control is effective or ineffective. Since managers do in fact engage in control activities, they are responsible for effective control—control which helps achieve organizational objectives.

THE CONTROL PROCESS

Since controlling is a universal management function, the basic process of controlling is the same no matter what is being controlled. In this section the steps in the control process are described and the techniques of application are identified.

[2]Harold Koontz and Cyril O'Donnell, *Essentials of Management* (New York: McGraw-Hill Book Co., 1974), p. 361.

Steps in the control process

As Figure XVII-4 indicates, the basic control process always involves three steps: (1) developing criteria, (2) measuring performance, and (3) correcting deviations.

FIGURE XVII-4
Control process

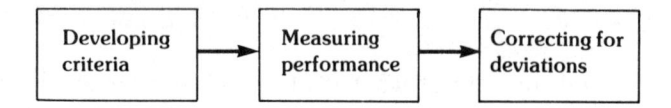

```
┌─────────────┐     ┌─────────────┐     ┌─────────────┐
│ Developing  │ ──▶ │ Measuring   │ ──▶ │ Correcting  │
│ criteria    │     │ performance │     │ for         │
│             │     │             │     │ deviations  │
└─────────────┘     └─────────────┘     └─────────────┘
```

Control criteria. Control criteria are the reference points against which actual performance can be compared. The purpose of control is to assure that goals set in planning are achieved. Unless there are criteria against which performance can be evaluated, control is impossible. Thus, the development of control criteria are necessary first steps in controlling.

Controlling and planning are very closely related. Control criteria stem directly (or should) from goals set in the planning process. In fact, when performance goals of the type discussed in the "Planning" reading (Block V) are established, these goals become the major criteria for evaluating performance. So the first step in the control process actually takes place in planning. This is the basis of the familiar statement that "something that has not been planned cannot be controlled."

While the performance goals set in planning are the major criteria by which actual results are evaluated, more specific criteria may be needed for day-to-day control of performance. For example, performance goals are useful in determining after-the-fact what has happened, but some way of evaluating progress toward goals along the way is usually needed.

These more specific control criteria need to be developed from the performance goals themselves. Specific criteria can take many different forms. They may in some cases be stated in units of output in terms of similar performance requirements on many types of jobs. Control criteria may also be stated as the performance of a particular activity by a particular date. When plans to achieve performance objectives are developed according to the approach suggested in the "Planning" reading, the activities identified become specific performance criteria.

In summary, the question that needs to be answered by all managers when developing control criteria is, "What can I look at or what information do I need in order to know whether or not what is actually being achieved will result in the attainment of the goals set in planning?" It is fairly obvious that the question is best answered during the planning process. Managers should not wait until they are ready to check on performance before deciding how such checks can be made.

Measuring performance. The second step in controlling is measuring actual results to determine if performance is proceeding according to plan. Many people believe that this is the most difficult part of controlling because it is not easy to measure performance on many types of jobs. It is probably closer to the truth to say measuring performance itself is not too difficult if some measuring scale of performance has been developed. Measuring performance begins with the identification of a measuring scale for performance in the particular area. Actually, this step in controlling involves two separate phases—collecting data and comparing the performance data with the control criteria developed in the first step in the control process.

In the reading dealing with "Planning" (Block V), the concept of performance standards was explained as an approach to setting good measurable performance goals. Performance standards were defined as yardsticks or measuring scales by which performance in an area could be measured. These same standards can be used in the control process as a way of measuring actual performance. As stated previously, part of the measuring process—developing a scale for measuring performance—results from good performance of the planning function.

The second phase of measuring performance is using the scale to actually measure performance. This usually means deciding what data is needed to measure performance on the scale of standard developed and then developing some system or method of actually collecting the necessary data.

The last phase of measuring is comparing the measurements of actual performance with the control criteria to see how they match up. If criteria are well developed and if standards and measuring systems are also well developed, comparisons are usually not hard. Occasionally such things as statistical analysis may be needed in making comparison in areas such as quality control; but for the most part, comparison of actual results to criteria can be done by simply looking at the two sets of data.

Correcting for deviations. The final step in the control process is correcting for any deviations found between actual and planned performance. This step in the control process is actually both a decision-making and action-taking step.

Correcting for deviations begins with an analysis and decision about what is wrong and what action needs to be taken to bring performance into line. This is a fancy way of saying that managers need to know what is wrong or why performance deviated before they can decide what needs to be done to bring it back into line. Determining what's wrong and what needs to be done may require some investigation and analysis. The point is that corrective action needs to be aimed at the real cause of the problem, otherwise it will probably do little or no good.

The second part of taking corrective action and, in our opinion, one of the more important parts of the entire control process is initiating corrective action. This usually means getting someone to change or modify their job behavior. Ultimately, all types of performance are the result of people's behavior. Taking corrective action then becomes a matter of influencing and helping people do the work necessary to bring performance into line with planned expectations.

The importance of this part of controlling cannot be over-emphasized. All of the previous steps in control can be performed well—good criteria can be developed, good data gathering systems can be used, good methods of comparison can be used, thorough analysis of the causes of deviations can result in good decisions to be implemented—but they are of little value until people actually implement the corrective action. So implementing correction action is a crucial step in the control process and considerable attention is devoted to the practical application of this step later on.

Control techniques

The control process is always implemented through the use of techniques and methods. No matter what is being controlled, the basic process is always the same, but different techniques and methods are more appropriate for controlling some types of situations than for others. One of the decisions managers must make in implementing the control process is what techniques and methods should be used.

The techniques and methods of implementing the control process are most often described and explained in rather general fashion as they relate to the total control process. It seems more meaningful to us to understand control techniques and methods in terms of each of the three steps in the control process. That is, most control techniques and methods seem to be either criteria techniques, measuring techniques, or corrective techniques. So the discussion here is organized around the three types of techniques.

Criteria techniques. Criteria techniques are those techniques and methods dealing with the establishment of criteria against which measurements of actual performance can be compared. The more useful criteria techniques are budgets, work standards, and activity networks. As pointed out earlier in the discussion, control criteria stem from the planning process. In fact, many of the criteria used in control are direct products of planning such as budgets, activity networks, and time schedules. Other criteria, such as work standards, are developed from goals and objectives set in the planning process.

Budgets are probably one of the most widely-used control criteria. Simply stated, a budget is a numerical statement of what is expected to happen in the future. Budgets can be in dollars, units of product, work-hours, or some other quantifiable result. Thus, budgets of various types can be used to establish a "picture" of what is supposed to happen and then actual results can be compared to this "picture."

Work standards are another commonly-used control criteria, at lower organization levels and especially in production line type situations. In such cases, work standards are set in many different ways (from past history, through motion-and-time study, by methods study, etc.), but ultimately they are derived from the goals developed in planning and if followed will result in the achievement of the objectives to which they are related.

Activity networks and time schedules of the type discussed in the "Planning" reading (Block V) also are useful control criteria in many situations. These networks and timetables are actually "blueprints" of what is supposed to happen in connection with the achievement of a specific objective. As a criteria this "blueprint" of what should happen is used as a bench mark to see how well activities are progressing toward the achievement of the objective.

These are only a few of the more important and more widely useful control criteria techniques. They are not appropriate for all types of situations. Managers need to select the control criteria that fit the situations that they need to control and these criteria need to be linked to the goals and objectives established in planning. Developing performance standards in planning and establishing control criteria provides a basis for control; but data, which fit the standards, can be used to compare actual performance to the criteria, still have to be collected.

Measuring techniques. Measuring techniques are the ways that the data on actual performance are collected. Data on actual performance can be collected in a number of ways. Some of the more useful ways are reports, direct observation, and formal appraisal of employee performance.

Reports on operations (from both higher and lower levels in the organization) are one of the more important ways of gathering data on actual performance. The important thing to keep in mind is that the right data be collected. The right data are performance data of the type needed to compare performance in the particular area with the criteria developed. That is, the data collected need to be comparable to the criteria and meaningful in terms of evaluating performance.

Direct observation is probably the most widely-used method of collecting performance data. And there is nothing wrong with this method, if managers are careful to observe the right things. When using this method to gather performance data, it is extremely easy to lose sight of what data are really needed and focus on data that are not really comparable to the control criteria. Such data tend to hinder rather than help in controlling performance. For example, it is easy to fall into the trap of observing how subordinates are doing their job (inputs) rather than what they are getting accomplished (outputs).

A third widely-used method of measuring performance or gathering performance data is employee performance evaluations. This usually involves the manager completing a standardized form on each subordinate's performance. The conduct of such evaluations can generate data useful in determining whether performance is proceeding according to plans if care is taken to focus such evaluation on useful data for assessing the progress toward achievement of organizational goals.

Measuring techniques are ways of gathering data to be compared to criteria. If good criteria have been established and if good data are collected, comparing the two sets of data to uncover deviations is not too difficult. Correcting for deviations is another matter entirely.

Correcting techniques. Correcting for any deviations found between planned and actual performance really involves two things—deciding what needs to be done and then taking action on that decision. There are some techniques which are useful in the performance on one or both of these two steps in correcting for deviations. They include such things as problem-solving, interviewing, and counseling. These are all techniques that are useful in either using the abilities of people to help determine what is wrong and/or influencing subordinates to do the things necessary to bring performance into line. We believe that this step in the control process is probably the most crucial and it is discussed in detail in the section on "Control in practice."

The control process involves three steps: (1) developing criteria, (2) measuring performance, and (3) correcting for deviations. All three steps are actually practiced through the use of particular techniques and methods.

CHARACTERISTICS OF GOOD CONTROL

No matter what is being controlled or what techniques are used, to be most effective, control systems need to have certain characteristics. We believe that to be effective, controls must be economical, must report deviation promptly, must focus on important aspects of performance, must be understandable, and must be accepted by the people who use them. These characteristics of good control can be viewed as guidelines to developing control systems and/or as criteria by which control systems can be evaluated for effectiveness.

Controls must be economical

It should go without saying that controls should be economical. The purpose of control is to assure the achievement of organization objectives and realistically, controls must be worth the cost. It is foolish to use more resources in controlling some activity than the activity itself would generate. This may seem like "common sense," but situations where managers spend a great deal of their time and considerable organizational resources controlling insignificant things are not too hard to find. Managers should always consider both the benefits and the cost of control and select the techniques and methods of control that result in the greatest benefits for the least costs in time and money.

Controls should report deviations promptly

A second characteristic of good control is that it reports deviations soon enough to make correction possible. Almost everyone has heard the old saying, "There is 20/20 vision in hindsight." Controls which report deviations after it is too late to correct for the deviations are of little value.

Ideally, controls would predict potential deviations before they occur. This would be the best of all possible worlds because it would allow the prevention of deviations. Unfortunately, it is difficult and often practically impossible to establish these types of controls. The best that can be done is to establish a system which will report the deviations soon enough to correct them. So when developing controls, managers need to ask and answer the question, "How quickly will this let me know whether actual performance matches planned performance?"

Controls need to focus on important aspects of performance

The third characteristic of good control is that it focuses on aspects of performance that are important. Controlling performance toward the achievement of objectives is a matter of developing standards and measuring performance. This characteristic deals with what will be measured and what will actually be controlled.

It is generally not possible for managers to concentrate their control efforts solely on the final objective. This is likely to wind up being only looking back to see if the objective was achieved. Control needs to be exercised during the process of achievement to assure that the objective is achieved. This requires that managers make some decisions (primarily in the criteria development process) about what will really be controlled.

The real question that must be answered is, what can be measured to determine if performance is proceeding according to plan? Stated another way, controls should focus on those aspects of performance that are critical to the achievement of the objectives and on those aspects of performance that are good indications of the progress toward goal achievement. It does little good to control things that have little effect on the achievement of objectives or things which provide little indication of whether goals will be achieved or not.

Deciding what to control is a situational matter. It can only be done well by analyzing the objective being sought and what needs to be done to achieve it. If activity schedules of the type discussion in the "Planning" reading were developed, they can be used to help identify aspects of performance that are critical to the achievement of the objective. Therefore, this guideline indicates that those things that really have a significant effect on the objective or objectives should be concentrated on.

Controls should be understandable

The fourth characteristic of good controls is that they are understandable to the people who will be using them. The best control systems in the world are of little value unless people understand them well enough to be able to use them. Controls which are not understood are not likely to be used effectively.

Certainly managers should understand the controls that they use, but it is just as important for subordinates to understand also. Ultimately, much of the corrective action required in control will actually be implemented by subordinates. Unless they also understand the controls, they are not likely to be able to implement corrective action in the most effective way. In short, effective implementation of corrective actions needs to be based on an understanding of why the action is being taken.

Controls must be accepted

Related to the above characteristic is the one that controls need to be accepted by the people who use them. Acceptance is not necessarily required, people can be forced to use and implement control systems. However, acceptance of controls affects motivation to use the controls appropriately. And the most effective control results when people are motivated to use the control system. So managers should strive not to force use of control systems, but to motivate people to use the needed control systems.

Acceptance of control systems on the part of employees depends on their understanding of the system and their understanding of the need for the system. One way of gaining such acceptance is to help employees understand the need for the system and the system itself. We find that true understanding promotes acceptance.

In summary, good control systems have five major characteristics:

1. They are economical.
2. They report deviations promptly.
3. They focus on important aspects of performance.
4. They are understandable.
5. They are accepted by the people who must use them.

CONTROL IN PRACTICE

Effective performance of the controlling function requires an understanding of the basic control process and of the techniques of control. Thus, control at any level involves implementing, through various techniques, the steps of developing criteria, measuring performance, and taking corrective action. Control winds up being the control of people. While managers perform the entire control process and use many of the control techniques described earlier, it is our experience that much of a manager's day-to-day control involves determining what corrective action is needed. It is also our belief that much of the performance of the control function takes place through such activities as disciplining, problem solving, and counseling. Obviously, these types of activities involve interpersonal communication. In many cases, the objective is to help employees understand why something needs to be done and in other cases the primary purpose is to collect information and ideas. So in our opinion much day-to-day control depends heavily on what might be called problem-solving in the broad sense. Managers can improve their controlling by developing skills in this area.

SUMMARY

Control is making sure that what happens is what was supposed to happen. It is important because it influences what is achieved and also because it is the base for further planning. Controlling is a major part of managing and it is every manager's responsibility to control.

The basic control process is the same everywhere. It involves developing criteria against which actual performance can be compared, measuring performance, and correcting for deviations. All three of the steps in the control process are implemented through the use of techniques.

Good control systems have several characteristics. They are economical, they report deviations promptly, they center on important aspects of performance, they are understandable, and they are accepted by the people who use them. These characteristics can serve as criteria when developing control systems.

Much day-to-day managerial control involves the development of mutual understanding with employees to get them to change their behavior and implement corrective action.

PREWORK QUESTIONS

Based on the material in "Controlling," select the best and most complete answer for the following questions. Select only one answer even though others are not wrong. If you are unsure of your choice, it is better to leave it blank. Once you have completed the questions, transfer your individual answers to the Prework Answer Sheet (p. 195) under the column marked *Individual answers*.

Individual answers

Team answers

_____ 1. Controlling is:

    a. The end point in the management process.
    b. A negative function in the management process.
    c. Not performed by all managers.
    d. Closely related to and an extension of the planning function.

_____ 2. The basic control process:

    a. Depends on feedback on performance.
    b. Is the same in all organizations at all levels.
    c. Focuses solely on results achieved.
    d. Takes place at the top of the organization.

_____ 3. Control criteria:

    a. Stem directly from performance areas, standards, and objectives.
    b. Focus primarily on people.
    c. Are not too important if managers plan well.
    d. Are the most important parts of the control process.

_____ 4. Measuring actual performance:

    a. Is easy if control criteria are well developed.
    b. Is a matter of collecting data consistent with control criteria.
    c. Is the easiest part of controlling.
    d. Is a matter of checking to see if objectives are being achieved.

_____ 5. Correcting for deviations:

    a. Almost always involves influencing and helping people change their behavior.
    b. Is closely related to planning.
    c. Involves deciding what needs to be done and then getting people to do it.
    d. Is the last step in the control process.

_____ 6. Control techniques:

    a. Are the vehicles through which the steps in control are implemented.
    b. Such as budgets, focus on the entire control process.
    c. Are generally more useful at higher organizational levels than at lower organizational levels.
    d. Are the fourth step in the control process.

7. Control sytems are:

    a. Good if they do not cost too much.
    b. Good if they control the right things.
    c. Good if people accept them.
    d. No better than the people who use them.

8. Gaining acceptance of control systems:

    a. Is not absolutely essential.
    b. Promotes effective use of the control system.
    c. Is a matter of explaining controls fully.
    d. Can be done even if people do not understand the system.

9. Much day-to-day managerial control:

    a. Is checking up on people's work.
    b. Can be done by observation.
    c. Involves effective interpersonal communication.
    d. Is through the use of budgets and reports.

10. In the final analysis, controlling is:

    a. Controlling people.
    b. An impersonal part of managing.
    c. Making sure that people do what they are supposed to.
    d. The same as planning and directing put together.

SESSION INTRODUCTION

This session will focus on creating an understanding of the control function by drawing on the control experience, the text material, and a lecture.

SESSION OVERVIEW

Step 1: Teamwork on prework (30 min.).
Step 2: Scoring individual and team answers and comparing team effectiveness (10 min.).
Step 3: Increasing team effectiveness (30 min.).
Step 4: Lecture and discussion (30 min.).
Step 5: Self-evaluation and individual learnings.

Step 1: Teamwork on prework (30 min.)

As prework, you answered a 10-item multiple-choice test on "Controlling." Each team is to identify the single best answer for each question. The text is not to be used during the discussion but you may use your prework answers. Team answers are to be recorded on the Prework Answer Sheet (p. 195) under the column *Team answers*.

You will have 30 minutes to arrive at team answers through discussion and analysis. At that time the individual and team answers will be scored to determine how effectively each team operated. The scoring system reflects the degree of commitment to team answers. Each correct answer receives 10 points. Items unanswered are worth 0 points. An incorrect answer results in -10 points. Thus, the score is calculated by taking the number correct, subtracting the number incorrect, and multiplying by 10.

This step should be completed by _____ .

Step 2: Scoring individual and team answers and comparing team effectiveness scores (10 min.)

Using the Prework Answer Sheet, score your individual and team answers based on the correct responses distributed to you. A simple procedure to follow is to record the correct answers in the column *Correct answers*. Where the given and correct answers match, put +10 in the *Points* column. Where no answer is given, record 0 points and, where the given and correct answers do not match, put -10 in the *Points* column. By totalling the points, the individual and team score can be determined.

Individuals and teams can be compared based on their scores. However, individuals come to teams with varying degrees of preparation and knowledge. As a result, the final score may not reflect how information was shared and how decisions were made during the team discussion. To take this into account a *Team effectiveness score* can be determined.

At least one team member should complete the Team Effectiveness Score sheet (p. 196), according to the following steps:

a. Determine the average individual score by adding the individual scores and dividing by the number of team members.
b. Subtract the average individual score from the team score to determine a gain or loss. A positive number indicates the team arrived at a higher score than the average of what individuals arrived at working separately. A loss, or negative number, indicates that team discussion and agreement resulted in a lower score than the individuals did working alone.

c. Determine the possible improvement by subtracting the average score from the perfect score of 100. This number represents how many points of improvement were possible through team discussion and agreement.
d. Determine team effectiveness by dividing the gain (+) or loss (−) by the possible improvement and multiplying by 100. Once all teams have completed the scoring, the average individual, team, and team effectiveness scores will be collected and posted.

Step 3: Increasing team effectiveness (30 min.)

A. Individual work.

To prepare for a team discussion, complete the following items. Allow all team members to finish before moving to the teamwork.

1. What have you learned about yourself as you have operated in this team?

2. What would you like to change to be a more effective team member?

B. Teamwork.

1. On a voluntary basis, each team member is to share their responses to the above two questions.
2. Each team member may ask (optional) "What are some other things I could to to be a more effective member?"

Step 4: Lecture and discussion (30 min.)

Step 5: Self-evaluation and individual learnings

Spend some "alone" time and think about what occurred during the last experience. Focus in on two or three things that affected you or that seemed significant to you. These may be positive or negative elements of the experience. What learnings can you draw from this reflection and what does this mean to you? Don't be concerned about what you ought to have learned, but rather focus on what you did learn and what it means to you. Based on your reflection of the experience, jot down your responses to the following questions:

1. What were your major learnings from the experience?

2. What implications do your learnings have for you as an individual?

3. What implications do your learnings have for you as a manager?

4. What questions do you have as a result of your experience, reflection, and learnings?

5. What implications will your learnings have on your future experiences?

PREWORK ANSWER SHEET

Questions	Individual answer	Individual points*	Correct	Team points*	Team answer
1					
2					
3					
4					
5					
6					
7					
8					
9					
10					
Individual score			Team score		

*Blanks—(no answer given)—receive 0 points; where correct and given answers match +10 points; where correct answer and given answers do not match −10 points.

TEAM EFFECTIVENESS SCORE SHEET

Individual scores

1. _____
2. _____
3. _____
4. _____
5. _____
6. _____
7. _____
8. _____

Average individual score

(A) (_____) ÷ (_____) = _____
    Total individual scores   No. members

Team score Less average individual score

(B) _____

Perfect score   100

(C) Less average individual score

Team effectiveness

(D) (_____) ÷ (_____) = (_____) × 100 = _____ %
    Gain (+) or loss (−)   Possible improvement

196   Basic management: An experience-based approach

Block XVIII

Control experience—Performance review

GOAL

Gain practical skills in interviewing, counseling, and reviewing subordinates.

PREWORK ASSIGNMENT

None.

SESSION INTRODUCTION

Controlling involves comparing performance with desired results and taking any needed corrective action. A great deal of controlling occurs through interviewing, counseling, and reviewing subordinates. The next activity will provide you the opportunity to practice and build your skills in this area.

SESSION OVERVIEW

Step 1: Role playing (50 min.).
Step 2: General discussion (10–30 min.).

Step 1: Role Playing (50 min.)

Form into triads and assume the roles of A, B, or C (a different letter for each triad member). Prepare for role playing by following the instructions at the top of the Role Instructions Sheet that matches your triad role letter—A, B, or C. Do not read the other role sheets.

Each role-playing session is conducted for 7 minutes. Three minutes is spent in reviewing each session. A total of three role-playing sessions are conducted.

Step 2: General Discussion (10–30 min.)

Participants discuss learnings, applications, etc.

Role instructions—A

You will engage in three role-playing situations. Each situation represents a manager interacting with a subordinate on a work-related problem or a performance review. A third person will act as observer. In the first situation, you will be the manager; the second situation, the observer; and in the third situation, the subordinate. In the manager role you have the opportunity to increase your skills in interviewing, counseling, and conducting a performance review. To maximize this opportunity, really push yourself to stretch using the tools you have learned. In the superior or subordinate role, it is important that you just be yourself as you would be in the situation. As observer you can be most helpful by giving constructive feedback.

You will be given time just prior to each role-playing session to silently prepare for the session. Based on your understanding of the role, you will have 7 minutes to role play. During the 7 minutes, you are to just be yourself in that situation. After each role-playing session, you will be given 3 minutes to review the session for learnings.

First session. Spend the next 5 minutes silently preparing for the first session.

Role: You are the newly-appointed manager of a textile plant. Your plant employs about 450 skilled and semi-skilled workers who operate on two shifts. You have four supervisors on each shift who have two foremen each who supervise the line workers. You were one of the packing supervisors prior to being promoted to plant manager. You have known for some time that your peer on the other shift, who is now your subordinate, has had below-satisfactory performance. As you have interacted with him/her, you are well aware that he/she has all the technical and managerial skills necessary to be a superior performer, yet his/her department does mediocre to poor. He/she used to work on the shift following your shift and as you stayed over, you have observed that he/she schedules work poorly, is cool to subordinate foremen, hasn't kept the previous plant manager informed of problem areas until they have become crises, and has on occasion coerced line workers into working overtime against their wishes. But still, you have seen him/her at times operate highly effectively, which confuses you.

When you were promoted, you knew that this supervisor was going to be your most significant management problem since the rest of the plant is the gem of the industry. You have been acting as plant manager now for two full months and the packing supervisor's performance has not altered from your experience with her/him as a peer. You have great concern about him/her because she/he seems so dissatisfied and not motivated. You realize that his/her dissatisfaction and poor motivation is caused behavior, not something that reflects something beyond your control. Since you have been plant manager, the plant is even doing better than in the past. You are really pleased with everything except the packing supervisor's department. It seems to be doing no better, and if anything, it is doing worse. You have asked the packing supervisor to stop by your office for a discussion about the performance in her/his department.

Remember, you know that the packing supervisor has the ability to do a "top notch" job and you want to get this one "sore spot" solved. You are confused and frustrated with his/her behavior.

Reviewing this session: As a manager use the following questions as a guide for reviewing the interview:

1. What seemed to be most helpful for you in creating understanding?
2. During the interview what seemed to hinder understanding?
3. How would you expect the subordinate to perform after the interview?
4. Ask the subordinate and observer things you could do that would be helpful in this situation.

Second session. Spend three minutes silently preparing for the second session.

Role: In this situation you are to act as an observer. You can be most helpful to the other two participants by giving constructive feedback when the role playing is completed. Pay particular attention to the following during the interview and afterwards share your answers and reasons for the answers with the participants:

1. What things seemed to help create understanding? What seemed to hinder the creation of understanding?
2. How would you expect the subordinate to perform after the interview?
3. What suggestions do you have to give the manager to improve skills in this area?

Third session. Spend four minutes silently preparing for the third session.

Role: You are a skilled maintenance worker in a manufacturing operation. You have been a skilled maintenance worker for numerous years and pride yourself as having fantastic diagnostic and terrific repair skills. When a machine breaks down, you jump right in, diagnose the problem, and get it back in operation so that workers don't lose money due to down-time. Many workers are your personal friends and they all depend on you to keep their machines in top running order.

Recently, your boss has casually mentioned that some of the machines seem to break down very soon after the original repair. And she/he has asked if you think that you could have made the necessary repairs while you had it disassembled for other reasons. It is quite clear to you that to do so would take a terrific amount of time in inspecting all the parts in your repair room for defects. Also, as the machines have gotten older and worn, the probability of this happening is greater, which is no fault of yours. You have tried the idea of the close inspection to detect other things which may go wrong, but it just takes entirely too much time to go through all the parts in these old machines. You would rather diagnose a problem and get the machine in operation so that the company and the employee don't lose valuable dollars.

Remember, you pride yourself in your skills and believe strongly that your approach is the best one.

Reviewing the session: As the subordinate, use the following questions as the basis for reviewing the interview:

1. What seemed most helpful to you in creating an understanding?
2. What seemed to have hindered understanding during the interview?
3. Did you feel better-off or worse-off after the interview?
4. How would you predict your performance to be after the interview?

Role instructions—B

You will engage in three role-playing situations. Each situation represents a manager interacting with a subordinate on a work-related problem or a performance review. A third person will act as observer. In the first situation, you will be the subordinate; the second situation, the manager; and in the third situation, the observer. In the manager role, you have the opportunity to increase your skills in interviewing, counseling, and conducting a performance review. To maximize this opportunity, really push yourself to stretch using the tools you have learned. In the superior or subordinate role, it is important that you just be yourself as you would be in the situation. As observer, you can be most helpful by giving constructive feedback.

You will be given time just prior to each role-playing session to silently prepare for the session. Based on your understanding of the role you will have 7 minutes to role play. During the 7 minutes, you are to just be yourself in that situation. After each role-playing session, you will be given 3 minutes to review the session for learnings.

First session. Spend the next 5 minutes silently preparing for the first session.

Role: You are the packing supervisor at a textile plant. The plant employs about 450 line workers on two shifts. There are four supervisors on each shift each of whom has two foremen who directly supervise the line workers. You have been the packing supervisor for about eight years. The current plant manager was appointed just two months ago and used to be your peer on the shift preceding the one you operate on. He/she has asked you to come in and talk about the performance in your department, which you know is just mediocre.

During the last three years, you have had two plant managers, both of whom have offered you little support. They have pushed you to accept objectives to which you have had no commitment, been unwilling to provide you with extra help that you have felt essential due to an increase in product mix, and have seemed to have kept the better job applicants for other departments. The performance evaluation, and wage and salary administration are tied to the goals that you believe are unfair. You just don't see the necessity to "bust your butt" for something that you don't think you can accomplish anyway. Your manager has asked you to see him/her and you expect to get the same speech from her/him that you have gotten before—that you just have a lot of ability both technically and managerially and need to develop the right attitude. Deep down you know it's a lot more than your attitude. You used to be the best packing supervisor in the industry as far as anybody could tell.

Remember, you can do a good job, but you have been treated very unfairly before and believe it will happen this time.

Processing: As the subordinate, use the following questions as the basis for reviewing the interview:

1. What seemed most helpful to you in creating an understanding?
2. What seemed to have hindered understanding during the interview?
3. Did you feel better-off or worse-off after the interview?
4. How would you predict your performance to be after the interview?

Second session. Spend 3 minutes silently preparing for the second session.

Role: You are the supervisor of a group of head nurses who manage other nurses. You are very concerned about one of your head nurses. Over the last couple of years, she/he has had low performance, failed to do many of the jobs assigned, and brings almost all decisions to committee meetings in order to get out of the decisions. You feel you must call her/him in for discussion. You are to the point of telling her/him that if she/he doesn't correct her/his performance you will have to terminate her/his employment since there is no position to which to demote her/him. You have called her/him in to talk over her/his performance.

Remember, this is the last chance for the head nurse. You are prepared to fire him/her if definite improvements are not made.

Reviewing this session: As a manager, use the following questions as a guide for reviewing the interview:

1. What seemed to be most helpful for you in creating understanding?
2. During the interview what seemed to hinder understanding?
3. How would you expect the subordinate to perform after the interview?
4. Ask the subordinate and observer for things you could do that would be helpful in this sort of situation.

Third Session. Spend 4 minutes silently preparing for the third session.

Role: In this situation, you are to act as an observer. You can be most helpful to the other two participants by giving constructive feedback when the role playing is completed. Pay particular attention to the following during the interview and afterwards share your answers and reasons for the answers with the participants:

1. What things seemed to help create understanding? What seemed to hinder the creation of understanding?
2. How would you expect the subordinate to perform after the interview?
3. What suggestions do you have to give the manager to improve skills in this area?

Role instructions—C

You will engage in three role-playing situations. Each situation represents a manager interacting with a subordinate on a work-related problem or a performance review. A third person will act as observer. In the first situation, you will be the observer; the second situation, the subordinate; and in the third situation, the manager. In the manager role, you have the opportunity to increase your skills in interviewing, counseling, and conducting a performance review. To maximize this opportunity, really push yourself to stretch using the tools you have learned. In the superior or subordinate role, it is important that you just be yourself as you would be in the situation. As observer, you can be most helpful by giving constructive feedback.

You will be given time just prior to each role-playing session to silently prepare for the session. Based on your understanding of the role you will have 7 minutes to role play. During the 7 minutes, you are to just be yourself in that situation. After each role-playing session, you will be given 3 minutes to review the session for learnings.

First session. Spend 5 minutes silently preparing for the first session.

Role: In this situation, you are to act as an observer. You can be most helpful to the other two participants by giving constructive feedback when the role playing is completed. Pay particular attention to the following during the interview and afterwards share your answers and reasons for the answers with the participants.

1. What things seemed to help create understanding? What seemed to hinder the creation of understanding?
2. How would you expect the subordinate to perform after the interview?
3. What suggestions do you have to give the manager to improve skills in this area?

Second session. Spend 3 minutes silently preparing for the second session.

Role: You are a head nurse. You have been a head nurse over several other nurses for too long. You just don't have any interest in supervising people anymore. It seems to cause you so much anxiety that you literally lose sleep at night when you go home. You would really love to get out of being in your current position. You have been considering taking a demotion to a nurse's job until you retire. You would leave the hospital but it is too close to retirement and will just cost you entirely too much to leave now. Your work is not super, but it has been satisfactory and you really don't think you can push yourself to do any more. Satisfactory should be enough for what you get paid. Your boss has called you in for a talk.

Remember, you are really tired of supervising people and you think you are doing satisfactory work. You don't want to retire but you do want a demotion.

Reviewing this session: As the subordinate, use the following questions as the basis for reviewing the interview:

1. What seemed most helpful to you in creating an understanding?
2. What seemed to have hindered understanding during the interview?
3. Did you feel better-off or worse-off after the interview?
4. How would you predict your performance to be after the interview?

Third session. Spend 4 minutes silently preparing for the third session.

Role: You are a maintenance supervisor in a manufacturing plant. A skilled maintenance worker in your department is coming in for an annual review. He/she is by far the best maintenance worker you have ever experienced in terms of being able to diagnose machine problems and quickly repair them so that the operators can rapidly begin work again. This is important to the workers since they are on a piece-rate pay system. But during the last six months you have had a problem in that her/his repairs seem to be short lived. That is, she/he immediately jumps in and repairs the machine but it doesn't seem long before something goes wrong with the machine, which would have been easily fixed while it was disassembled for the original repair. Numerous times you have spoken to her/him about this, but it seems to be recurring as you review the maintenance records. You are about to have your annual review with her/him and plan to discuss this matter. She/he has got to understand that this cannot go on since it is costing the company and the employees many dollars in down-time.

Remember, you feel strongly that the maintenance worker has got to change his/her practices.

Reviewing this session: As manager, use the following questions as a guide for reviewing the interview:

1. What seemed to be most helpful for you in creating understanding?
2. During the interview, what seemed to hinder understanding?
3. How would you expect the subordinate to perform after the interview?
4. Ask the subordinate and observer for things you could do that would be helpful in this sort of situation.

Block XIX

Integrating the management function

GOALS

1. Experience the total management process.
2. Gain skills in planning, organizing, directing, and controlling.

PREWORK ASSIGNMENT

None.

SESSION INTRODUCTION

Performing the management process involving planning, organizing, directing, and controlling. This experience will give you the opportunity to engage in performing and assessing all of the functions. Additionally, it provides you the opportunity to integrate and increase skills associated with the total process.

SESSION OVERVIEW

Step 1: Planning and organizing for production (45 min.).
Step 2: Directing the production (20 min.).
Step 3: Performance review session (30 min.).
Step 4: Reviewing the experience (20 min.).
Step 5: Cross-team exchange and discussion (10 min.).
Step 6: Individual development goal setting (15 min.).
Step 7: Sharing goals (10 min.).
Step 8: Discussion (10 min.).
Step 9: Evaluation (optional).

Step 1: Planning and organizing for production (45 min.)

Each team is to create an organization to produce shipping containers according to the requirements in Blocks VII and XIII. However, instead of receiving market requirements from the Brasan Brokerage Company, each organization is to maximize profits during a 20-minute production period while meeting the requirements as laid out in Blocks VII and XIII.

To stimulate an operating organization, one person should be designated as the top person. The organization may be put together in any way after that but no manager may have more than two subordinates. Only the bottom layer of the organization may actually manufacture the containers.

During the next two steps, "Directing the production" and "Performance review session," communication must follow the chain of command established in planning and organizing for production. That is, each person can only report to his/her superior or direct his/her subordinates.

You have until _____ to complete planning and organizing for the 20-minute production period.

Step 2: **Directing the production** (20 min.)

Each team has 20 minutes in which to produce shipping containers in order to maximize the profits of their organization.

Step 3: **Performance review session** (30 min.)

Using the profit statement in Block VII, calculate total profits.

Each superior now is to conduct a private performance review session with their subordinates.

Step 4: **Reviewing the experience** (20 min.)

    A. Individual work.

To get maximum learning from our experience, we must review our experiences and draw conclusions from them. To prepare for a team discussion, complete the following questions or statements as an individual during the next minutes. Allow all team members to finish before moving to the teamwork.

1. Think about what occurred during the last experience. Focus in on one or two things that affected you or that seemed significant to you. These may be positive or negative elements of the experience. What learnings can you draw from this reflection and what does this mean to you? Don't be concerned about what you ought to have learned, but rather focus on what you did learn and what it means to you.

2. What impact did the planning have on controlling?

3. How did the required organization structure influence how leadership was exercised?

4. List some things you have learned about yourself as a manager or worker.

5. Which of its functions would you most like to improve upon?

6. Based on this and other experiences, what are some things that you would like to improve on in your back-home situation?

B. Teamwork.

As a team, discuss and complete the following items. The best learning will occur if all team members will share their ideas and feelings in the discussion.

1. Discuss the individual responses to the above questions.

2. a. The team is to prepare a brief report to be given to the other teams which includes the general focus on what people learned about themselves as managers and what they expect to improve on in the back-home situation.
   b. Select a spokesperson to present the team's report in the next step.

Step 5: Cross-team exchange and discussion (10 min.)

Each team makes a report to the other teams and open discussion follows.

Step 6: Individual development goal setting (15 min.)

Growth and development occur through a process of understanding oneself in having a desire to change. This process can be accelerated by systematically setting specific development goals.

Silently reflect back on the experiences that you have had in the various sessions that you have been involved in. You may want to flip through and review your "Self-evaluation and individual learnings" sheets for some of the sessions. Based on the things that you have learned about yourself, set some specific development goals to increase your managerial effectiveness. The goals will be more constructive if they are specific, measurable, involve you directly, or time bounded and ones that you feel responsible for accomplishing. (Example: I will complete a "to do" list by 9:00 a.m. every day for the next two months.)

Set your own individual development goals by completing the following statement several times:

My development goals are to . . .

Step 7: **Sharing learnings and goals** (20 min.)

Team members are to share one or two of their more significant goals. During this time you may want to have the benefit of other critiques of your goals in terms of their being specific, measurable, and time bounded. You may also get some additional ideas for goals as you participate in the discussion.

Step 8: **Discussion** (10 min.)

Step 9: **Self-evaluation** (optional)

Index

A

Abilities, 130
Achievement, 132, 134
Activities, 60
    assignment of; see Job assignments
    complexity, 88
    coordination, 86
    degrees of interrelation, 88
    determination of, 52-53
    grouping, 82-83, 92-96, 98
    relationship between, 53-55
    sequencing, 53-55, 60
    timing, 55-56
Activities differences, 11
Activity-authority relationships, 8, 83, 89
Activity networks, 53-55, 60, 186
    related activities, 54
    related and unrelated activities, 54
    time frame, 55
Activity schedules, 188
Administration, 135
Administrivia, 2
Allen, Louis A., 151 n
Appreciation, 132
Assembly phase, 105-8
Assignment of job activities; see Job assignments
Assumptions about work behavior, 127-29
    needs and, 133
Authority, 84, 89-92, 99
    application of concepts of, 92
    decentralized, 157
    defined, 89
    delegation of; see Delegation of authority
    number of relationships, 92
    rights of, 89
    types, 91-92
    use as leadership style, 154, 156
Authority relationships, 84
Autocratic leadership, 156

B

Barnett, Rosalind C., 5 n
Barriers to effective communication, 24-27, 30
Behavior, 129-35
    abilities, 130
    assumptions about, 127-29
        needs and, 133
    defined, 130
    goals, 130
    model of, 129-30
    needs causing, 129-30
    rational and selfish, 130
Behaviorism, 137
Blake, Robert R., 157, 162
Blueprints, 186
Body language, 26, 31
Bounded group decision, 155-56
Brainstorming, 137
Branch managers, 177-80
Branch office, 177-80
Budgets, 186

C

Calero, Henry H., 26 n
Carrot and stick approach, 133
Channels of communication, 23
Chartier, Myron R., 27 n, 28 n, 29
Clarity of expression, 27-30, 32
Codes, 23
Common frame of reference, 28
Communication, 9, 21-38
    awareness of, 5
    barriers to, 24-27, 30
    bottleneck of, 22
    defined, 21, 29, 31
    degree of effectiveness, 22
    effectiveness, 21, 30
    elements, 27-30
    job assignments, 112
    management and, 21-24
    process of, 23-24
    purpose, 23
    taking it for granted, 25, 30
    tendency to evaluate, 26-27, 30
Communication skill, 11-14, 16, 24, 29
Company policy, 135
Congruent communication, 29
Consensus taking, 153
Construction materials, 207-12
Contingency theory, 162-63, 166
Controlling, 2, 8-10, 14-15, 22, 82, 109, 181-96
    acceptance, 189, 191
    basic process, 182-87, 189-90
    branch office, 177-80
    characteristics of good control, 182, 187-89, 191
    correcting deviations, 184-85, 190
    correcting techniques, 187
    criteria, 184, 190
    criteria techniques, 186
    defined, 181-82, 189-90
    developing criteria, 184
    economical, 187
    effective performance of, 189
    focus on important aspects of performance, 188
    importance of, 183
    measuring performance, 184-85, 190
    measuring techniques, 186-87
    nature of, 182-83, 191
    negative view of, 182
    performance review, 197-202
    performance standards, 185
    practical aspects, 182, 189
    primary focus of, 183
    report of deviations, 188
    responsibility for, 183
    steps in process of, 184-85
    techniques of, 185-87, 190
    understandability, 188
Cooperation, 153
Coordination, 86, 95
    need for, 97
Coping with emotions, 27, 29-30, 32
Correcting for deviations, 184-85, 190
Correcting techniques of controlling, 187
Counseling, 9, 187
Criteria techniques of controlling, 186
Customer departmentation, 95

D

Davis, Keith, 22 n
Decision-making, 89
Decision-making authority, 91
Decisions
    bounded group, 155-56

Decisions—Cont.
   making, announcing, and selling of, 155
   tentative, 155
Decoding process, 24
Delegation of authority, 8-9, 82-83, 86, 89-90, 96-98, 100
   amount of, 88-89, 97
   clarity of, 88-89
   level of subordinate ability, 97
   nature of activities involved, 97
   needs for coordination, 97
   power source, 91
   results expected, 97
Democratic leadership, 157
Departmentation, 92-95
Diagnosing, 153
Dignity, needs for, 132
Direct observation of performance, 186-187
Directing, 2, 7-9, 14-15, 22, 82, 109-22, 181
   assigning job activities, 110, 112-13, 115-16
   defined, 109-10, 117
   developing understanding and agreement, 110, 113-14, 117
   importance of, 110-11
   influence objective of, 110-11
   job-well-done conference, 110, 113, 115-17
   nature of, 110-11, 115-16
   pattern assembly, 105-8
   problem solving techniques, 123-26
   process, 111, 151
   purpose, 109, 116
   responsibility for, 111
Directives, 114-15, 124
Dissatisfiers, 135, 139-40
   importance of, 135
Division of work, 85-86, 92, 99; *see also* Specialization of work
   application of principle of, 86

E

Education, 11, 13
Educational managers, 11
Effective communication, 21, 30
Effective leadership, 151-53, 164
Effective management, 11-14, 16
Effective performance, 11-13
Elaborating, 153
Emery Air Freight, 137
Emotions, coping with, 27, 29-30
Employee-centered managers, 161
Employee performance evaluation, 186-87
Employees' personal objectives, achievement of, 111
Encoding, 23
Encoding process, 24
Encouraging, 153
Equipment departmentation, 92, 95
Esteem needs, 132
Evaluating, 153
Executives, 6, 11
   planning responsibility of, 45
Experiences; *see end of each chapter*
Experimentation, 2
Expressing group feeling, 153

F

Face-to-face communication, 9, 112-13
Face-to-face contact, 89
Facial expressions, 23
Feedback, 24, 29
   leadership styles, 173-75
Fiedler, Fred E., 162-63
Fire-fighting, 44-45
Focus on useful skills, 2
Following, 153
Forecasting, 49
Formal appraisal of employee performance, 186-87
Foulkes, Fred K., 137
Frame of reference, 24, 29
Freedom, 132
Functional authority, 91, 99-100
   disadvantage of, 91
Functional departmentation, 92-94
Functional relationships, 91-92
Functions, 8-11
   defined, 8
   importance of, 10-11
   performance of, 10
   sequence of, 10
Future conditions, anticipation of, 49

G

Gatekeeping, 153
Geographical departmentation, 95
Gestures, 23
Gibb, Jack R., 151-52 n
Giving information, 153
Goals, 2, 130, 137-38
   activity, 130
   conditions, 130
   establishment, 8
   objects, 130
Grid theory; *see* Managerial grid
Grouping of activities, 8-9, 82-83, 92-96, 98
   assigning activities, 95-96
   departmentation, 92-95
Growth and advancement, 134

H

Hackman, J. Richard, 127 n
Haney, William V., 22 n
Hanson, Phillip C., 28 n
Harmonizing, 153
Hayakawa, S. I., 25 n
Herzberg, Frederick, 133, 135-38
Hierarchy of needs, 131-33, 135-36, 139
Hierarchy of objectives, 50

I

Ideas, 24
Identification of performance areas, 47-48
Improving managerial performance, 13-14
Independence, 132
Individual learnings; *see end of each chapter*
Influence on employees, 110-11
Information, 24
Initiating activity, 153
Inputs, 187
Instructor, getting acquainted with, 2
Integrated plans, 56
Integrating management function, 203-6
International office building, 39-42
Interpersonal interaction, 9, 12, 109
Interpersonal relations, 135
Interviewing, 187

J

Job activity groupings, 89; *see also* Grouping of activities
Job assignments, 8, 95-96, 110, 112-13, 115-16
   communication of, 112
   objective in, 112
Job-centered managers, 161
Job creation, 84
Job descriptions, 112
   contents, 112
   good, 112
   written, 112, 116
Job dissatisfaction, 133-34
Job enrichment, 136-38, 140
   changing nature of jobs, 136
   methods of, 136
   problem-solving goal-setting approach, 136-37
   work territories approach, 137
Job satisfaction, 133-34
Job-well-done conference, 110, 113, 115-17
   aspects of, 113
   contribution of job, 113, 115
   defined, 113
   methods of job, 113, 115
   objectives of, 113, 115
   results expected, 113, 115
Jones, John E., 25 n
Jourard, Sidney, 28

K

Katz, Robert L., 12 n, 24
Knowledge, 12, 14
Koontz, Harold, 183 n

L

Language, 23-24
Lassey, William R., 153 n
Leader-subordinate relations, 162-63
Leadership, 2, 9, 110, 151-71
   consideration, 162
   contingency theory, 162-63, 166
   definition, 152
   effectiveness, 151-53, 164
   employee-centered, 161
   essence, 152
   functions, 153
   implications of, 152
   initiating structure, 162
   job-centered, 161
   maintenance functions, 153
   nature of, 151-53, 163, 165
   possible independence of dimensions of, 162
   styles; *see* Leadership styles
   task functions, 153
   traditional view of, 151-52
Leadership role, 111

Leadership styles, 111, 151, 153-60, 164, 166
    authority, use of, 154
    autocratic, 156
    bonded group decision, 155-56
    continuum, 154, 162
    democratic, 157
    dimensions of, 157
    feedback on, 173-75
    limited group autonomy, 156
    managerial grid, 157-60, 162, 165
    managers make and announce decision, 155
    managers sell decision, 155
    participative, 156-57
    sale and inquiry, 155
    specific, 155-57
    survey of ideas, 155
    tentative decisions, 155
Learning model, 2
Learnings; *see end of each chapter*
Letters, 24
Levels of ability, 85, 88, 97
Likert, Rensis, 161
Limited group autonomy, 156
Line authority, 91, 99
Line relationships, 91
Listening (active), 27, 29-32
Listening checks, 114-15, 124
Listening skills, 24
Long-range activities, 11

M

McGregor, Douglas, 128-29, 133, 136, 138-39
McMurry, Robert N., 109 n
Maintenance functions, 153
Management, 5-20
    communication and, 21-24
    defined, 5-6, 8, 14-15
    effectiveness, 11-14, 16
    functions, 8-11
        defined, 8
    importance of, 6-7
    levels of, 6
    nature, 7-11
    organizations, 5-7
    performance of function, 10
    process of, 7-10
        defined, 8, 14
    role of, 6-7
    sequence of function, 10
    understanding of, 2, 5
Managerial grid, 157-60, 162, 165
Managerial leadership, 151; *see also* Leadership
Managerial skill, 11-14, 16
Managers
    categories of, 6
    control responsibility, 183
    defined, 6
    directing responsibility of, 111
    employee-centered, 161
    job-centered, 161
    organizing responsibility, 83-84
    planning responsibility, 45-46
Marketing department, 84
Maslow, A. H., 131, 133, 135-36, 138-39
Massarik, Fred, 152 n
Measuring techniques of controlling, 186-87

Memos, 24
Message, 23-24
Methods Time Measurement, 96
Meyers, M. Scott, 136
Microwave tower, 67-71
Mixed departmentation, 95
Mixed message, 25-26
Motivation, 2, 9, 85-86, 110-11, 127-29, 133, 138
    assumptions about work behavior, 127-29
    needs and, 133
    goals, 137-38
    job enrichment, 136-38, 140
    needs; *see* Needs
    practical aspects, 135-38
    reinforcement theory, 137-38, 140
    Vroom's Expectancy Model, 137-38, 140
Mouton, Jane S., 157, 162
Mutual understanding and agreement, 113-15
    directives for, 114-15
    listening checks, 114-15
    open-ended question, 114-15
    summarizing, 114-15

N

Need satisfiers, 133-35
    importance of, 135
Needs, 129-30, 138
    assumptions of work behavior and, 133
    common, 131-33
    defined, 130
    esteem, 132
    hierarchy of, 131-33, 135-36, 139
    motivating, 131
    physiological, 131-32
    safety, 132
    self-realization, 132
    social, 132
    threatened, 132-33
    unsatisfied, 131
    work as source of satisfaction of, 133
Negative recognition, 137
Nierenberg, Gerald I., 26 n
Noise, 24
Nonverbal communication, 25-26, 30
Norms, 2

O

Objectives, 59
    achieving through planning, 60
    activities associated with, 52-53
    challenging, 51
    characteristics of, 51
    conversion into realities, 110
    defined, 50
    function, 50
    hierarchy of, 50
    job assignment, 112
    job-well-done conference, 113, 115
    measurable, 51
    planning to achieve, 43-44, 51-56
    relative importance of, 51
    setting of, 43-44, 46-51; *see also* Setting objectives
    time dimension, 51
Occupational specialization, 95

O'Donnell, Cyril, 183
Office managers, 11
Ohio State University studies on leadership effectiveness, 162, 166
One-time special projects, 56
Open-ended questions, 114-15, 123
Openness, 2
Oral assignments, 112
Oral communication, 24
Oral face-to-face job and task assignments, 112
Oral symbols, 23
Organization
    defined, 73
    management in, 5-7
Organization chart for branch office, 177
Organization structure, 83-84
    defined, 89
    hypothetical, 90
Organizational objectives, achievement of, 111
Organizing, 2, 7-9, 14-15, 22, 81-104, 109-110, 181
    basic concepts of, 82, 84-92, 98
    defined, 81, 98
    delegating authority, 82-83, 89-90, 96-98, 100
    grouping activities, 82-83, 92-96, 98
    importance of, 82-83
    nature of, 82-84, 98
    on-going process, 84
    overall purpose, 100
    process, 83
    production, 73-80, 147-50
    purpose, 8
    responsibility for, 83-84
    shipping containers, 73-80, 147-50
    simulation, 73-80, 147-50
Orientation, 1-3
    getting acquainted with instructor, 2
    teamwork, 1-2
Outputs, 187
Oxford Dictionary, 25

P

Participation, 2
Participative leadership, 156-57
Pattern assembly, 105-8
Paul, William J., 136 n
Perception, 24
Performance
    assessment of, 48-49
    determining standards of, 48
    evaluation, 9, 48-49
    identification of areas of, 47-48
Performance areas, 47-48, 51, 59
Performance goals, 184
Performance measurement, 184-185, 190
Performance objectives; *see* Objectives
Performance review of control experience, 197-202
Performance standards, 48, 51, 59, 185
    adequacy of, 88
    determination of, 48
Personality traits, 11
Physiological needs, 131-32
Pictures, 23
Planning, 2, 7-8, 14-15, 22, 43-65, 109-10, 181, 184
    achieving objectives, 43-44, 51-56, 60
    constraints, 57

Planning—Cont.
    defined, 44
    end point of process, 56
    importance of, 43-45, 59
    importance to other functions, 45
    integration of plans, 56
    international office building, 39-42
    master time schedule, 56
    microwave tower, 67-71
    nature of, 43-46
    orientation of, 8
    practical considerations, 43-44, 57-58
    process of, 46, 59
    responsibility for, 45-46
    setting objectives, 43-44, 46-51
    special purpose plans, 56
    uncertainty, reduction of, 44-45
Policies, rules and procedures, 57
Positive reinforcement, 137-38, 140
Power, 89-90
    defined, 109
    force of, 90
    sources of, 90-91
Power position, 163
Problem-solving, 9, 187
Problem-solving goal-setting approach, 136-37
Problem-solving techniques, 123-26
    directives, 124
    listening checks, 124
    open-ended question, 123
    summarizing, 124
Process departmentation, 92, 95
Product departmentation, 92, 94
Production line managers, 11
Production organization simulation, 73-80, 147-50

R

Receivers of messages, 24
Receiving skills, 24, 27
Recognition, 132, 134, 137
Reik, T., 29
Reinforcement theory, 137-38
Reports on operations, 186
Responsibility, 2, 84, 91, 134
    delegation of, 91
Roethlesberger, Fritz, 27 n
Rogers, Carl R., 27 n
Role-playing situations, 197-202
Roles
    leadership, 111
    management, 6-7
Routine projects, 56

S

Safety needs, 132
Salary, 135
Sales managers, 11
Satisfier-Dissatisfier Theory, 133, 139-40
    basic assumptions of, 133
Satisfiers, 133-34, 139-40
    importance of, 135
Sattler, William M., 25
Schmidt, Warren, 154, 162
Seeking information, 153

Self-concept, 27, 30-31
Self-disclosure, 27-28, 30, 32
Self-evaluation; see end of each chapter
Self-fulfillment needs, 132
Self-realization needs, 132
Self-respect, 132
Sending skills, 24, 27
Senses of human beings, 23
Sequencing activities, 53-55, 60
Sesame Street, 82
Setting objectives, 43-44, 46-51, 59
    anticipating future conditions, 49-50
    assessing present situation, 46-49
    determining performance standards, 48
    evaluating present performance, 48-49
    identification of performance areas, 47-48
    steps in, 46
Setting standards, 153
Shipping containers, 73-80, 137, 147-50
Short-range activities, 11
Sight, 23
Simulation of production organization, 73-80, 147-50
Sirota, David, 137
Situational decision, 89
Skills, 11-14, 16
    relative importance of, 13
Skinner, B. F., 137
Smell, 23
Social needs, 132
Sound, 23
Span of management
    broad, 87
    effects on structure, 87-88
    factors affecting, 88-89
    levels of management, number of, 88
    limitations, 87
    managers, number of, 88
    narrow, 87
    practical aspects, 89
    size, 87-88
Span of supervision, 84, 86-89, 99
Special purpose plans, 56
Specialization of work, 84-86, 92, 99
    general benefits of, 85
    limitations, 85-86
    specific benefits of, 85
Staff assistance, availability of, 88-89
Staff authority, 91, 100
Staff relationships, 91
Stating opinions, 153
Status, 132
Status symbols, 25
Stereotypes, 25
Subdepartments, 92
Subordinate ability, 88
Summarizing, 114-15, 124, 153
Superior-subordinate relationships, 91, 111
Supervision, 135
Supervisors, 6, 11
    planning responsibility of, 45
Supervisory ability, 88
Survey of ideas, 155
Symbolic communication, 25-26, 30-31
Symbols, 23-24

T

Tagiuri, Renatu, 5 n
Tannerbaum, Robert, 152 n, 154, 162
Task accomplishment, 153
Task assignments, 112
Task functions, 153
Task structure, 162-63
Taste, 23
Teams, 1
    effectiveness of; see end of each chapter
    formation of, 1
    interview of partner in, 1
    introduction of partner to, 2
Teamwork, 82, 153
Teamwork skills, 2
Technical skill, 11-14, 16
Tension, 129
    reducing, 153
Tentative decisions, 155
Territorial departmentation, 92, 95
Theory X assumptions of work behavior, 128-29, 135-36, 138-39
    needs and, 133
Theory Y assumptions of work behavior, 128-29, 135-36, 138-39
    needs and, 133
Third ear, 29
Time departmentation, 92, 95
Time-and-motion study, 96
Time schedules, 186
Timing activities, 55-56
Togetherness, 153
Tones of voice, 23
Touch, 23
Training, 11, 13
Transactional Analysis (TA), 27
Transfer of information, 21; see also Communication
Trust, 2, 28

U

Uncertainty, planning to reduce, 44-45
Understanding, 12, 27, 29
Uniformity, need for, 91-92
Unity of command, 84, 86, 99
University of Michigan studies on leadership effectiveness, 161-62, 166

V

Verbal communication, 25-26, 30-31
Visual channel, 23
Vroom, Victor H., 138
Vroom's Expectancy Model, 137-38, 140

W

Wants and desires, 130
Words, 23
Work, 134
Work standards, 186
Work territories, 137
Working conditions, 135
Written communication, 24
Written job descriptions, 112, 116
    contents of, 112
Written symbols, 23

CONSTRUCTION MATERIALS FOR BLOCKS VII AND XIII

Block VII
3 sheets of 6¾" squares
3 sheets of 7½" squares

Block XIII
10 sheets of 6¾" squares
10 sheets of 7½" squares

6¾" square

6¾" square

6¾" square

6¾" square

6¾" square

6¾" square

6¾" square

6¾" square

6¾" square

6¾" square

6¾" square

6¾" square

6¾" square

7½" square

7½" square

7½" square

7½" square

7½" square

7½" square

7½" square

7½" square

7½" square

7½" square

7½" square

7½" square

7½" square

CONSTRUCTION MATERIALS FOR BLOCKS IV, VI, AND IX

Block IV

International Office Building-1 sheet (9 patterned panels)

Block VI

Microwave Tower-3 sheets (27 plain panels)

Block IX

Pattern Assembly-3 sheets (27 plain panels)

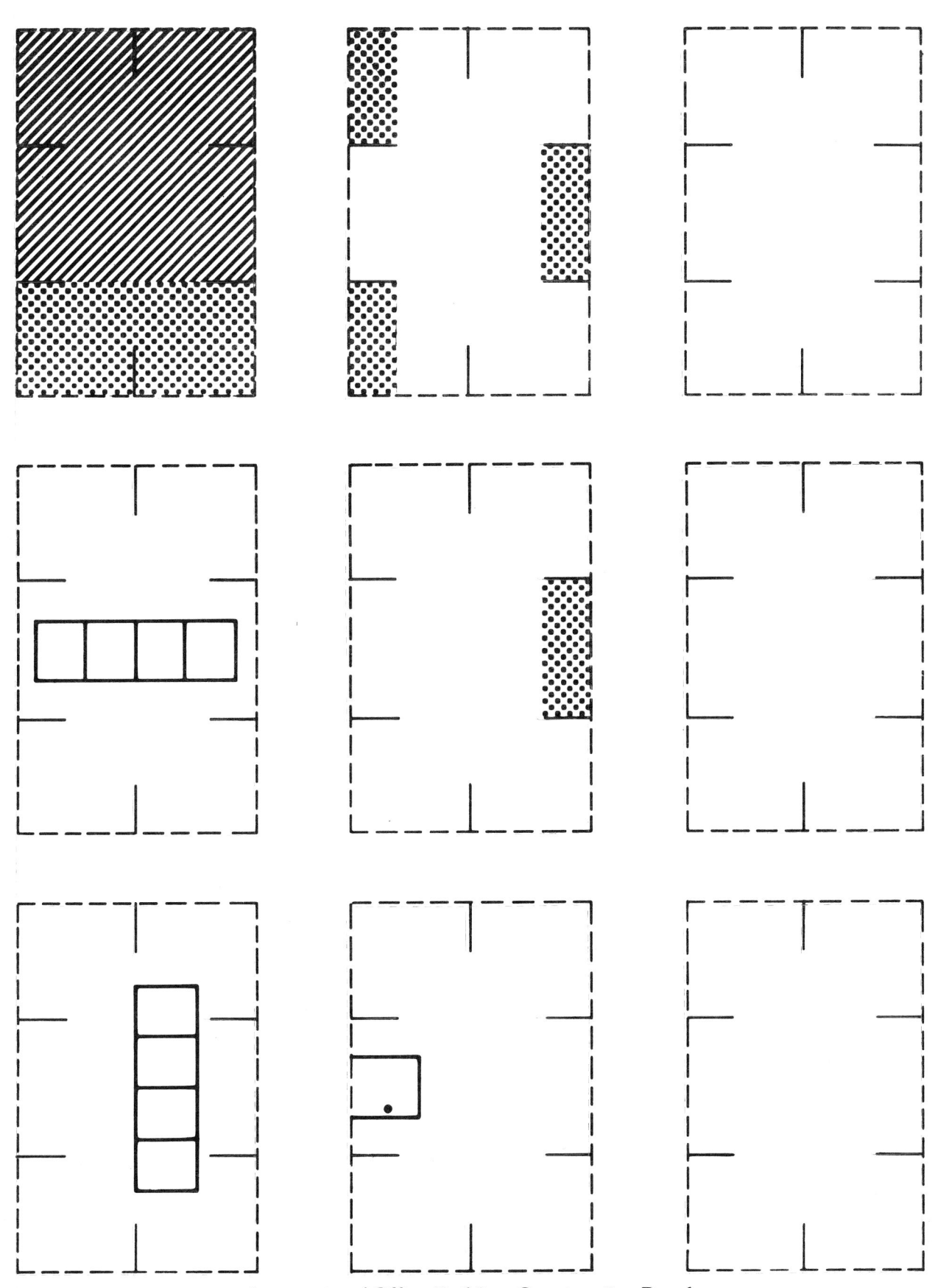

International Office Building Construction Panels

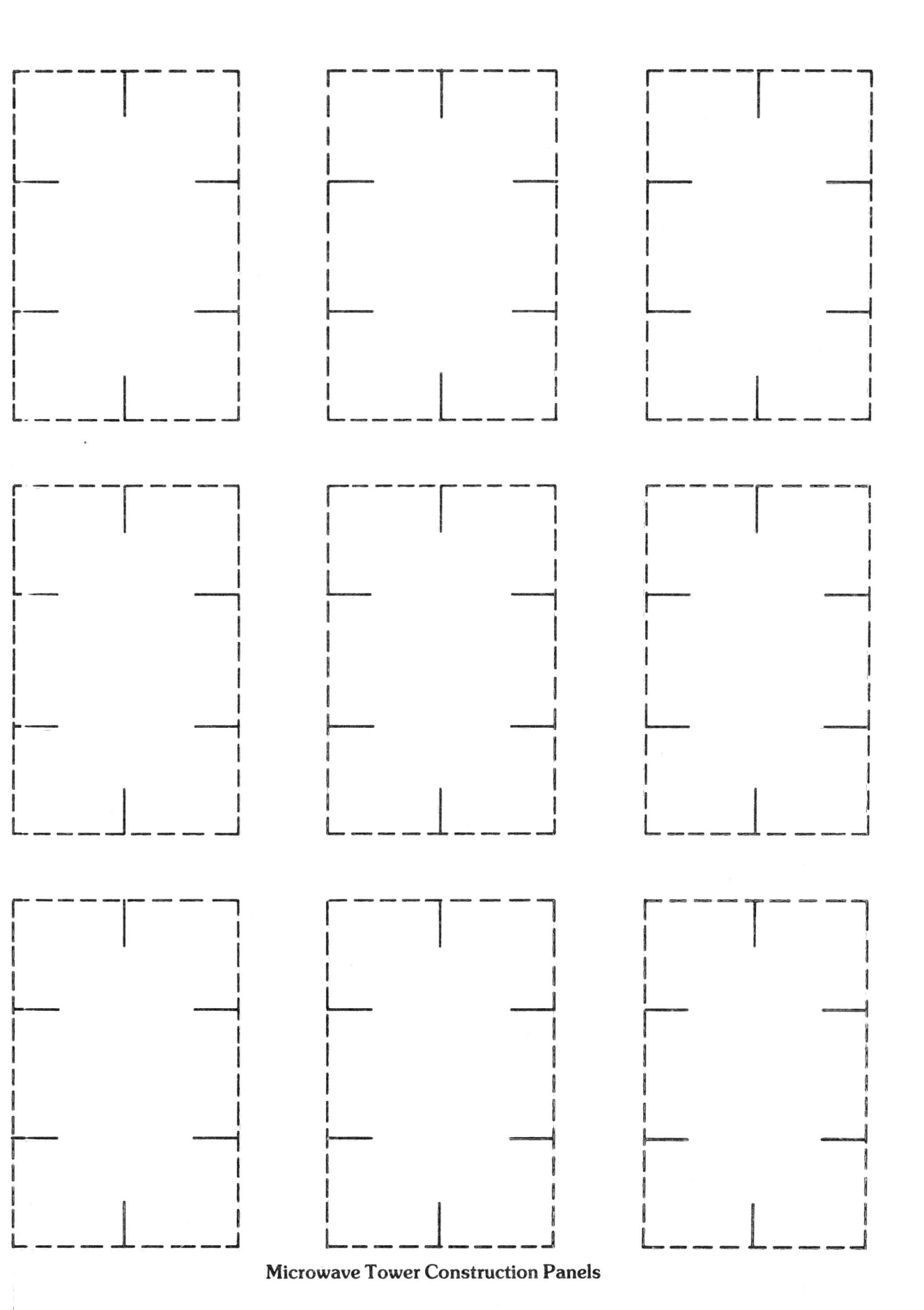

Microwave Tower Construction Panels

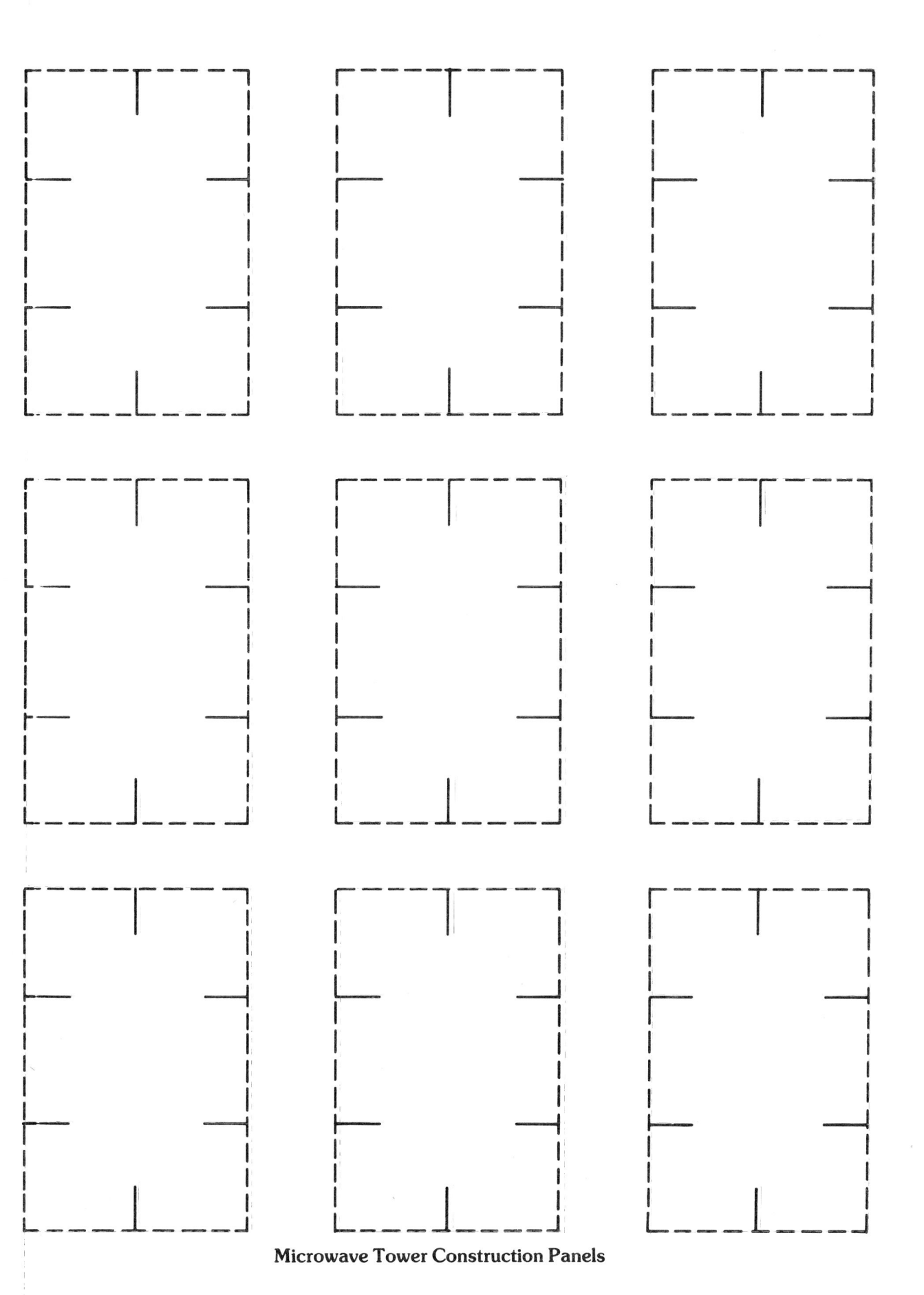

Microwave Tower Construction Panels

Microwave Tower Construction Panels

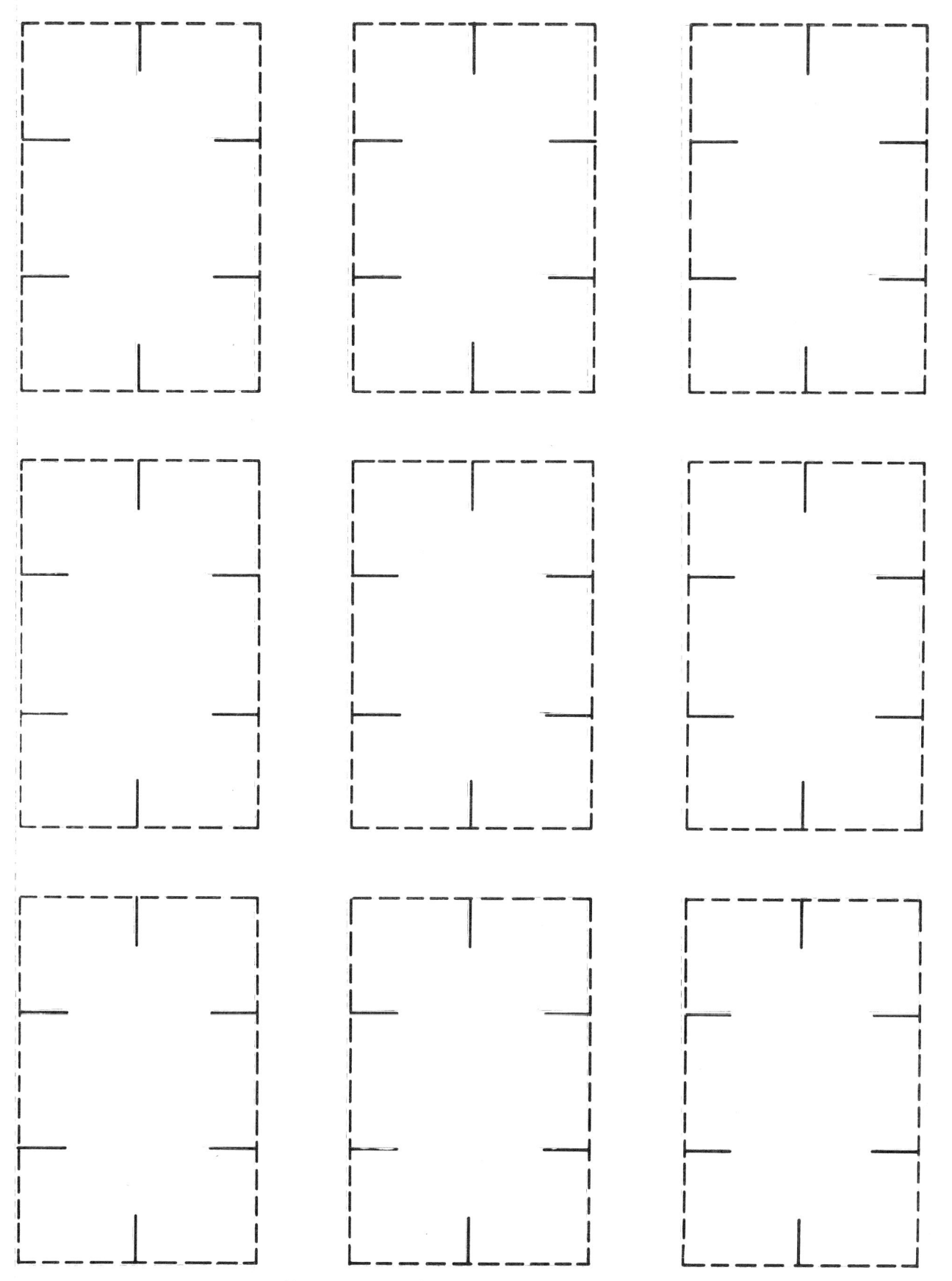

Pattern Assembly Construction Panels

Pattern Assembly Construction Panels

Pattern Assembly Construction Panels